# The
# Planned
# Vegetable
# Garden

# The Planned Vegetable Garden

Leslie Godfrey

J. M. Dent & Sons Ltd

LONDON MELBOURNE TORONTO

First published 1979
© Leslie Godfrey 1979
All rights reserved. No part of this publication
may be reproduced, stored in a retrieval system,
or transmitted, in any form or by any means,
electronic, mechanical, photocopying, recording or
otherwise, without the prior permission of
J. M. Dent & Sons Ltd.

Phototypeset in 11 on 13pt Bembo by
Trident Graphics Ltd, Reigate, Surrey
Printed in Great Britain by
Billings Ltd, London, Guildford & Worcester for
J. M. Dent & Sons Ltd
Aldine House, Welbeck Street, London

British Library Cataloguing in Publication Data

Godfrey, Leslie
    The planned vegetable garden.
    1. Vegetable gardening
    I. Title
    635      SB322

ISBN 0–460–04401–X

# Contents

# Introduction

Every year we spend literally millions of pounds on vegetable seeds, composts, fertilisers, insecticides, cloches and other sundries to grow our own vegetables. It's a basic desire and the pictures on the seed packets give us hope that this year we will get big firm cabbages, fat straight carrots, crisp lettuces, ripe golden onions and pounds and pounds of long tender runner beans.

But what happens? At the end of the season half the gardeners in the country are as disappointed with their crops as they were last year, and the year before, and the year before that. Many of them give up growing vegetables altogether, not knowing quite why they failed – which is a pity, because there is no reason at all why those gardeners couldn't grow the crops they dreamed about. There's nothing wrong with them or with their abilities.

It's not the gardeners that are at fault, it's their gardens. There is something radically wrong with over half the vegetable gardens in the country. Take a train journey and look out of the window. Compare the farmers' fields with the private gardens that back on to the railway line. What do you see? The farmers and market gardeners have whole fields full of good looking cabbages, Brussels sprouts, potatoes, runner beans, peas and other crops. Sometimes the weather is against them and they lose a crop; but that's rare. Normally they make a good profit. But what about the private gardens? How often do you see vegetables in them as good as those in the farmers' fields? Perhaps one in ten. There's nothing unusual about gardens that back on to railway lines except that they give us a chance to be nosey. I suspect that other private gardens are the same.

Many of them suffer from what our forefathers called 'Soil Sickness'. If your plot won't grow vegetables as good as the pictures on the seed packets the chances are that your garden suffers from some sort of 'soil sickness' too. Fortunately it can be cured and the remedies are not too painful. Let me tell you about them.

# 1. The Planned Vegetable Garden

## THE AIMS OF THIS BOOK

1. To help you restore the soil in your vegetable garden if it has become worn out and grows poor crops.
2. If you have a good fertile soil to suggest ways in which you can keep it so.
3. To give each of your vegetables the conditions they need to grow into fine healthy specimens.
4. To give you detailed sowing and rotation plans that will help to keep diseases under control without the use of too many insecticides: there are plans to suit different sized vegetable gardens, from 10 ft by 10 ft to 40 ft by 40 ft, and these plans are the result of work done on plots in normal garden conditions.
5. Above all it sets out to make it easy for you to grow vegetables as good as the pictures on the seed packets or in the seed catalogues.

### A word about seed catalogues

The firms that market seeds and plants are much the same as any other companies. They have products to sell and profits to make and they advertise and market their wares in a way they consider will give them the best possible sales. Most of them are very ethical people and many seed catalogues give very reliable advice and information. But it does seem that there are just a few companies who want to part us from our money by making claims that are a little extravagant. So do take what you are told in advertisements and catalogues with a pinch of salt – with a common sense question mark in your mind. Whatever anyone says it isn't easy to grow bananas in your back garden in Balham and I don't think you should try.

However, if your garden gets plenty of light it is easy to grow good vegetables. You can grow some of them more cheaply than you can buy them. With many others you'll be growing them for the taste, not the value, because you'll be growing varieties that you just can't get in the shops – with a flavour that you just can't buy.

## WHAT ARE VEGETABLES?
## WHERE HAVE THEY COME FROM?

I don't want to get involved in the age-old argument as to whether a tomato is a fruit or a vegetable. For my money it's a fruit that is used as a vegetable. Vegetables are, broadly speaking, those herbaceous plants that are used by man for food. He may find them growing wild but normally he cultivates them. Sometimes he grows the plants for their roots, sometimes for their stems and leaves and with others it's for their seed containers or seeds.

Where have these plants come from? In many cases the origins of our vegetable plants are lost in the mists of time but it seems that the cucumber came from northern India, beetroots from the Mediterranean countries, carrots from Britain and Europe, the potato and the tomato from the Americas; and while broad beans were being eaten by the lake dwellers of Switzerland in the Bronze Age the ancient Egyptians accorded divine honours to one variety of onion. And surely they were right to do so. The noble onion is one of the earliest of cultivated plants and has been grown from time immemorial in almost all of the temperate zones of the world.

Our ancestors discovered our vegetable plants over a span of thousands of years in quite different parts of the world, and yet we wish to grow them side by side in one small plot in Brighton, or Birmingham, or Bolton. Would it not be reasonable to assume that these plants might need quite different growing conditions? Well of course they do need different conditions but not too different. Man with his ingenuity has, over the centuries, been breeding and selecting varieties of these vegetable plants so that they will grow virtually side by side and flourish in our marvellous climate.

Yes, our marvellous climate. Not perhaps what we would always wish it to be during our summer holidays, but from the vegetable growers' point of view it is almost ideal in most years. Our Emerald Isle is set in a silver sea warmed by the Gulf Stream and watered by the rain clouds from the Atlantic, giving us the conditions in which to grow a wider variety of vegetable plants than most other countries in the world, with exotic tomatoes and cucumbers growing close to hardy swedes and leeks.

But to get the best from our plot these different vegetables do need somewhat different growing conditions, in spite of the selecting and reselecting of strains of plants that has gone on. With a little thought and planning we can give them the conditions they need and they in turn will reward us with bigger and better roots, leaves, stems, seeds or seed pods . . . whichever it is that we are after.

## WHAT DIFFERENT CONDITIONS DO PLANTS NEED?

When we look at the individual needs of different plants it is like looking at the separate pieces of an interesting but complex jig-saw puzzle. Let's have a look at some of those pieces.

Some plants, runner beans and marrows, for example, need plenty of compost or manure at their roots to produce a worthwhile crop. With these plants our 'crop' is the seed-pot or 'fruit'.

But with carrots and parsnips it's good roots we want and if we plant them in manure or compost the roots will grow forked and misshapen. On the other hand if we put carrots and parsnips in a poor soil we'll get a very poor crop. We have to plant them in a soil that's been manured for a previous crop and has then been deeply dug. We'll then get the good straight roots we're after.

Other plants that like well-manured ground are members of the cabbage family. Most of us refer to them as brassicas. The family is a very large and important one with the botanical name *Cruciferae* and includes Brussels sprouts, broccoli, kale, cauliflowers, kohl rabi and close relations like swedes, turnips and radishes. All these brassicas will do well in ground that's been freshly manured but although swedes and turnips may look as if they've done well in that fresh manure, when you come to eat them they'll have a rank or 'earthy' taste and not the delicate flavour that you really want. So swedes and turnips need to be grown in ground that has been manured for a previous crop and not in fresh manure or compost.

We also have to consider whether our plants need an 'alkaline' or an 'acid' soil. Fortunately that's not too complex as most vegetables need a soil that's almost neutral, neither acid nor alkaline but just between the two. Unless they are chalky most soils tend to be acid and the constant application of compost or manure does, in itself, make soils acid. So we generally have to apply some form of lime to the surface of the soil from time to time to correct this and produce those 'neutral' conditions our plants need.

But just to be difficult not all plants like lime. Tomatoes and marrows like a slightly acid soil and potatoes will be scabby if they come in contact with fresh lime. So these crops must be grown on land that has been limed in previous years for other crops.

However, members of the cabbage family think lime is marvellous stuff. It sweetens the soil and helps to prevent diseases like club-root that cabbages can be prone to.

We've also got to consider what *part* of the plant it is that we're going to eat. With lettuce and cabbage it will be the leaves, with carrots and parsnips the roots and with peas and beans the seeds or seed-pods. Different food elements in the soil have an effect on these different parts of the plant so we'll have to give some thought to this. For instance, tomato plants with big leaves and small fruit look fine but I'm sure you'd prefer a plant with small leaves and big tomatoes.

These are just some of the pieces of the jig-saw puzzle that we'll need to fit together properly.

Why don't we just decide on the ideal growing conditions for each vegetable, allocate it its place in the garden and then grow it year after year in the same place? In fact we can do just that with a few vegetables and they'll do quite well. Some gardeners grow onions in the same place year after year and get good crops, but for most vegetables it just won't do. Like the rest of the plant and animal kingdom, vegetables suffer from pests and diseases. If these pests or diseases get a hold they can stay in the soil and reinfect the plants in following years, and this can also happen to the onion with a disease called 'white rot'.

Most of us have had it happen in our own gardens or seen it happen in friends' gardens – marvellous crops the first two or three years and then deterioration sets in as the diseases get a hold. After five years or so all the work of digging, planting, thinning and hoeing results in poor crops. Very disheartening. It has happened since man first started cultivating crops – but it doesn't have to be like that.

## WHY CROP ROTATION?

Our ancestors used to leave some of their fields and plots to 'lie fallow' each year. They knew that if they continually grew the same plants in the same place year after year something would happen to the soil and they'd get poor crops. They called it 'soil sickness' and found that leaving part of the land to lie fallow each year, with no crops on, helped to cure this soil sickness – like taking a rest when you're ill.

What had happened was that the soil had either become deficient in the nutrients the plants needed or it had become diseased – probably both. Leaving the soil to rest for a year improved it, but it wasn't really necessary. And we certainly don't want to leave any of our vegetable plots to lie fallow. So how do we avoid 'soil sickness'? How do we avoid our soil becoming diseased?

**We rotate our crops.** Different diseases affect different plants, or rather families of plants. 'Club-root', which is a well-known disease of the cabbage family will have no effect on, say, potatoes, and potato blight will not damage runner-beans. So provided we know which botanical family a plant belongs to we can work out a system of crop rotation to ensure that no member of a plant family is grown in the same soil more than once in three years, or preferably four.

This rotation plan will give plant diseases a chance to die out. If your vegetable garden gets plenty of light but it won't grow good crops it may have become impoverished and disease ridden. Strict adherence to a crop rotation plan is essential to restore it to health and fertility. If you have a new plot then proper crop rotation will prevent many pests and diseases getting a hold.

## SO WHAT MUST WE DO?

1. We must plan our work, and then work our plan.
2. We must follow a system of crop rotation so that diseases do not build up in the soil.
3. We must plan our vegetable garden so that we give compost or manure to those plants that need it and then follow on the next year with plants that like ground that's been manured for a previous crop.
4. We must have a controlled liming programme to keep the soil at the correct state for each crop. But we should not apply lime as a matter of routine, only when tests have shown that it is needed.
5. We can even get one crop to improve the soil for the next one. Peas and beans have nodules on their roots. These nodules contain helpful bacteria which extract nitrogen from the air. If we leave the roots in the ground after the crop is cleared the nitrogen can be beneficial to 'leaf crops' subsequently planted in the same place.
6. We must plan our layout in such a way that tall crops like runner beans do not overshadow shorter ones.
7. Some crops such as Brussels sprouts, Savoy cabbages and leeks will need to stay in the ground during the winter months. It will be helpful if they can be planted near each other so that when we

come to do the winter digging we haven't got odd rows of winter crops in each plot. If the plot that contains the 'winter crops' can be the same one in which we grow the root crops the following year then we won't need to manure it and it can be the last one to be dug over after the winter crops are out of the way.

Well, those are some of the pieces of the jig-saw puzzle; add a few others such as the need to have a continuous supply of crops throughout the year without a glut one month and a shortage the next, put them all together and a picture of your cropping and sowing plan will emerge.

In fact I've put the picture together for you and set out detailed cropping and sowing plans for different sized plots. Let's have a careful look at the basic principles and at the four course rotation.

## PLANT GROUPS AND THE ROTATION SYSTEM

First we need to arrange our plants into groups. There are many methods of classifying them:

> By the botanical group or 'plant family' to which they belong.
> By their cultivation needs. Carrots, for instance, have different needs from cabbages.
> By the season in which they grow – spring crops or winter crops.
> By whether we cook them or eat them raw – main vegetables or salad crops.
> By whether we just use them for flavouring – herbs.
> By the way they grow – climbing, tall or short.
> By the diseases that affect them.
> By the part of them that we eat – root crops, leaf crops or seed crops.

And no doubt you may think of others.

For our rotation system we need to classify vegetables in such a way that all the plants in one group have the same general cultivation needs as each other and that any plant diseases left in the soil from one plant group will not affect other plant groups in following years. We want these diseases to die out and we do it by depriving them for a period of the plants on which they live.

I have classified over forty varieties of vegetables into four main groups.

## Potato Group
Capsicums (sweet peppers)
Courgettes
Cucumber (outdoors)
Lettuce (late)
Marrows
Melons (outdoors)
Potatoes
Seakale beet (Swiss chard)
Spinach beet
Sweet corn
Tomatoes

## Legumes Group
Legumes
- Broad beans
- French beans
- Haricot beans
- Peas
- Runner beans

Celeriac
Celery
Jerusalem artichokes
Lettuce (mid season)
Parsley

## Onions and Brassicas
Brassicas
- Broccoli
- Brussels sprouts
- Cabbage
- Cauliflowers
- Chinese cabbage
- Kale
- Kohl rabi
- Radishes

Garlic
Leeks
Onions
Shallots
Spring onions

## Roots Group
Beetroot
Carrots
Chicory (sugar loaf)
Endive
Parsnips
Radishes (early)
Salsify
Scorzonera
Spinach
Swedes
Turnips

In general the members of a particular 'plant family' are in the same group, but there are exceptions. Turnips, radishes and swedes are brassicas but they are included in the Roots Group because they have different cultivation needs from the leaf-type brassicas such as cabbage. But we must ensure in drawing up our sowing plans that they never follow on in the same ground as the leaf-type brassicas, otherwise we might get some diseases being passed on. **This makes it important to keep strictly to the sowing plans.**

A rotation system that is sometimes recommended is based on only three groups – roots, legumes and brassicas – but this isn't specific enough. It doesn't classify plants according to 'plant families' and may lead to members of the same family following each other in the same ground year after year. Under such crude classifications you might get tomatoes following potatoes, and turnips and swedes following the

*15*

leaf brassicas and radishes, thereby losing some of the benefits of crop rotation.

The manuring and liming programme can also get confusing under a three group system.

Keep the plants in the groups specified, make sure that the rows go where suggested in the Master Plans and you will avoid members of the same plant family following each other in the same ground. You will get the benefit of much healthier crops year after year.

## Perennial plants

The crops included in the Master Plans are raised from seeds or young plants each year, but you may also have room in your garden for some 'perennial' vegetable crops. Crops like perpetual or 'Welsh' onions, chives, mint and other herbs which require modest amounts of space and may perhaps be grown in odd corners of the flower border. (See the section on 'Herbs' on page 191.)

Globe artichokes and asparagus are among the aristocrats of vegetables and are not difficult to grow, but they do need their own separate permanent beds. And what garden is complete without its rhubarb patch? Information on growing artichokes, asparagus and rhubarb will be found in the section 'Culture of Individual Crops'.

# 2. Explaining the Master Plans

Farmers can fairly easily keep to rotation systems because they are growing a limited number of crops and have enough land to move these crops round as necessary.

The vegetable gardener is in a different situation. He may wish to grow thirty or more different types of vegetables in a very limited space, and keeping to a strict rotation system to avoid pests and diseases building up in the soil is a complex problem. No wonder many gardeners don't bother.

But it is essential that you do bother if you want healthy crops year after year. So the Master Plans have dealt with these complexities for you. They give you exact plans of where to grow each of your vegetables in all four years of the rotation system. The Master Plans are based on the assumption that you can divide your vegetable garden into four areas of about the same size but if you only have room for one small plot or two small plots this is also catered for. In fact if you have just a small area of say 10 ft by 10 ft it is still worth following a rotation system. (See page 71.)

## WHERE SHALL WE PUT OUR PLOTS?

The vegetable garden must be sited right out in the open where it will get the greatest amount of light. Almost all gardens are surrounded by hedges, walls, fences or perhaps even trees.

### Trees
If you try to grow vegetables under the shade of trees you'll be very disappointed in the results; your crops will be small and unhealthy. The roots of trees extend at least as far as the span of the branches and the tree may also have large tap roots, going down under it. All the roots are taking plant nutrients from the soil as well as copious amounts of water, so your vegetables won't stand much chance.

 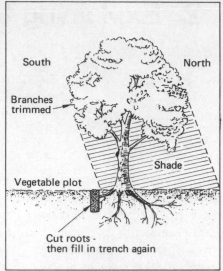

It is possible to grow vegetables on the SOUTH side of a large tree, but you may have to trim back any low growing branches; and to stop the tree robbing your plot of moisture and plant food it might be worth digging a trench 3 ft deep and cutting through some of the roots. Keep this trench at least 8 ft from the trunk and only go part way round the tree, otherwise you might make it unstable and possibly dangerous. Certainly if a large tree is anywhere near a house do get expert advice before cutting through its roots or lopping its branches. It might even be better to have it taken down altogether, although it's usually a sad thing for a tree, that may have taken over fifty years to grow, to disappear from the landscape.

## Walls
A mixed blessing. The south side of a wall is ideal for growing plants especially those, like tomatoes, that love the sun. But if you plant close to the NORTH side of a wall your plants will be tall and 'weedy' as they struggle towards the light.

## Fences
The same things in general apply to fences, but they can be a bit draughty, especially through that gap at the bottom. So during the growing season fill it in . . . but not with soil as that could cause the fence to rot. Use planks of wood, some old tiles or plastic sheeting.

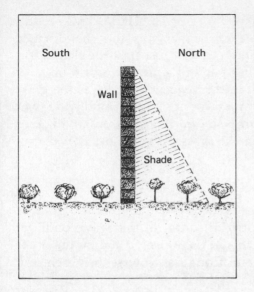
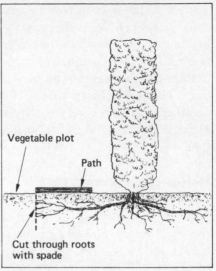

Remove them during the winter so that the bottom of the fence gets a good airing.

## Hedges

Usually good to look at but, like trees, they do rob the soil of plant foods and water. So keep your vegetable plots a few feet away from them. In fact the sensible thing is to have the path between the hedge and the plot – this makes it easier to trim the hedge anyway. Then, when you're digging the plot, make sure you cut through any hedge roots that protrude beyond the path. Have the path about 1 ft away from the hedge, more if the hedge is a tall one and is likely to cast a shadow on your vegetable plot.

## Paths

They can be made of many things – gravel, cinder, concrete, tarmac – and quite often you just have to put up with what you've got. If you have any choice I suggest the most convenient is paving slabs. They're relatively easy to lay, can be taken up and relaid without too much trouble and, perhaps best of all, they are ideal for a 'planned garden' as it is so easy to measure the distance between rows by checking the known measurements of the slabs. Lay them on a foundation of sharp sand or ash.

By the way, modern paving slabs are 'metric' and what looks like a

2 ft wide slab may in fact measure 600 mm or 1 ft 11⅝ in. This needn't cause any problems because you can either measure the distance between your rows of seeds in millimetres, or just treat the slab as if it were 2 ft wide, with half of it being 1 ft and a quarter of it 6 in.

Possibly the worst type of path in the vegetable garden is the grass one. The wheelbarrow makes a mess of it, it gets muddy in wet weather, you can't very easily dump soil on it when you are digging and the edges get ragged. So keep the grass paths for the flower garden.

## Points of the compass

As each of our vegetable plants needs the greatest amount of light it is best for the rows to run from north to south. In this way you'll get the sunshine on one side of the plants in the morning and on the other side in the afternoon. If the rows run from east to west then each row of plants will shade the one behind.

But if your garden has a definite slope in one direction you'll find it

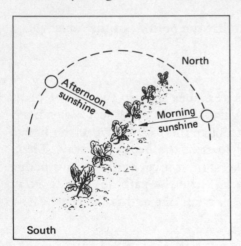

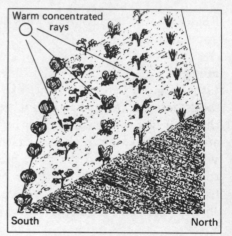

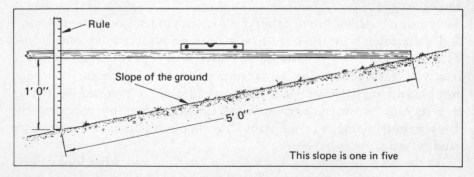

much easier in working your plot if the rows run across the slope and not up and down hill. So if the plot slopes towards the south this means the rows will run from east to west, but this is no problem as the southern tilt of the land will prevent one row of plants from shading another. In fact that slope to the south will give you a warmer plot and earlier crops and is probably the ideal site. You should certainly sow from east to west on a south-facing slope if the gradient is one in five or more. The gradient can easily be checked with a spirit level, a length of wood and a rule. So run your rows from north to south unless your garden has a definite tilt to the south, in which case run the rows from east to west.

## THE PLOTS

The vegetable garden is divided into four plots. These will probably be in the same part of the garden but there is no reason why they shouldn't be in quite different places – even two at home and two on the allotment. One group of vegetables is grown in each plot and then in subsequent years the groups move on into different plots until by Year 5 they are back where they started. This gives time for pests and diseases to die out before any group of plants occupy the same soil again

| Year 1 | Year 2 | Year 3 | Year 4 |
|--------|--------|--------|--------|
| Plot A | Plot B | Plot C | Plot D |
| Potato Group | Legumes Group | Onions & | Roots Group |
| Legumes Group | Onions & |    Brassicas | Potato Group |
| Onions & |    Brassicas | Roots Group | Legumes Group |
|    Brassicas | Roots Group | Potato Group | Onions & |
| Roots Group | Potato Group | Legumes Group |    Brassicas |

and then in Year 5 back to Year 1, to begin again.

By the way, if starting at Year 1 in the Master Plans means that a particular crop will be grown yet again in the same place then start your rotation at Year 2, or 3, or 4; whichever is the best starting place for *your* garden.

21

If your plots are laid out in a 'square' then label them like this.

Right

| | |
|---|---|
| A | B |
| D | C |

*Not like this.*

Wrong

| | |
|---|---|
| A | B |
| C | D |

In future years it will make it much easier to remember what has to go where.

## THE PLANS

There are three Master Plans to choose from.

### The Large Master Plan

This has four plots each 20 ft wide.

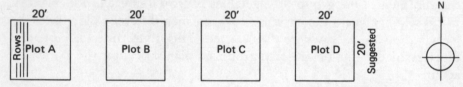

The suggested length of row is also 20 ft but this can be increased or decreased according to the space you have available.

If your vegetable rows are 20 ft long and the area available is square, the space needed would be 44 ft by 46 ft including 2 ft wide paths. (The dotted line is an imaginary line between two adjoining plots.)

Or if you have a long narrow space you would need 86 ft by 24 ft.

Make sure the rows run north to south. But you may well have two plots at home and two on the allotment, or separated in some way.

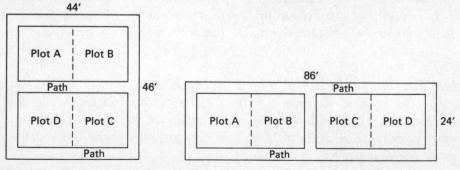

## The Medium Master Plan

This has four plots each 15 ft wide.

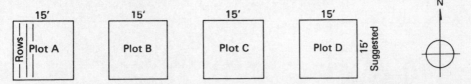

The suggested length of row is 15 ft but this can of course be varied to suit your own garden.

If your vegetable rows are 15 ft long and your garden is square you will need a space 34 ft by 36 ft including 2 ft wide paths.

Or if your garden is long and narrow you would need 66 ft by 19 ft.

Again make sure the rows run north to south. And, of course, your four plots may be quite separate or in some other layout.

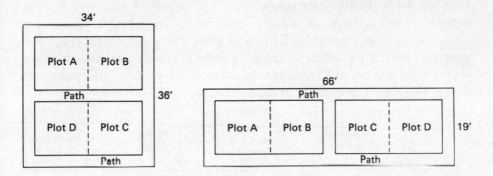

## The Small Master Plan

This has four plots each 10 ft wide.

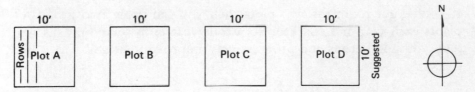

The suggested length of row is 10 ft but this may be varied to suit the space available.

If your vegetable rows are 10 ft long and your garden is square the space needed will be 24 ft by 26 ft including 2 ft paths.

If your garden is long and narrow you will need 46 ft by 14 ft.

Your four plots may be quite separate or in some other layout, but make sure the rows run north to south.

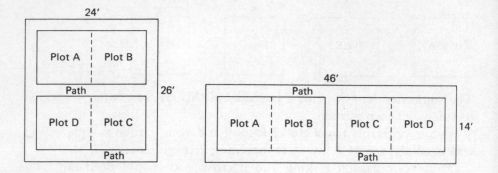

## The Little Plot

But you might only have space for *one* plot, say 15 ft by 15 ft, or just 10 ft by 10 ft. In this case grow just one group of plants each year instead of trying to grow a bit of everything or trying to grow the same things year after year. This will give you good crops year after year but they'll be different crops. Surely it's better to have a good crop of something different than a very poor crop of the same old thing. Suggested cropping details are on pages 72–3.

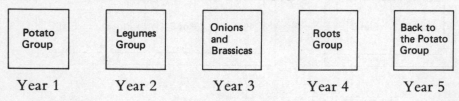

## Two Little Plots

If you've got room for two plots then you can grow two groups of plants each year and still keep to a four year crop rotation. This will give you good crops and progressively improve your soil. Do it like this:

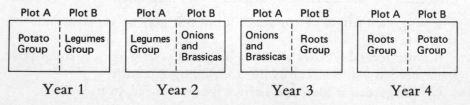

And then in Year 5 go back to Year 1 and start again.

Follow the Medium Master Plan if the plots are 15 ft wide and the Small Master Plan if they are 10 ft wide.

## Three Little Plots

If you have room for three small plots, but not four, you can still keep to a four year crop rotation by doing this:

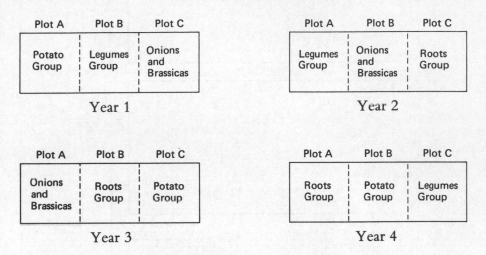

| Plot A | Plot B | Plot C |
|---|---|---|
| Potato Group | Legumes Group | Onions and Brassicas |

Year 1

| Plot A | Plot B | Plot C |
|---|---|---|
| Legumes Group | Onions and Brassicas | Roots Group |

Year 2

| Plot A | Plot B | Plot C |
|---|---|---|
| Onions and Brassicas | Roots Group | Potato Group |

Year 3

| Plot A | Plot B | Plot C |
|---|---|---|
| Roots Group | Potato Group | Legumes Group |

Year 4

In Year 5 start again at Year 1.

Use the Medium Master Plan if the plots are 15 ft wide and the Small Master Plan if they are 10 ft wide.

The whole secret of success is to **keep to the rotation plan year after year after year.**

## YOUR MASTER PLAN

First make a rough plan of your garden. This is a great help in deciding which Master Plan to choose and ensuring that you leave room for essentials like the compost bins. If you have a total area available for your vegetable garden of say, 42 ft long by 35 ft wide and your garden runs roughly north to south your layout would perhaps look like this. (Remember, to avoid shading each other the rows of vegetables **must** run north to south – unless the garden has a definite tilt to the south, in which case run them from east to west.)

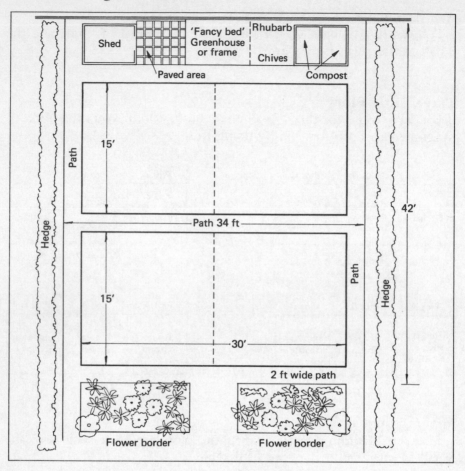

## Shed

If you need a garden shed make sure it's sited so that you won't hit it with the wheelbarrow when turning the corner and so that there is easy access through the doorway. The paved area will be useful for storing things that don't need to go under cover, perhaps the wheelbarrow, cloches or incinerator – but don't light it near the shed.

## 'Fancy bed'

When we look through the catalogues or seed displays there's often something that takes your 'fancy'. You might like to have a space to grow such things, or of course use the room for a garden frame or a greenhouse.

## Compost bins

These are essential. Site them so that they are easy to load and unload. See the section on 'Composts'.

## Rhubarb

What a good return a couple of rhubarb crowns (roots) give. They need a good soil so plant them near the compost bins so that you remember to give them a few forkfuls every year. Rhubarb leaves make an excellent aphid killer, too, the recipe is on page 216.

## Herbs

No garden is complete without herbs. Plant some chives in front of the rhubarb. Put some mint roots in good soil in an old bucket that's got holes in the bottom for drainage and bury it up to its rim in a shady spot near the back door. (This will give you a handy supply but stop the mint taking over the whole flower garden.) You can plant other herbs straight into the flower garden and very pleasant they look too; plants like sage, rosemary and thyme. See the section 'Cultivation of Individual Crops'.

## NOW CHOOSE YOUR MASTER PLAN

The layout opposite would exactly suit the Middle Master Plan, but select the one that best fits YOUR garden:

The Large Master Plan and Seed Ordering Guide are on pages 28–41.
The Middle Master Plan and Seed Ordering Guide are on pages 42–56.
The Small Master Plan and Seed Ordering Guide are on pages 57–71.

# 3. The Large Master Plan

**Four plots each 20 ft wide**

The lines on the plans are exactly where the drills for the seeds should be made, and the distances given are those between one drill and the next. In the case of the peas a drill 6 in. wide should be taken out.

Give the plants the distance apart in the rows that the seed packet says. This is very important with brassicas – better to have ten good plants than fifteen poor ones.

**Note:** if you want to grow something different see the list of 'Alternative Crops' on page 74.

## POTATO GROUP

| | |
|---|---|
| 1'0'' | ———— Outdoor Tomatoes ———— 1'0'' |
| 2'6'' | Marrows • • • • • • • • 2'0'' |
| | • • • • Sweet • 2'0'' |
| 3'0'' or Courgettes • • • • • • • 2'0'' |
| | • • Corn • • 2'0'' |
| 2'6'' 2'0'' • 1'6'' • • • 2'0'' |
| | ———— Seakale Beet ———— |
| 1'9'' | |
| | ———— Early Potatoes ———— |
| 1'9'' | Followed by Lettuce |
| | ———— Early Potatoes ———— |
| 2'0'' | |
| | ———— Maincrop Potatoes ———— |
| 2'0'' | |
| | ———— Maincrop Potatoes ———— |
| 2'0'' | |
| | ———— Maincrop Potatoes ———— |
| 1'6'' | |

Suggested length of rows 20ft

## LEGUMES GROUP

| | |
|---|---|
| 1'0'' | ———— Lettuce ———— |
| 9'' | ———— Lettuce ———— |
| 9'' | ———— Lettuce ———— |
| 1'6'' | |
| | ———— Tall Broad Beans ———— |
| 9'' | ———— Tall Broad Beans ———— |
| 2'3'' | |
| | ———— French Beans ———— |
| 9'' 40 Celery – | |
| 9'' plants | ———— French Beans ———— 1'6'' |
| 9'' | ———— French Beans ———— 1'6'' |
| 2'0'' 5'6'' | |
| | ———— Dwarf Broad Beans ———— |
| 1'0'' | ———— Dwarf Broad Beans ———— |
| 2'0'' | |
| 6'' | ———— Dwarf Peas ———— |
| 1'9'' | |
| | ———— Runner Beans ———— |
| 1'3'' | ———— Runner Beans ———— |
| 1'0'' | |
| 6'' | ——— Parsley ——— Early Lettuce ——— |

20'

Suggested length of rows 20ft

## POTATO GROUP

NOVEMBER TO JANUARY: dig and manure. Don't put any manure under the tomatoes or they'll be all leaf, but put some extra under the marrows and sweet corn.

FEBRUARY: don't spread any lime. The plants don't need it and it would make the potatoes scabby.

The tomatoes are kept well away from the potatoes: potatoes might survive a touch of potato blight but the tomatoes wouldn't – it could devastate them in a week.

The plan allows for six bush marrows but only grow four if your soil is rich.

Use the first row of early potatoes as soon as they're ready – to give the seakale room to develop. You can grow some lettuce where they've been. Spread a little lime before you sow the seed but keep it off the other crops.

The sweet corn is grown in a 'block' to assist pollination.

## LEGUMES GROUP

NOVEMBER: dig and manure the whole plot. Put plenty of manure under where the runner beans and celery will be.

FEBRUARY: lime to achieve a pH reaction of 6.5. This group follows the potatoes from last year so the soil will almost certainly need liming but do check with a lime testing kit.

The two varieties of broad beans are kept well apart so that if blackfly attack one lot it won't necessarily spread to the others. If the broad beans are out of the ground by mid July try a late sowing of more French beans in the vacant space.

Runner beans are best grown beside a path – less shading of other plants and they're easier to attend to – so in some years the Master Plan reverses the sowing order of this group.

Sow the lettuce half a row at a time or choose several varieties that mature at different times.

Leave the pea and bean roots in the soil when you clear away the crops – their nodules will help to supply nitrogen for the brassicas next year.

The word 'manure' means any type of compost or organic manure. See the chapter on 'Manure, Compost and Fertilisers'.

Most soils are too acid and need applications of lime to achieve the correct pH level. The right level of acidity can make a big difference to your crops. If you garden on chalk, however, you probably won't need to add lime. So buy a simple lime testing kit and check your soil each year – it's worth it.

## ONIONS & BRASSICAS

| Spacing | Crop |
|---|---|
| 1'0" | Leeks |
| 1'0" | Leeks |
| 1'0" | Leeks |
| 1'0" | |
| 6" 6" | Onions |
| 6" 6" | Onions |
| | Onions |
| 1'0" | Shallots |
| 1'0" | Kohl Rabi |
| 1'0" | Savoy Cabbage |
| 1'0" | Radish |
| 1'0" | Spring Onions |
| 2'0" | Followed by Savoy Cabbage |
| | Broccoli – 'Calabrese' |
| 1'3" | Kohl Rabi |
| 1'3" | Brussel Sprouts |
| 1'6" | Summer Cabbage |
| 2'0" | Followed by Winter Radish |
| 1'0" | Broccoli – 'Purple Sprouting' |

Suggested length of rows 20ft

## ROOTS GROUP

| Spacing | Crop |
|---|---|
| 1'0" | Swede |
| 9" | Early Radish |
| 9" | Swede |
| 1'6" | Turnips |
| 1'0" | Followed by Spinach or Lettuce |
| 1'6" | Turnips |
| | Spinach Beet |
| 1'6" | Parsnips |
| 1'0" | Parsnips |
| 1'0" | Parsnips |
| 1'0" | Carrots |
| 1'0" | Carrots |
| 1'0" | Carrots |
| 1'0" | Carrots |
| 1'0" | Beetroot |
| 1'0" | Beetroot |
| 1'0" | Beetroot |
| 1'0" | Beetroot |
| 1'0" | Sugar Loaf Chicory |
| 1'0" | |

20'

Suggested length of rows 20ft

NOVEMBER: dig and manure the whole plot. Put plenty of manure under the leeks.

FEBRUARY: lime the soil to achieve a pH reaction of 6.5–7.0. These plants need an almost neutral soil and lime helps to control club root.

All these plants like a rich soil. The brassicas follow the peas and beans from last year so they'll benefit from those nitrogen fixing nodules.

The plan has been arranged so that the kohl rabi and summer cabbage are out of the way by the time the broccoli, sprouts and Savoys need plenty of room. If the spring onions are still in the ground when you put out the Savoys just pull enough to make room for each plant then use the rest as the Savoys start to grow.

NOVEMBER TO FEBRUARY: dig the plot as soon as it is clear of crops from the previous year but don't add any manure as it would make the parsnips and carrots 'fork' and spoil the taste of the swedes and turnips.

FEBRUARY: lime only if the pH reaction has fallen below 6.0.

Although potatoes are sometimes referred to as a 'root' crop they are not included with this group as they need different soil conditions. This group will benefit from the manure given to the brassicas and onions the previous year – deep digging is all that is required.

Turnips and swedes are brassicas so do sow them where shown so that they don't follow where other brassicas have been in previous years. If the turnips are out of the ground by mid July you can sow some spinach or lettuce in their place.

# THE LARGE MASTER PLAN:
## Total Layout for 'Long' Gardens: Year 1

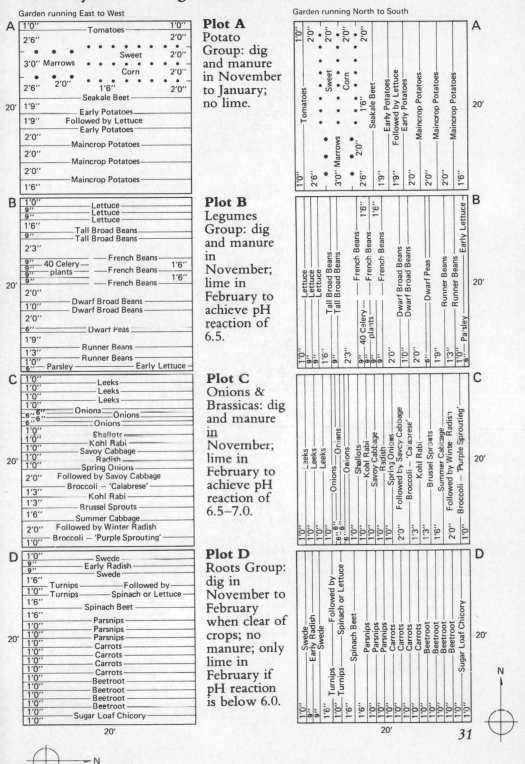

Garden running East to West

Garden running North to South

**Plot A**
Potato Group: dig and manure in November to January; no lime.

**Plot B**
Legumes Group: dig and manure in November; lime in February to achieve pH reaction of 6.5.

**Plot C**
Onions & Brassicas: dig and manure in November; lime in February to achieve pH reaction of 6.5–7.0.

**Plot D**
Roots Group: dig in November to February when clear of crops; no manure; only lime in February if pH reaction is below 6.0.

# THE LARGE MASTER PLAN:
## Total Layout for 'Long' Gardens: Year 2

Garden running East to West | Garden running North to South

**A**

6" — Parsley — Early Lettuce
1'0"
1'3" — Runner Beans
1'9" — Runner Beans
6" — Dwarf Peas
2'0"
1'0" — Dwarf Broad Beans
2'0" — Dwarf Broad Beans
20'
9" — French Beans — 1'6"
9" — 40 Celery — French Beans
9" — plants — French Beans — 1'6"
2'3"
9" — Tall Broad Beans
9" — Tall Broad Beans
1'6" — Lettuce
9" — Lettuce
9" — Lettuce
1'0"

## Plot A
Legumes Group: dig and manure in November; lime in February to achieve pH reaction of 6.5.

*(North to South view: Lettuce, Lettuce, Lettuce, Tall Broad Beans, Tall Broad Beans, French Beans 1'6", French Beans, French Beans, 40 Celery plants, Dwarf Broad Beans, Dwarf Broad Beans, Dwarf Peas, Runner Beans, Runner Beans, Parsley, Early Lettuce; measurements 1'0", 9", 1'6", 9", 2'3", 9", 9", 9", 2'0", 1'0", 2'0", 6", 1'9", 1'3", 1'0", 6")*

**B**

1'0" — Leeks
1'0" — Leeks
1'0" — Leeks
1'0"
6" 6" — Onions — Onions
6" 6" — Onions
1'0" — Shallots
1'0" — Kohl Rabi
1'0" — Savoy Cabbage
1'0" — Radish
1'0" — Spring Onions
2'0" — Followed by Savoy Cabbage
1'3" — Broccoli – 'Calabrese'
1'3" — Kohl Rabi
1'6" — Brussel Sprouts
— Summer Cabbage
2'0" — Followed by Winter Radish
1'0" — Broccoli – 'Purple Sprouting'

## Plot B
Onions & Brassicas: dig and manure in November; lime in February to achieve pH reaction of 6.5–7.0.

*(North to South view: Leeks, Leeks, Leeks, Onions, Onions, Onions, Shallots, Kohl Rabi, Savoy Cabbage, Radish, Spring Onions, Followed by Savoy Cabbage, Broccoli – 'Calabrese', Kohl Rabi, Brussel Sprouts, Summer Cabbage, Followed by Winter Radish, Broccoli – 'Purple Sprouting'; measurements 1'0", 1'0", 1'0", 1'0", 6" 6", 6" 6", 1'0", 1'0", 1'0", 1'0", 1'0", 2'0", 1'3", 1'3", 1'6", 2'0", 1'0")*

**C**

1'0" — Swede
9" — Early Radish
9" — Swede
1'6"
1'0" — Turnips — Followed by
1'0" — Turnips — Spinach or Lettuce
1'6"
1'6" — Spinach Beet
1'0" — Parsnips
1'0" — Parsnips
1'0" — Parsnips
1'0" — Carrots
1'0" — Carrots
1'0" — Carrots
1'0" — Carrots
1'0" — Beetroot
1'0" — Beetroot
1'0" — Beetroot
1'0" — Beetroot
1'0" — Sugar Loaf Chicory

## Plot C
Roots Group: dig in November to February when clear of crops; no manure; only lime in February if pH reaction is below 6.0.

*(North to South view: Swede, Early Radish, Swede, Turnips, Turnips, Followed by Spinach or Lettuce, Spinach Beet, Parsnips, Parsnips, Parsnips, Carrots, Carrots, Carrots, Carrots, Beetroot, Beetroot, Beetroot, Beetroot, Sugar Loaf Chicory; measurements 1'0", 9", 1'6", 1'0", 1'6", 1'6", 1'0", 1'0", 1'0", 1'0", 1'0", 1'0", 1'0", 1'0", 1'0", 1'0", 1'0", 1'0")*

**D**

1'0" — Tomatoes — 1'0"
2'6" — 2'0"
— Sweet — 2'0"
3'0" Marrows — Corn — 2'0"
2'6" — 2'0" — 1'6" — 2'0"
— Seakale Beet
20' 1'9"
1'9" — Early Potatoes
— Followed by Lettuce
— Early Potatoes
2'0"
— Maincrop Potatoes
2'0"
— Maincrop Potatoes
2'0"
— Maincrop Potatoes
1'6"

## Plot D
Potato Group: dig and manure in November to January; no lime.

*(North to South view: Tomatoes, Sweet Corn, Marrows, Seakale Beet, Early Potatoes, Followed by Lettuce, Early Potatoes, Maincrop Potatoes, Maincrop Potatoes, Maincrop Potatoes; measurements 1'0", 2'6", 3'0" Marrows, 2'6", 2'0", 1'9", 1'9", 2'0", 2'0", 1'6")*

*32*          20'                    20'

N

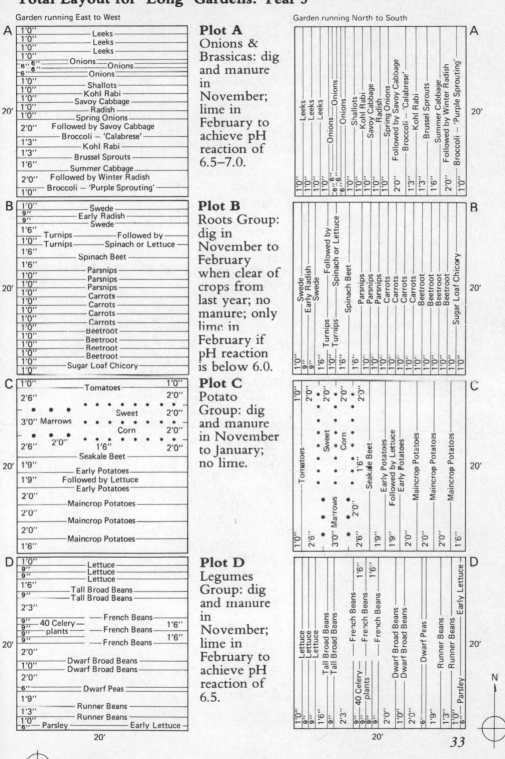

Garden running East to West

**Plot A**
Onions & Brassicas: dig and manure in November; lime in February to achieve pH reaction of 6.5–7.0.

**Plot B**
Roots Group: dig in November to February when clear of crops from last year; no manure; only lime in February if pH reaction is below 6.0.

**Plot C**
Potato Group: dig and manure in November to January; no lime.

**Plot D**
Legumes Group: dig and manure in November; lime in February to achieve pH reaction of 6.5.

Garden running North to South

# THE LARGE MASTER PLAN:
## Total Layout for 'Long' Gardens: Year 4

Garden running East to West

Garden running North to South

**A**

| | |
|---|---|
| 1'0" | Swede |
| 9" | Early Radish |
| 9" | Swede |
| 1'6" | Turnips ———— Followed by |
| 1'0" | Turnips ———— Spinach or Lettuce |
| 1'6" | |
| 1'6" | Spinach Beet |
| 1'0" | Parsnips |
| 1'0" | Parsnips |
| 1'0" | Parsnips |
| 1'0" | Carrots |
| 1'0" | Carrots |
| 1'0" | Carrots |
| 1'0" | Carrots |
| 1'0" | Beetroot |
| 1'0" | Beetroot |
| 1'0" | Beetroot |
| 1'0" | Beetroot |
| 1'0" | Sugar Loaf Chicory |
| 1'0" | |

20'

**Plot A**
Roots Group: dig in November to February as soon as clear of crops from last year; no manure; only apply lime in February if pH reaction is below 6.0.

**A**

Swede · Early Radish · Swede · Turnips · Turnips · Spinach Beet · Parsnips · Parsnips · Parsnips · Carrots · Carrots · Carrots · Carrots · Beetroot · Beetroot · Beetroot · Beetroot · Sugar Loaf Chicory · Followed by Spinach or Lettuce

(1'0" · 9" · 9" · 1'6" · 1'0" · 1'6" · 1'6" · 1'0" · 1'0" · 1'0" · 1'0" · 1'0" · 1'0" · 1'0" · 1'0" · 1'0" · 1'0" · 1'0" · 1'0")

20'

**B**

| | | |
|---|---|---|
| 1'0" | Tomatoes | 1'0" |
| 2'6" | | 2'0" |
| | · · · · · · · | 2'0" |
| 3'0" Marrows | · · · · Sweet | 2'0" |
| | · · · · Corn | 2'0" |
| 2'6" | 2'0" · · · · 1'6" | 2'0" |
| 1'9" | Seakale Beet | |
| 1'9" | Early Potatoes | |
| 2'0" | Followed by Lettuce / Early Potatoes | |
| 2'0" | Maincrop Potatoes | |
| 2'0" | Maincrop Potatoes | |
| 1'6" | Maincrop Potatoes | |

20'

**Plot B**
Potato Group: dig and manure in November to January; no lime.

**B**

Tomatoes · Marrows · Sweet Corn · Seakale Beet · Early Potatoes · Followed by Lettuce · Early Potatoes · Maincrop Potatoes · Maincrop Potatoes · Maincrop Potatoes

(1'0" · 2'0" · 2'0" · 2'0" · 2'0" · 2'0" · 1'9" · 1'9" · 2'0" · 2'0" · 2'0" · 1'6")

20'

**C**

| | |
|---|---|
| 6" 1'0" | Parsley ———— Early Lettuce |
| 1'3" | Runner Beans |
| 1'9" | Runner Beans |
| 6" | Dwarf Peas |
| 2'0" | |
| 1'0" | Dwarf Broad Beans |
| 2'0" | Dwarf Broad Beans |
| 9" 9" 9" | 40 Celery plants ———— French Beans 1'6" / French Beans / French Beans 1'6" |
| 2'3" | |
| 9" | Tall Broad Beans |
| 1'6" | Tall Broad Beans |
| 9" | Lettuce |
| 9" | Lettuce |
| 1'0" | Lettuce |

20'

**Plot C**
Legumes Group: dig and manure in November; lime in February to achieve pH reaction of 6.5.

**C**

Lettuce · Lettuce · Lettuce · Tall Broad Beans · Tall Broad Beans · French Beans 1'6" · French Beans 1'6" · French Beans · 40 Celery plants · Dwarf Broad Beans · Dwarf Broad Beans · Dwarf Peas · Runner Beans · Runner Beans · Parsley · Early Lettuce

(1'0" · 9" · 9" · 1'6" · 9" · 2'3" · 9" · 9" · 9" · 2'0" · 1'0" · 2'0" · 6" · 1'9" · 1'3" · 1'0" · 6")

20'

**D**

| | |
|---|---|
| 1'0" | Leeks |
| 1'0" | Leeks |
| 1'0" | Leeks |
| 1'0" | Onions |
| 6" 6" | Onions ———— Onions |
| 6" 6" | Onions |
| 1'0" | Shallots |
| 1'0" | Kohl Rabi |
| 1'0" | Savoy Cabbage |
| 1'0" | Radish |
| 1'0" | Spring Onions |
| 2'0" | Followed by Savoy Cabbage |
| 1'3" | Broccoli – 'Calabrese' |
| 1'3" | Kohl Rabi |
| 1'6" | Brussel Sprouts |
| | Summer Cabbage |
| 2'0" | Followed by Winter Radish |
| 1'0" | Broccoli – 'Purple Sprouting' |

20'

**Plot D**
Onions & Brassicas: dig and manure in November; lime in February to achieve pH reaction of 6.5–7.0.

**D**

Leeks · Leeks · Leeks · Onions · Onions · Onions · Shallots · Kohl Rabi · Savoy Cabbage · Radish · Spring Onions · Followed by Savoy Cabbage · Broccoli – 'Calabrese' · Kohl Rabi · Brussel Sprouts · Summer Cabbage · Followed by Winter Radish · Broccoli – 'Purple Sprouting'

(1'0" · 1'0" · 1'0" · 1'0" · 6" 6" · 6" 6" · 1'0" · 1'0" · 1'0" · 1'0" · 1'0" · 2'0" · 1'3" · 1'3" · 1'6" · 2'0" · 1'0")

20'

20'

N

# THE LARGE MASTER PLAN:
## Total Layout for a 'Square' Garden: Year 1

**A**

| | | |
|---|---|---|
| 1'0" | ———— Outdoor Tomatoes ———— | 1'0" |
| 2'6" | | 2'0" |
| 3'0" | Bush Marrows or Courgettes · · · Sweet · · · Corn | 2'0" / 2'0" / 2'0" |
| 2'6" | 2'0" · · 1'6" · · · · | 2'0" |
| 1'9" | ———— Seakale Beet ———— | |
| 1'9" | ———— Early Potatoes ———— Followed by Lettuce ———— Early Potatoes ———— | |
| 2'0" | ———— Maincrop Potatoes ———— | |
| 2'0" | ———— Maincrop Potatoes ———— | |
| 2'0" | ———— Maincrop Potatoes ———— | |
| 1'6" | | |

20'

**B**

| | |
|---|---|
| 6" 1'0" | Parsley ———— Early Lettuce ———— |
| 1'3" | Runner Beans — Runner Beans — |
| 1'9" | |
| 6" | ———— Dwarf Peas ———— |
| 2'0" | |
| 1'0" | Dwarf Broad Beans — Dwarf Broad Beans — |
| 2'0" | |
| 9" | ———— French Beans ———— |
| 9" | 40 Celery- — French Beans — 1'6" |
| 9" | plants — French Beans — 1'6" |
| 2'3" 6'0" | |
| 9" | Tall Broad Beans — Tall Broad Beans — |
| 1'6" | |
| 9" | — Lettuce — |
| 9" | — Lettuce — |
| 1'0" | — Lettuce — |

20'

20'

**D**

| | |
|---|---|
| 1'0" | ———— Swede ———— |
| 9" | ———— Early Radish ———— |
| 9" | ———— Swede ———— |
| 1'6" | Turnips |
| 1'0" | Followed by Spinach or Lettuce |
| 1'6" | Turnips |
| 1'6" | — Spinach Beet — |
| 1'0" | — Parsnips — |
| 1'0" | — Parsnips — |
| 1'0" | — Parsnips — |
| 1'0" | — Carrots — |
| 1'0" | — Carrots — |
| 1'0" | — Carrots — |
| 1'0" | — Carrots — |
| 1'0" | — Beetroot — |
| 1'0" | — Beetroot — |
| 1'0" | — Beetroot — |
| 1'0" | — Beetroot — |
| 1'0" | — Sugar Loaf Chicory — |

20'

**C**

| | |
|---|---|
| 1'0" | — Leeks — |
| 1'0" | — Leeks — |
| 1'0" | — Leeks — |
| 1'0" | — Leeks — |
| 6" 6" | — Onions — |
| 6" 6" | — Onions — |
| 6" 6" | — Onions — |
| 1'0" | — Shallots — |
| 1'0" | — Kohl Rabi — |
| 1'0" | — Savoy Cabbage — |
| 1'0" | — Radish — |
| 1'0" | Spring Onions |
| 2'0" | Followed by Savoy Cabbage |
| 1'3" | — Broccoli – 'Calabrese' — |
| 1'3" | — Kohl Rabi — |
| 1'6" | — Brussel Sprouts — |
| 1'6" | — Summer Cabbage — |
| 2'0" | Followed by Winter Radish |
| 1'0" | Broccoli – 'Purple Sprouting' — |

N

## Plot A
Potato Group: dig and manure November to January; no lime.

## Plot D
Roots Group: dig in November to February when clear of crops; no manure; only lime in February if pH reaction is below 6.0.

## Plot B
Legumes Group: dig and manure November; lime in February to achieve pH reaction of 6.5.

## Plot C
Onions & Brassicas: dig and manure November; lime in February to achieve pH reaction 6.5–7.0.

# THE LARGE MASTER PLAN:
## Total Layout for a 'Square' Garden: Year 2

**A**

- 6" Parsley — Early Lettuce
- 1'0" Runner Beans
- 1'3" Runner Beans
- 1'9"
- 6" Dwarf Peas
- 2'0"
- 1'0" Dwarf Broad Beans
- Dwarf Broad Beans
- 2'0"
- 9" 40 Celery plants — French Beans — 1'6"
- 9" French Beans — 1'6"
- 9" French Beans
- 2'3" 6'0"
- Tall Broad Beans
- 9" Tall Broad Beans
- 1'6"
- Lettuce
- 9" Lettuce
- 9" Lettuce
- 1'0"

20'

**B**

20'

- 1'0" Leeks
- 1'0" Leeks
- 1'0" Leeks
- 1'0" Onions
- 6" 6" Onions
- 6" 6" Onions
- 1'0" Shallots
- 1'0" Kohl Rabi
- 1'0" Savoy Cabbage
- 1'0" Radish
- 1'0" Spring Onions
- 2'0" Followed by Savoy Cabbage
- Broccoli – 'Calabrese'
- 1'3" Kohl Rabi
- 1'3" Brussel Sprouts
- 1'6" Summer Cabbage
- 2'0" Followed by Winter Radish
- Broccoli – 'Purple Sprouting'
- 1'0"

20'

**D**

- 1'0" Outdoor Tomatoes 1'0"
- 2'6" 2'0"
- 3'0" Bush Marrows or Courgettes — Sweet Corn 2'0" 2'0"
- 2'6" 2'0" 1'6" 2'0"
- Seakale Beet
- 1'9" Early Potatoes — Followed by Lettuce
- 1'9" Early Potatoes
- 2'0" Maincrop Potatoes
- 2'0" Maincrop Potatoes
- 2'0" Maincrop Potatoes
- 1'6"

**C**

20

- 1'0" Swede
- 9" Early Radish
- 9" Swede
- 1'6" Turnips
- 1'0" Followed by Spinach or Lettuce
- 1'6" Turnips
- Spinach Beet
- 1'6" Parsnips
- 1'0" Parsnips
- 1'0" Parsnips
- 1'0" Carrots
- 1'0" Carrots
- 1'0" Carrots
- 1'0" Carrots
- 1'0" Beetroot
- 1'0" Beetroot
- 1'0" Beetroot
- 1'0" Beetroot
- 1'0" Sugar Loaf Chicory
- 1'0"

N

## Plot A
Legumes Group: dig and manure November; lime in February to achieve pH reaction of 6.5.

## Plot D
Potato Group: dig and manure November to January; no lime.

## Plot B
Onions & Brassicas: dig and manure November; lime in February to achieve pH reaction of 6.5–7.0.

## Plot C
Roots Group: dig in November to February when clear of crops; no manure; no lime unless pH reaction has fallen below 6.0.

# THE LARGE MASTER PLAN:
## Total Layout for a 'Square' Garden: Year 3

**A**

| | |
|---|---|
| 1'0" | Leeks |
| 1'0" | Leeks |
| 1'0" | Leeks |
| 1'0" | Leeks |
| 6", 6" | Onions |
| 6", 6" | Onions |
| | Onions |
| 1'0" | Shallots |
| 1'0" | Kohl Rabi |
| 1'0" | Savoy Cabbage |
| 1'0" | Radish |
| 1'0" | Spring Onions |
| 2'0" | Followed by Savoy Cabbage |
| | Broccoli – 'Calabrese' |
| 1'3" | Kohl Rabi |
| 1'3" | Brussel Sprouts |
| 1'6" | Summer Cabbage |
| 2'0" | Followed by Winter Radish |
| 1'0" | Broccoli – 'Purple Sprouting' |

20'

**B**

| | |
|---|---|
| 1'0" | Swede |
| 9" | Early Radish |
| 9" | Swede |
| 1'6" | Turnips |
| 1'0" | Followed by Spinach or Lettuce |
| 1'6" | Turnips |
| | Spinach Beet |
| 1'6" | Parsnips |
| 1'0" | Parsnips |
| 1'0" | Parsnips |
| 1'0" | Carrots |
| 1'0" | Carrots |
| 1'0" | Carrots |
| 1'0" | Carrots |
| 1'0" | Beetroot |
| 1'0" | Beetroot |
| 1'0" | Beetroot |
| 1'0" | Beetroot |
| 1'0" | Sugar Loaf Chicory |
| 1'0" | |

20'     20'

**D**

| | |
|---|---|
| 1'0" | Lettuce |
| 9" | Lettuce |
| 9" | Lettuce |
| 1'6" | |
| 9" | Tall Broad Beans |
| | Tall Broad Beans |
| 2'3" | |
| | French Beans |
| 9", 9" | 40 Celery — French Beans — 1'6" |
| 9" | plants — |
| 9" | French Beans — 1'6" |
| 2'0", 6'0" | |
| 1'0" | Dwarf Broad Beans |
| | Dwarf Broad Beans |
| 2'0" | |
| 6" | Dwarf Peas |
| 1'9" | |
| 1'3" | Runner Beans |
| | Runner Beans |
| 1'0", 6" | Parsley — Early Lettuce |

**C**

| | |
|---|---|
| 1'0" | Outdoor Tomatoes — 1'0" |
| 2'6" | 2'0" |
| 3'0" | Bush Marrows / or Courgettes — Sweet Corn — 2'0" 2'0" |
| 2'6" | 2'0" 2'0" |
| 1'9" | Seakale Beet |
| 1'9" | Early Potatoes / Followed by Lettuce / Early Potatoes |
| 2'0" | Maincrop Potatoes |
| 2'0" | Maincrop Potatoes |
| 2'0" | Maincrop Potatoes |
| 1'6" | |

20'

—N

## Plot A
Onions & Brassicas: dig and manure November; lime in February to achieve pH reaction 6.5–7.0.

## Plot B
Roots Group: dig November to February when clear of crops; no manure; no lime unless pH reaction has fallen below 6.0.

## Plot D
Legumes Group: dig and manure November; lime in February to achieve pH reaction of 6.5.

## Plot C
Potato Group: dig and manure November to January; no lime.

# THE LARGE MASTER PLAN:
## Total Layout for a 'Square' Garden: Year 4

**A**

| | |
|---|---|
| 1'0" | Swede |
| 9" | Early Radish |
| 9" | Swede |
| 1'6" | Turnips |
| 1'0" | Followed by Spinach or Lettuce |
| 1'6" | Turnips |
| | Spinach Beet |
| 1'6" | Parsnips |
| 1'0" | Parsnips |
| 1'0" | Parsnips |
| 1'0" | Carrots |
| 1'0" | Carrots |
| 1'0" | Carrots |
| 1'0" | Carrots |
| 1'0" | Beetroot |
| 1'0" | Beetroot |
| 1'0" | Beetroot |
| 1'0" | Beetroot |
| 1'0" | Sugar Loaf Chicory |
| 1'0" | |

20'

**B**

| | | |
|---|---|---|
| 1'0" | Outdoor Tomatoes | 1'0" |
| 2'6" | | 2'0" |
| 3'0" | Bush Marrows or Courgettes — Sweet Corn | 2'0" |
| 2'6" | 2'0" 1'6" | 2'0" |
| | Seakale Beet | |
| 1'9" | Early Potatoes | |
| 1'9" | Followed by Lettuce / Early Potatoes | |
| 2'0" | Maincrop Potatoes | |
| 2'0" | Maincrop Potatoes | |
| 2'0" | Maincrop Potatoes | |
| 1'6" | | |

20'

**D**

| | |
|---|---|
| 1'0" | Leeks |
| 1'0" | Leeks |
| 1'0" | Leeks |
| 1'0" | Onions |
| 6",6" | Onions |
| 6",6" | Onions |
| 1'0" | Shallots |
| 1'0" | Kohl Rabi |
| 1'0" | Savoy Cabbage |
| 1'0" | Radish |
| 1'0" | Spring Onions |
| 2'0" | Followed by Savoy Cabbage |
| | Broccoli – 'Calabrese' |
| 1'3" | Kohl Rabi |
| 1'3" | Brussel Sprouts |
| 1'6" | Summer Cabbage |
| 2'0" | Followed by Winter Radish |
| 1'0" | Broccoli – 'Purple Sprouting' |

20'

**C**

| | | |
|---|---|---|
| 1'0" | Lettuce | |
| 9" | Lettuce | |
| 9" | Lettuce | |
| 1'6" | | |
| 9" | Tall Broad Beans | |
| | Tall Broad Beans | |
| 2'3" | | |
| 9" | French Beans | 1'6" |
| 9" | 40 Celery plants — French Beans | |
| 9" | | 1'6" |
| 9" | French Beans | |
| 2'0" 6'0" | | |
| 1'0" | Dwarf Broad Beans | |
| | Dwarf Broad Beans | |
| 2'0" | | |
| 6" | Dwarf Peas | |
| 1'9" | | |
| | Runner Beans | |
| 1'3" | Runner Beans | |
| 1'0" 6" | Parsley — Early Lettuce | |

N

## Plot A
Roots Group: dig in November to February when clear of crops; no manure; no lime unless pH reaction has fallen below 6.0.

## Plot D
Onions & Brassicas: dig and manure November; lime in February to achieve pH reaction of 6.5–7.0.

## Plot B
Potato Group: dig and manure November to January; no lime.

## Plot C
Legumes Group: dig and manure November; lime in February to achieve pH reaction of 6.5.

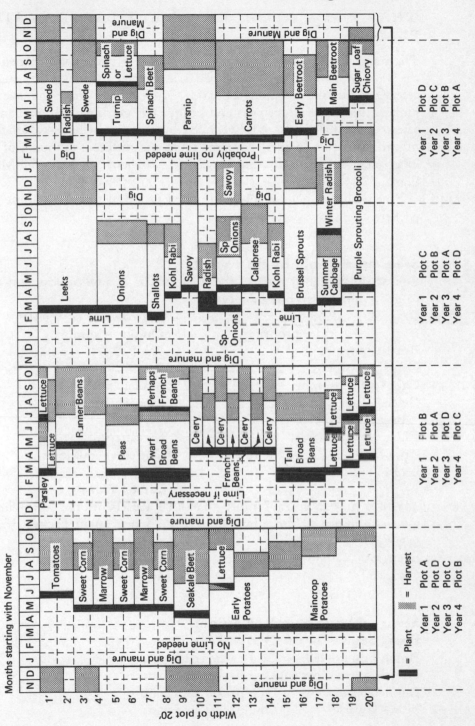

## WHAT SEEDS TO ORDER FOR THE LARGE MASTER PLAN

The number of seeds that a supplier puts in a packet will depend on the variety, its cost of production and its size. Some seeds, such as celery, are as fine as grains of sand. Others range from the size of a pinhead up to the larger peas and beans. The germination rate can also affect the number of seeds we need but seedsmen have to abide by minimum requirements. Different firms put different amounts of seed in a packet but the following should be sufficient for the Large Master Plan.

You will find helpful advice in seed catalogues and on some seed packets.

### Seeds usually sold by the packet

One small packet of each of these should be enough unless you want to grow more than one variety:

Broccoli – calabrese
Broccoli – purple sprouting
Brussels sprouts
Cabbage – Savoy
Cabbage – summer
Celery – self blanching
  or American green
Chicory – sugar loaf
Kohl rabi
Leeks

Marrows or courgettes
Onions – spring
Parsley
Parsnip
Seakale beet
Spinach beet
Swede
Sweet corn
Tomato – outdoor
Turnip
Winter radish

You'll probably want more than one variety of the following to give continuity of cropping, but keep to one small packet of each variety:

Beetroot
Carrot

Lettuce
Radish

### Seeds sold by volume or weight

Broad beans – dwarf  One packet or $\frac{1}{4}$ pint
Broad beans – tall  One packet or $\frac{1}{4}$ pint
French beans – dwarf  One packet or $\frac{1}{4}$ pint
Runner beans  One packet or $\frac{1}{4}$ pint
Peas – dwarf  One packet or $\frac{1}{4}$ pint

| Onion sets* | 2 lb: this should give 240 sets planted 4–6 in. apart. |
| Shallots* | 2 or 3 lb: you'll need 40 shallots planted 6 in. apart. |
| Potatoes – early* | 7 lb: you'll need 40 potatoes planted 1 ft apart. |
| Potatoes – main* | 7 lb: you'll need 36 potatoes planted 1 ft 6 in. apart |

*These weights are approximate as the size of the 'seed' will vary.

## Plants

You may wish to get plants of the following instead of raising them from seed:

| Beans – French | 54 plants | Marrows or courgettes | 6 plants |
| Beans – runner | 52 plants | Sweet corn | 24 plants |
| Celery – self blanching | 40 plants | Tomatoes – outdoor | 13 plants |
| Leeks | 120 plants | Any of the brassicas | |

## Alternatives

If you decide to grow any of the 'alternatives' listed on page 74 a small packet of any of the following will suffice:

Capsicum (peppers)
Cauliflower
Celeriac
Chinese cabbage
Corn salad
Cucumber – outdoor
    or ridge
Curly kale (borecole)
Endive
Haricot beans
Melons – cantaloupe
Salsify
Scorzonera
Spinach

GARLIC: one small 'clove' is used for each plant and you get about eight garlic cloves to the oz.

JERUSALEM ARTICHOKES: these are grown from tubers. Twenty tubers (enough for one 20 ft row) would weigh about 2 lb depending on size.

See the 'Sowing and Harvesting Guide' on page 83.

# 4. The Medium Master Plan

## Four plots each 15 ft wide

This plan is based on the Large Master Plan except that the Brussels sprouts and tall broad beans have been omitted as they need a lot of room. Otherwise it includes all the vegetables in the larger plan – thirty different kinds – but less of them. If you want to grow something different there is a list of 'Alternative Crops' on page 74.

The lines on the plans are exactly where the drills for the seeds should be made and the distances given are those between one drill and the next. Take out a 6 in. wide drill for the peas.

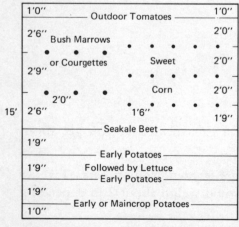

## POTATO GROUP

NOVEMBER TO JANUARY: dig and manure the plot where this group are to go but don't put any manure under the tomatoes. Put any extra manure under the marrows.

FEBRUARY: don't spread any lime – the potatoes and tomatoes don't like it.

## First plot (15' × 15')

```
1'0"  ──────── Lettuce ────────
9"    ──────── Lettuce ────────
1'6"                            2'0"
9"   28 Celery ─── French Beans ───
9"    plants                     1'3"
9"           ─── French Beans ───
1'6"   5'6"                     2'0"
15'  ──── Dwarf Broad Beans ────
1'0"  ──── Dwarf Broad Beans ────
2'0"
6"   ──────── Dwarf Peas ────────
1'9"
1'3"  ──────── Runner Beans ───────
1'0"  ──────── Runner Beans ───────
6"   ── Parsley ──────── Early Lettuce ──
```

## Second plot (15')

```
9"    ──────── Leeks ────────
1'0"  ──────── Leeks ────────
1'0"
6"   ──────── Onions ────────
6"   ──────── Onions ────────
6"   ──────── Onions ────────
1'0"  ──────── Shallots ───────
1'3"  ──────── Kohl Rabi ───────
15'  1'3"  Spring Onions
          Followed by Savoy Cabbage
1'3"  ──────── Kohl Rabi ───────
1'3"  ── Broccoli – 'Calabrese' ──
1'3"  ──── Summer Cabbage ────
1'3"  Followed by Winter Radish
          ── Summer Cabbage ──
1'3"  ── Broccoli – 'Purple Sprouting' ──
6"   ──────── Radish ────────
```

## Third plot (15' × 15')

```
1'0"  ──────── Swede ────────
9"    ──── Early Radish ────
9"    ──────── Swede ────────
1'6"  ──────── Turnips ───────
1'0"  Followed by Spinach or Lettuce
          ──── Turnips ────
1'6"  ──── Spinach Beet ────
1'6"  ──────── Parsnips ───────
15'  1'0"  ──────── Parsnips ───────
1'0"  ──────── Carrots ────────
1'0"  ──────── Carrots ────────
1'0"  ──────── Beetroot ───────
1'0"  ──────── Beetroot ───────
1'0"  ──── Sugar Loaf Chicory ────
1'0"
                15'
```

## LEGUMES GROUP

NOVEMBER: dig and manure the whole plot where you are going to plant this group. Put plenty of manure where the runner beans and celery will be planted.

FEBRUARY: lime the plot, if necessary, to achieve a pH reaction of 6.5.

## ONIONS & BRASSICAS

NOVEMBER: dig and manure the whole plot where these are to go.

FEBRUARY: lime the ground to achieve a pH reaction of 6.5–7.0.

## ROOTS GROUP

NOVEMBER TO FEBRUARY: dig the plot ready for this group as soon as it's clear of the previous year's brassica crops. Don't add any manure as it would make the roots 'fork'.

FEBRUARY ONWARDS: lime any ground that is dug and do the rest as it becomes available, but only lime if the pH reaction has fallen below 6.0.

## ROTATION AND CROPPING SYSTEM FOR THE MEDIUM MASTER PLAN

Treat the garden year as starting in November. Keep exactly to the spacings shown on the plans.

You need four plots, each 15 ft wide. Label them A B C and D and sow the plant groups as shown, making sure the rows run north to south.

### Year 1

Plot A — Potato Group

Plot B — Legumes Group

Plot C — Onions and Brassicas

Plot D — Roots Group

PLOT A: the potatoes are kept well away from the tomatoes to prevent the spread of disease. Once the early potatoes are out of the way sow some lettuce in their place.

PLOT B: the runner beans have been put beside a path so that they are easy to attend to. If the broad beans are out of the way by late July sow some more French beans in their place.

PLOT C: pull just enough spring onions to make way for each Savoy plant and then use the rest as you need them. Sow winter radish once you've used the summer cabbage.

PLOT D: if the turnips have been used by July sow some lettuce or spinach in their place.

### Year 2

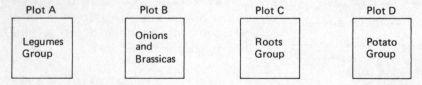

Plot A — Legumes Group

Plot B — Onions and Brassicas

Plot C — Roots Group

Plot D — Potato Group

The same plots are still labelled A B C and D but the plant groups move along one as shown. The rows must still run north to south.

PLOT A: if the move puts the runner beans between two adjoining plots then turn the whole plan over, as it were, to get them alongside a path so that they are easy to look after. But don't do this with any other plant group.

PLOT B: the broccoli and Savoy cabbages need plenty of room to develop but the crops grown between them will be out of the way in plenty of time to give them that space.

## Year 3

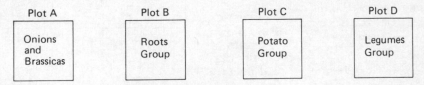

| Plot A | Plot B | Plot C | Plot D |
|--------|--------|--------|--------|
| Onions and Brassicas | Roots Group | Potato Group | Legumes Group |

The plant groups move along again.

PLOT B: when you come to dig the plot in November it will still contain the Savoys and purple sprouting broccoli from last year. Make sure you don't disturb their roots but dig where you can. Complete the digging once they are out of the way. You will still be able to sow this year's seeds at the right time.

## Year 4

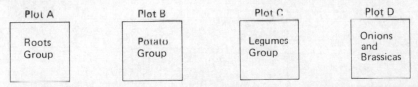

| Plot A | Plot B | Plot C | Plot D |
|--------|--------|--------|--------|
| Roots Group | Potato Group | Legumes Group | Onions and Brassicas |

The plots are still A B C D but the plant groups move along once again.

## Year 5

Go back to Year 1 and start the rotation sequence all over again.

# THE MEDIUM MASTER PLAN:
## Total Layout for 'Long' Gardens: Year 1

Garden running East to West

Garden running North to South

**Plot A**
Potato Group: dig and manure in November to January; no lime.

Plot A (East to West):
- 1'0" — Outdoor Tomatoes — 1'0"
- 2'6" Bush Marrows — 2'0"
- 2'9" or Courgettes — Sweet Corn — 2'0", 2'0", 2'0"
- 15' 2'6" — 2'0" — 1'6" 1'9"
- 1'9" — Seakale Beet
- 1'9" — Early Potatoes
- 1'9" Followed by Lettuce — Early Potatoes
- 1'9" — Early Potatoes or Maincrop — 1'0"

Plot A (North to South):
Outdoor Tomatoes, Bush Marrows, or Courgettes, Sweet, Corn, Seakale Beet, Early Potatoes, Followed by Lettuce, Early Potatoes, Early Potatoes or Maincrop
Measurements: 1'0", 2'0", 2'0", 2'0", 2'0", 1'6", 1'9", 2'6", 2'9", 2'6", 1'9", 1'9", 1'9", 1'0" — 15'

**Plot B**
Legumes Group: dig and manure in November; lime in February to achieve pH reaction of 6.5.

Plot B (East to West):
- 1'0" — Lettuce
- 9" — Lettuce
- 1'6" — 2'0"
- 9" 28 Celery — French Beans
- 9" plants — French Beans — 1'3"
- 9"
- 1'6" 5'6" — 2'0"
- 1'0" — Dwarf Broad Beans
- Dwarf Broad Beans
- 2'0"
- 6" — Dwarf Peas
- 1'9"
- 1'3" — Runner Beans
- 1'3" — Runner Beans
- 1'0"
- 6" Parsley — Early Lettuce

Plot B (North to South):
Lettuce, Lettuce, French Beans, French Beans, 28 Celery plants, Dwarf Broad Beans, Dwarf Broad Beans, Dwarf Peas, Runner Beans, Runner Beans, Parsley, Early Lettuce
Measurements: 1'0", 9", 1'6", 9", 9", 9", 1'6", 5'6", 1'0", 2'0", 6", 1'9", 1'3", 1'0", 6" — 15'
2'0", 1'3", 2'0"

**Plot C**
Onions & Brassicas: dig and manure in November; lime in February to achieve pH reaction of 6.5–7.0.

Plot C (East to West):
- 9" — Leeks
- 1'0" — Leeks
- 1'0"
- 6" — Onions
- 6" — Onions
- 1'0" — Shallots
- 1'3" — Kohl Rabi
- 1'3" — Spring Onions
- 1'3" Followed by Savoy Cabbage
- 1'3" — Kohl Rabi
- 1'3" — Broccoli – 'Calabrese'
- 1'3" — Summer Cabbage
- 1'3" Followed by Winter Radish
- 1'3" — Summer Cabbage
- Broccoli – 'Purple Sprouting'
- 6" — Radish

Plot C (North to South):
Leeks, Leeks, Onions, Onions, Shallots, Kohl Rabi, Spring Onions, Followed by Savoy Cabbage, Kohl Rabi, Broccoli – 'Calabrese', Summer Cabbage, Followed by Winter Radish, Summer Cabbage, Broccoli – 'Purple Sprouting', Radish
Measurements: 9", 1'0", 1'0", 6", 6", 1'0", 1'3", 1'3", 1'3", 1'3", 1'3", 1'3", 1'3", 1'3", 6" — 15'

**Plot D**
Roots Group: dig in November to February when clear of crops; no manure; only lime in February if pH reaction is below 6.0.

Plot D (East to West):
- 1'0" — Swede
- 9" — Early Radish
- 9" — Swede
- 1'6" — Turnips
- 1'0" Followed by Spinach or Lettuce
- 1'6" — Turnips
- Spinach Beet
- 15' 1'6"
- 1'0" — Parsnips
- 1'0" — Parsnips
- 1'0" — Carrots
- 1'0" — Carrots
- 1'0" — Beetroot
- 1'0" — Beetroot
- 1'0" — Sugar Loaf Chicory

Plot D (North to South):
Swede, Early Radish, Swede, Turnips, Followed by Spinach or Lettuce, Turnips, Spinach Beet, Parsnips, Parsnips, Carrots, Carrots, Beetroot, Beetroot, Sugar Loaf Chicory
Measurements: 1'0", 9", 9", 1'6", 1'0", 1'6", 1'6", 1'0", 1'0", 1'0", 1'0", 1'0", 1'0", 1'0" — 15'

15'

N

# THE MEDIUM MASTER PLAN:
## Total Layout for 'Long' Gardens: Year 2

Garden running East to West

Garden running North to South

**A**

| 6" | Parsley | Early Lettuce |
| 1'0" | | |
| 1'3" | Runner Beans | |
| | Runner Beans | |
| 1'9" | | |
| 6" | Dwarf Peas | |
| 2'0" | | |
| 1'0" | Dwarf Broad Beans | |
| | Dwarf Broad Beans | |
| 1'6" | | 2'0" |
| 9" | 28 Celery | French Beans |
| 9" | plants | 1'3" |
| 9" | | French Beans |
| 1'6" | 5'6" | 2'0" |
| | Lettuce | |
| 9" | Lettuce | |
| 1'0" | | |

15'

**Plot A**
Legumes Group: dig and manure in November; lime in February to achieve pH reaction of 6.5.

Garden running North to South columns (Plot A):
Lettuce — 1'0"
Lettuce — 9"
— 1'6"
French Beans — 9" 28 Celery / 9" plants
French Beans — 9"
— 1'6" 5'6"
Dwarf Broad Beans — 1'0"
Dwarf Broad Beans — 2'0"
Dwarf Peas — 6"
Runner Beans — 1'9"
Runner Beans — 1'3"
Parsley — 1'0"
Early Lettuce — 6"

**A** 15'

**B**

| 9" | Leeks |
| 1'0" | Leeks |
| 1'0" | |
| 6" | Onions |
| 6" | Onions |
| 1'0" | |
| 1'3" | Shallots |
| 1'3" | Kohl Rabi |
| 1'3" | Spring Onions |
| 1'3" | Followed by Savoy Cabbage |
| 1'3" | Kohl Rabi |
| 1'3" | Broccoli – 'Calabrese' |
| 1'3" | Summer Cabbage |
| 1'3" | Followed by Winter Radish |
| 1'3" | Summer Cabbage |
| 1'3" | Broccoli – 'Purple Sprouting' |
| 6" | Radish |

15'

**Plot B**
Onions & Brassicas: dig and manure in November; lime in February to achieve pH reaction of 6.5–7.0.

Garden running North to South columns (Plot B):
Leeks — 9"
Leeks — 1'0"
Onions — 1'0"
Onions — 6"
Shallots — 6"
Kohl Rabi — 1'3"
Spring Onions — 1'3"
Followed by Savoy Cabbage — 1'3"
Kohl Rabi — 1'3"
Broccoli – 'Calabrese' — 1'3"
Summer Cabbage — 1'3"
Followed by Winter Radish — 1'3"
Summer Cabbage — 1'3"
Broccoli – 'Purple Sprouting' — 1'3"
Radish — 6"

**B** 15'

**C**

| 1'0" | Swede |
| 9" | Early Radish |
| 9" | Swede |
| 1'6" | |
| | Turnips |
| 1'0" | Followed by Spinach or Lettuce |
| | Turnips |
| 1'6" | Spinach Beet |
| 1'6" | |
| 1'0" | Parsnips |
| 1'0" | Parsnips |
| 1'0" | Carrots |
| 1'0" | Carrots |
| 1'0" | Beetroot |
| 1'0" | Beetroot |
| 1'0" | Sugar Loaf Chicory |

15'

**Plot C**
Roots Group: dig in November to February when clear of crops; no manure; only lime in February if pH reaction is below 6.0.

Garden running North to South columns (Plot C):
Swede — 1'0"
Early Radish — 9"
Swede — 9"
Turnips — 1'6"
Followed by Spinach or Lettuce — 1'0"
Turnips — 1'6"
Spinach Beet — 1'6"
Parsnips — 1'0"
Parsnips — 1'0"
Carrots — 1'0"
Carrots — 1'0"
Beetroot — 1'0"
Beetroot — 1'0"
Sugar Loaf Chicory — 1'0"

**C** 15'

**D**

| 1'0" | Outdoor Tomatoes | 1'0" |
| 2'6" | | 2'0" |
| | Bush Marrows | |
| 2'9" | or Courgettes | Sweet 2'0" |
| | | Corn 2'0" |
| 2'6" | 2'0" | 1'6" 1'9" |
| | Seakale Beet | |
| 1'9" | | |
| | Early Potatoes | |
| 1'9" | Followed by Lettuce | |
| | Early Potatoes | |
| 1'9" | | |
| | Early Potatoes or Maincrop | |
| 1'0" | | |

15'

**Plot D**
Potato Group: dig and manure in November to January; no lime.

Garden running North to South columns (Plot D):
Outdoor Tomatoes — 1'0"
— 2'6"
Bush Marrows — 2'0"
or Courgettes — 2'9" / Sweet 2'0"
Corn — 1'6"
— 2'6" 2'0"
Seakale Beet — 1'9"
Early Potatoes — 1'9"
Followed by Lettuce — 1'9"
Early Potatoes — 1'0"
Early Potatoes or Maincrop

**D** 15'

15'

N

47

# THE MEDIUM MASTER PLAN:
## Total Layout for 'Long' Gardens: Year 3

**Garden running East to West**  ·  **Garden running North to South**

### Plot A
Onions & Brassicas: dig and manure in November; lime in February to achieve pH reaction of 6.5–7.0.

**A** (East to West)

| | |
|---|---|
| 9″ | Leeks |
| 1'0″ | Leeks |
| 1'0″ | |
| 6″ | Onions |
| 6″ | Onions |
| 1'0″ | Shallots |
| 1'3″ | |
| 1'3″ | ...ions |
| 1'3″ | Followed ... Savoy Cabbage |
| 1'3″ | Kohl Rabi |
| 1'3″ | Broccoli – 'Calabrese' |
| 1'3″ | Summer Cabbage |
| 1'3″ | Followed by Winter Radish |
| 1'3″ | Summer Cabbage |
| 1'3″ | Broccoli – 'Purple Sprouting' |
| 6″ | Radish |

15' (left margin)

**A** (North to South): 9″ Leeks · 1'0″ Leeks · 1'0″ Onions · 6″ Onions · 6″ Shallots · 1'0″ Kohl Rabi · 1'3″ Spring Onions · 1'3″ Followed by Savoy Cabbage · 1'3″ Kohl Rabi · 1'3″ Broccoli – 'Calabrese' · 1'3″ Summer Cabbage · 1'3″ Followed by Winter Radish · 1'3″ Summer Cabbage · 1'3″ Broccoli – 'Purple Sprouting' · 6″ Radish — 15'

### Plot B
Roots Group: dig in November to February when clear of crops; no manure; only lime in February if pH reaction is below 6.0.

**B** (East to West)

| | |
|---|---|
| 1'0″ | Swede |
| 9″ | Early Radish |
| 9″ | Swede |
| 1'6″ | Turnips |
| 1'0″ | Followed by Spinach or Lettuce |
| 1'6″ | Turnips |
| 1'6″ | Spinach Beet |
| 1'0″ | Parsnips |
| 1'0″ | Parsnips |
| 1'0″ | Carrots |
| 1'0″ | Carrots |
| 1'0″ | Beetroot |
| 1'0″ | Beetroot |
| 1'0″ | Sugar Loaf Chicory |

15'

**B** (North to South): 1'0″ Swede · 9″ Early Radish · 9″ Swede · 1'6″ Turnips · 1'0″ Followed by Spinach or Lettuce · 1'6″ Turnips · 1'6″ Spinach Beet · 1'0″ Parsnips · 1'0″ Parsnips · 1'0″ Carrots · 1'0″ Carrots · 1'0″ Beetroot · 1'0″ Beetroot · 1'0″ Sugar Loaf Chicory — 15'

### Plot C
Potato Group: dig and manure in November to January; no lime.

**C** (East to West): 1'0″ ... 1'0″ — Outdoor Tomatoes · 2'6″ Bush Marrows 2'0″ · 2'9″ or Courgettes — Sweet 2'0″ · Corn 2'0″ · 2'6″ 2'0″ 1'6″ 1'9″ — Seakale Beet · 1'9″ Early Potatoes · 1'9″ Followed by Lettuce · Early Potatoes · 1'9″ Early Potatoes or Maincrop · 1'0″

15'

**C** (North to South): 1'0″ Outdoor Tomatoes · 2'6″ Bush Marrows 2'0″ · 2'9″ or Courgettes · Sweet 2'0″ · Corn 1'6″ · 2'6″ 2'0″ Seakale Beet · 1'9″ Early Potatoes · 1'9″ Followed by Lettuce · 1'9 Early Potatoes · 1'0″ Early Potatoes or Maincrop — 15'

### Plot D
Legumes Group: dig and manure in November; lime in February to achieve pH reaction of 6.5.

**D** (East to West)

| | |
|---|---|
| 1'0″ | Lettuce |
| 9″ | Lettuce |
| 1'6″ | |
| 9″ 28 Celery | French Beans 2'0″ |
| 9″ plants | French Beans 1'3″ |
| 9″ | |
| 1'6″ 5'6″ | 2'0″ |
| 1'0″ | Dwarf Broad Beans |
| | Dwarf Broad Beans |
| 2'0″ | |
| 6″ | Dwarf Peas |
| 1'9″ | |
| 1'3″ | Runner Beans |
| 1'0″ | Runner Beans |
| 6″ | Parsley — Early Lettuce |

15'

**D** (North to South): 1'0″ Lettuce · 9″ Lettuce · 1'6″ · 9″ 28 Celery 2'0″ French Beans · 9″ plants 1'3″ French Beans · 9″ · 1'6″ 5'6″ 2'0″ Dwarf Broad Beans · 1'0″ Dwarf Broad Beans · 2'0″ Dwarf Peas · 6″ · 1'9″ Runner Beans · 1'3″ Runner Beans · 1'0″ Parsley · 6″ Early Lettuce — 15'

48

15'

N

# THE MEDIUM MASTER PLAN:
## Total Layout for 'Long' Gardens: Year 4

Garden running East to West

Garden running North to South

**Plot A**
Roots Group: dig in November to February when clear of crops; no manure; only lime in February if pH reaction is below 6.0.

### Plot A (East to West)

A — 15'

- 1'0" Swede
- 9" Early Radish
- 9" Swede
- 1'6" Turnips
- 1'0" Followed by Spinach or Lettuce
- Turnips
- 1'6" Spinach Beet
- 1'6" Parsnips
- 1'0" Parsnips
- 1'0" Carrots
- 1'0" Carrots
- 1'0" Beetroot
- 1'0" Beetroot
- 1'0" Sugar Loaf Chicory
- 1'0"

### Plot A (North to South) — 15'

Swede (1'0") | Early Radish (9") | Swede (9") | Turnips (1'6") | Followed by Spinach or Lettuce (1'0") | Turnips (1'6") | Spinach Beet (1'6") | Parsnips (1'6") | Parsnips (1'0") | Carrots (1'0") | Carrots (1'0") | Beetroot (1'0") | Beetroot (1'0") | Sugar Loaf Chicory (1'0")

**Plot B**
Potato Group: dig and manure in November to January; no lime.

### Plot B (East to West)

B — 15'

- 1'0" Outdoor Tomatoes 1'0"
- 2'6" Bush Marrows 2'0"
- 2'9" or Courgettes — Sweet 2'0"
- Corn 2'0"
- 2'6" 2'0" 1'6" 1'9"
- 1'9" Seakale Beet
- 1'9" Early Potatoes
- 1'9" Followed by Lettuce
- Early Potatoes
- 1'9" Early Potatoes or Maincrop
- 1'0"

### Plot B (North to South) — 15'

Outdoor Tomatoes (1'0" 2'0") | Bush Marrows (2'6") | or Courgettes (2'9") — Sweet Corn (2'0" 1'6") | Seakale Beet (2'6" 2'0") | Early Potatoes (1'9") | Followed by Lettuce (1'9") | Early Potatoes (1'9") | Early Potatoes or Maincrop (1'0")

**Plot C**
Legumes Group: dig and manure in November; lime in February to achieve pH reaction of 6.5.

### Plot C (East to West)

C — 16'

- 6" Parsley — Early Lettuce
- 1'0"
- 1'3" Runner Beans
- Runner Beans
- 1'9"
- 6" Dwarf Peas
- 2'0"
- 1'0" Dwarf Broad Beans
- Dwarf Broad Beans
- 1'6" 2'0"
- 9" 28 Celery — French Beans
- 9" plants
- 9" French Beans 1'3"
- 1'6" 5'6" 2'0"
- Lettuce
- 9" Lettuce
- 1'0"

### Plot C (North to South) — 15'

Lettuce (1'0") | Lettuce (9") | French Beans (1'6" 2'0") | French Beans (1'3") | 28 Celery plants (9" 9" 9") | Dwarf Broad Beans (1'6" 5'6" 2'0") | Dwarf Broad Beans (1'0") | Dwarf Peas (2'0") | Runner Beans (6") | Runner Beans (1'9") | Parsley (1'3") | Early Lettuce (1'0" 6")

**Plot D**
Onions & Brassicas: dig and manure in November; lime in February to achieve pH reaction of 6.5–7.0.

### Plot D (East to West)

D — 15'

- 9" Leeks
- 1'0" Leeks
- 1'0"
- 6" Onions
- 6" Onions
- 1'0" Shallots
- 1'3" Kohl Rabi
- 1'3" Spring Onions
- 1'3" Followed by Savoy Cabbage
- 1'3" Kohl Rabi
- 1'3" Broccoli – 'Calabrese'
- 1'3" Summer Cabbage
- 1'3" Followed by Winter Radish
- Summer Cabbage
- 1'3" Broccoli – 'Purple Sprouting'
- 6" Radish

15'

### Plot D (North to South) — 15'

Leeks (9") | Leeks (1'0") | Onions (1'0" 6") | Onions (6") | Shallots (1'0") | Kohl Rabi (1'3") | Spring Onions (1'3") | Followed by Savoy Cabbage (1'3") | Kohl Rabi (1'3") | Broccoli – 'Calabrese' (1'3") | Summer Cabbage (1'3") | Followed by Winter Radish (1'3") | Summer Cabbage (1'3") | Broccoli – 'Purple Sprouting' (1'3") | Radish (6")

49

# THE MEDIUM MASTER PLAN:
## Total Layout for a 'Square' Garden: Year 1

**A**

```
1'0"                                    1'0"
        ——— Outdoor Tomatoes ———
2'6"                                    2'0"
              •   •   •   •   •
   •  Bush Marrows      Sweet          2'0"
2'9"               •   •   •   •   •
   or Courgettes        Corn           2'0"
   •      •        •   •   •   •
         2'0"
2'6"              1'6"      •   •   •   1'9"
                 ——— Seakale Beet ———
1'9"
              ——— Early Potatoes ———
1'9"          Followed by Lettuce
              ——— Early Potatoes ———
1'9"
         ——— Early Potatoes or Maincrop ———
1'0"
```
15'

**B**

```
6"     ——— Parsley ——— Early Lettuce ———
1'0"           ——— Runner Beans ———
1'3"           ——— Runner Beans ———
1'9"
6"             ——— Dwarf Peas ———
2'0"
          ——— Dwarf Broad Beans ———
1'0"      ——— Dwarf Broad Beans ———
1'6"
                                        2'0"
9"                          ——— French Beans ———
9"  28 Celery                                  1'3"
9"    plants ———          ——— French Beans ———
1'6"   5'6"                              2'0"
9"             ——— Lettuce ———
              ——— Lettuce ———
1'0"
```
15'

**D**

```
1'0"
         ——— Swede ———
9"       ——— Early Radish ———
9"       ——— Swede ———
1'6"
              ——— Turnips ———
1'0"   Followed by Spinach or Lettuce
              ——— Turnips ———
1'6"
         ——— Spinach Beet ———
1'6"
              ——— Parsnips ———
1'0"          ——— Parsnips ———
1'0"          ——— Carrots ———
1'0"          ——— Carrots ———
1'0"          ——— Beetroot ———
1'0"          ——— Beetroot ———
1'0"     ——— Sugar Loaf Chicory ———
1'0"
```
15'

**C**

```
9"              ——— Leeks ———
1'0"            ——— Leeks ———
1'0"
6"              ——— Onions ———
6"              ——— Onions ———
6"              ——— Onions ———
1'0"
              ——— Shallots ———
1'3"
              ——— Kohl Rabi ———
1'3"           ——— Spring Onions ———
1'3"      Followed by Savoy Cabbage
              ——— Kohl Rabi ———
1'3"
         ——— Broccoli – 'Calabrese' ———
1'3"       ——— Summer Cabbage ———
1'3"      Followed by Winter Radish
              ——— Summer Cabbage ———
1'3"
6"       ——— Broccoli – 'Purple Sprouting' ———
6"            ——— Radish ———
```
15'

N

## Plot A
Potato Group: dig and manure in November to January; no lime.

## Plot D
Roots Group: dig in November to February when clear of crops; no manure; lime in February only if pH reaction is below 6.0.

## Plot B
Legumes Group: dig and manure in November; lime in February to achieve pH reaction of 6.5.

## Plot C
Onions & Brassicas: dig and manure in November; lime in February to achieve pH reaction of 6.5–7.0.

**A**

| | |
|---|---|
| 6" | Parsley ———————— Early Lettuce ————— |
| 1'0" | ———————— Runner Beans ———————— |
| 1'3" | ———————— Runner Beans ———————— |
| 1'9" | |
| 6" | ———————— Dwarf Peas ———————— |
| 2'0" | |
| 1'0" | ———— Dwarf Broad Beans ———— |
| | ———— Dwarf Broad Beans ———— |
| 1'6" | 2'0" |
| 9" | 28 Celery ———— French Beans ———— |
| 9" | plants ———— 1'3" |
| 9" | ———— French Beans ———— |
| 1'6" 5'6" | 2'0" |
| 9" | ———————— Lettuce ———————— |
| | ———————— Lettuce ———————— |
| 1'0" | |

15'

**B**

| | |
|---|---|
| 9" | ———————— Leeks ———————— |
| 1'0" | ———————— Leeks ———————— |
| 1'0" | ———————— Onions ———————— |
| 6" | ———————— Onions ———————— |
| 6" | ———————— Onions ———————— |
| 6" | |
| 1'0" | ———————— Shallots ———————— |
| 1'3" | ———— Kohl Rabi ———— |
| 1'3" | Spring Onions |
| 1'3" | Followed by Savoy Cabbage |
| 1'3" | ———— Kohl Rabi ———— |
| 1'3" | ———— Broccoli – 'Calabrese' ———— |
| 1'3" | Summer Cabbage |
| 1'3" | Followed by Winter Radish |
| 1'3" | Summer Cabbage |
| 6" | ———— Broccoli – 'Purple Sprouting' ———— |
| 6" | ———— Radish ———— |

15'     15'

**D**

| | |
|---|---|
| 1'0" | ———— Outdoor Tomatoes ———— 1'0" |
| 2'6" | 2'0" |
| | 2'0" |
| Bush Marrows | Sweet 2'0" |
| 2'9" or Courgettes | Corn 2'0" |
| 2'0" | |
| 2'6" | 1'6" 1'9" |
| 1'9" | ———— Seakale Beet ———— |
| | ———— Early Potatoes ———— |
| 1'9" | Followed by Lettuce |
| | ———— Early Potatoes ———— |
| 1'9" | |
| 1'0" | ———— Early Potatoes or Maincrop ———— |

**C**

| | |
|---|---|
| 1'0" | ———————— Swede ———————— |
| 9" | ———— Early Radish ———— |
| 9" | ———————— Swede ———————— |
| 1'6" | |
| | ———————— Turnips ———————— |
| 1'0" | Followed by Spinach or Lettuce |
| | Turnips |
| 1'6" | |
| | ———— Spinach Beet ———— |
| 1'6" | |
| 1'0" | ———— Parsnips ———— |
| 1'0" | ———— Parsnips ———— |
| 1'0" | ———— Carrots ———— |
| 1'0" | ———— Carrots ———— |
| 1'0" | ———— Beetroot ———— |
| 1'0" | ———— Beetroot ———— |
| 1'0" | Sugar Loaf Chicory ———— |
| 1'0" | |

15'

—N

## Plot A
Legumes Group: dig and manure in November; lime in February to achieve pH reaction of 6.5.

## Plot D
Potato Group: dig and manure in November to January; no lime.

## Plot B
Onions & Brassicas: dig and manure in November; lime in February to achieve pH reaction of 6.5–7.0.

## Plot C
Roots Group: dig in November to February when clear of crops; no manure; lime in February only if pH reaction is below 6.0.

# THE MEDIUM MASTER PLAN:
## Total Layout for a 'Square' Garden: Year 3

**A**

| | |
|---|---|
| 9" | ————— Leeks ————— |
| 1'0" | ————— Leeks ————— |
| 1'0" | |
| 6" | —————— Onions —————— |
| 6" | —————— Onions —————— |
| 6" | —————— Onions —————— |
| 1'0" | |
| | ————— Shallots ————— |
| 1'3" | |
| | ————— Kohl Rabi ————— |
| 1'3" | ————— Spring Onions ————— |
| 1'3" | Followed by Savoy Cabbage |
| | ————— Kohl Rabi ————— |
| 1'3" | |
| | ————— Broccoli – 'Calabrese' ————— |
| 1'3" | ————— Summer Cabbage ————— |
| 1'3" | Followed by Winter Radish |
| | ————— Summer Cabbage ————— |
| 1'3" | |
| 6" | ——— Broccoli – 'Purple Sprouting' ——— |
| 6" | ————— Radish ————— |

15'

**B**

15'

| | |
|---|---|
| 1'0" | ————— Swede ————— |
| 9" | ————— Early Radish ————— |
| 9" | ————— Swede ————— |
| 1'6" | |
| | ————— Turnips ————— |
| 1'0" | Followed by Spinach or Lettuce |
| | ————— Turnips ————— |
| 1'6" | |
| | ————— Spinach Beet ————— |
| 1'6" | |
| | ————— Parsnips ————— |
| 1'0" | |
| | ————— Parsnips ————— |
| 1'0" | |
| | ————— Carrots ————— |
| 1'0" | |
| | ————— Carrots ————— |
| 1'0" | |
| | ————— Beetroot ————— |
| 1'0" | |
| | ————— Beetroot ————— |
| 1'0" | |
| | ————— Sugar Loaf Chicory ————— |
| 1'0" | |

15'

**D**

| | |
|---|---|
| 1'0" | ————— Lettuce ————— |
| 9" | ————— Lettuce ————— |
| 1'6" | 2'0" |
| 9" | 28 Celery —— ——— French Beans ——— |
| 9" | plants —— 1'3" |
| 9" | ——— French Beans ——— |
| 1'6" | 5'6" 2'0" |
| | ——— Dwarf Broad Beans ——— |
| 1'0" | ——— Dwarf Broad Beans ——— |
| 2'0" | |
| 6" | ——— Dwarf Peas ——— |
| 1'9" | |
| | ——— Runner Beans ——— |
| 1'3" | ——— Runner Beans ——— |
| 1'0" | |
| 6" | — Parsley ——— Early Lettuce — |

15'

**C**

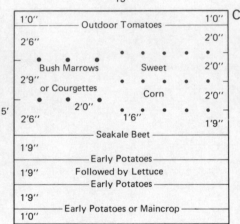

| | |
|---|---|
| 1'0" | ——— Outdoor Tomatoes ——— 1'0" |
| 2'6" | 2'0" |
| | Bush Marrows       Sweet    2'0" |
| 2'9" | or Courgettes                         2'0" |
| | Corn |
| 2'6" | 2'0"   1'6"        1'9" |
| | ——— Seakale Beet ——— |
| 1'9" | |
| | ——— Early Potatoes ——— |
| 1'9" | Followed by Lettuce |
| | ——— Early Potatoes ——— |
| 1'9" | |
| | ——— Early Potatoes or Maincrop ——— |
| 1'0" | |

N

## Plot A
Onions & Brassicas: dig and manure in November; lime in February to achieve pH reaction of 6.5–7.0.

## Plot B
Roots Group: dig in November to February when clear of crops; no manure; lime in February only if pH reaction is below 6.0.

## Plot D
Legumes Group: dig and manure in November; lime in February to achieve pH reaction of 6.5.

## Plot C
Potato Group: dig and manure in November to January; no lime.

# THE MEDIUM MASTER PLAN:
## Total Layout for a 'Square' Garden: Year 4

**A**

| | |
|---|---|
| 1'0" | Swede |
| 9" | Early Radish |
| 9" | Swede |
| 1'6" | Turnips |
| 1'0" | Followed by Spinach or Lettuce |
| | Turnips |
| 1'6" | Spinach Beet |
| 1'6" | Parsnips |
| 1'0" | Parsnips |
| 1'0" | Carrots |
| 1'0" | Carrots |
| 1'0" | Beetroot |
| 1'0" | Beetroot |
| 1'0" | Sugar Loaf Chicory |
| 1'0" | |

15'

**B** — 15'

| | | |
|---|---|---|
| 1'0" | Outdoor Tomatoes | 1'0" |
| 2'6" | | 2'0" |
| 2'9" | Bush Marrows / or Courgettes — Sweet / Corn | 2'0" / 2'0" |
| 2'0" | 1'6" | 1'9" |
| 2'6" | Seakale Beet | |
| 1'9" | Early Potatoes | |
| 1'9" | Followed by Lettuce / Early Potatoes | |
| 1'9" | Early Potatoes or Maincrop | |
| 1'0" | | |

**D** — 15'

| | |
|---|---|
| 9" | Leeks |
| 1'0" | Leeks |
| 1'0" | Onions |
| 6" | Onions |
| 6" | Onions |
| 6" | Onions |
| 1'0" | Shallots |
| 1'3" | Kohl Rabi |
| 1'3" | Spring Onions |
| 1'3" | Followed by Savoy Cabbage / Kohl Rabi |
| 1'3" | Broccoli — 'Calabrese' |
| 1'3" | Summer Cabbage |
| 1'3" | Followed by Winter Radish / Summer Cabbage |
| 1'3" | Broccoli — 'Purple Sprouting' |
| 6" | Radish |
| 6" | |

**C** — 15'

| | | |
|---|---|---|
| 1'0" | Lettuce | |
| 9" | Lettuce | |
| 1'6" | | 2'0" |
| 9" | 28 Celery — French Beans | |
| 9" | plants | |
| 9" | French Beans | 1'3" |
| 1'6" | 5'6" | 2'0" |
| | Dwarf Broad Beans | |
| 1'0" | Dwarf Broad Beans | |
| 2'0" | | |
| 6" | Dwarf Peas | |
| 1'9" | | |
| | Runner Beans | |
| 1'3" | Runner Beans | |
| 1'0" | Parsley — Early Lettuce | |
| 6" | | |

N

## Plot A
Roots Group: dig in November to February when clear of crops; lime in February only if pH reaction is below 6.0.

## Plot D
Onions & Brassicas: dig and manure in November; lime in February to achieve pH reaction of 6.5–7.0.

## Plot B
Potato Group: dig and manure in November to January; no lime.

## Plot C
Legumes Group: dig and manure in November; lime in February to achieve pH reaction of 6.5.

# THE MEDIUM MASTER PLAN ROTATION SEQUENCE

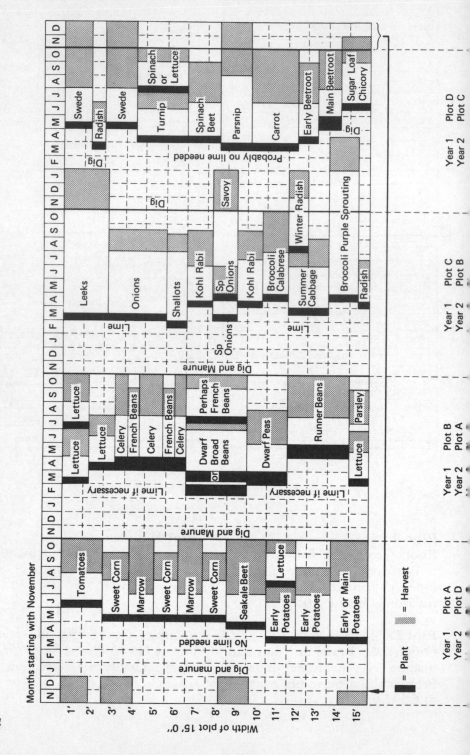

# WHAT SEEDS TO ORDER FOR THE MEDIUM MASTER PLAN

The number of seeds that a supplier puts in a packet will depend on the variety, its size and its cost and different firms put in somewhat different amounts. Seed potatoes, shallots and onion sets can also vary quite a bit in size so the following list is just given as a guide. Do read what it says on the seed packets. You will also find helpful advice in seed catalogues.

## Seeds usually sold by the packet
One small packet of each of these should be enough unless you want to grow more than one variety:

Beetroot – early (Boltardy)
Beetroot – maincrop
Broccoli – calabrese
Broccoli – purple sprouting
Cabbage – Savoy
Cabbage – summer
Carrot
Celery – self blanching or American green
Chicory – sugar loaf
Kohl rabi
Leeks
Lettuce – early

Lettuce – maincrop
Marrows or courgettes
Onions – spring
Parsley
Parsnip
Radish – early
Radish – main
Radish – winter
Seakale beet
Spinach beet
Swede
Sweet corn
Tomato – outdoor
Turnip

## Seeds usually sold by volume or weight
Broad beans – dwarf   One packet or ¼ pint
French beans – dwarf   One packet or ¼ pint
Runner beans   One packet or ¼ pint
Peas – dwarf   One packet or ¼ pint
Onion sets   1 lb: this should give 140 sets planted 4–6 in. apart.
Shallots   2 lb: this should give 30 shallots planted 6 in. apart.
Early potatoes   7 lb: you will need 40 potatoes planted 1 ft apart.

If you sow one row of maincrop potatoes then you'll get 5 lb of earlies and 2 lb maincrop.

## Plants

You may wish to obtain plants of the following instead of raising them from seed:

| | | | |
|---|---|---|---|
| Beans – French | 24 plants | Marrows or courgettes | 6 plants |
| Beans – runner | 40 plants | Sweet corn | 15 plants |
| Celery – self blanching | 28 plants | Tomatoes – outdoors | 10 plants |
| Leeks | 60 plants | Any of the brassicas | |

## Alternatives

If you want to grow any of the 'alternatives' listed on page 74 one small packet of any of the following will do:

| | |
|---|---|
| Capsicum (sweet peppers) | Endive |
| Cauliflower | Haricot beans |
| Celeriac | Melons – cantaloupe |
| Chinese cabbage | Salsify |
| Corn salad | Scorzonera |
| Cucumber – outdoor or ridge | Spinach |
| Curly kale (borecole) | |

GARLIC: one small clove is used for each plant. You get about eight garlic cloves to the oz.

JERUSALEM ARTICHOKES: these are grown from tubers. Fifteen tubers (enough for one 15 ft row) would weigh about 1½ lb depending on size.

See the 'Sowing and Harvesting Guide' on page 83.

# 5. The Small Master Plan

**Four plots each 10 ft wide**

This plan is based on the Large Master Plan except that those crops that need a lot of room have been excluded. The plan still includes eighteen different vegetables and will give a long season of supply. If you want to grow something that is not included in the plan have a look at the list of 'Alternative Crops' on page 74.

The lines of the plans are exactly where the drills for the seeds should be taken out and the distances given are those between one seed-drill and the next.

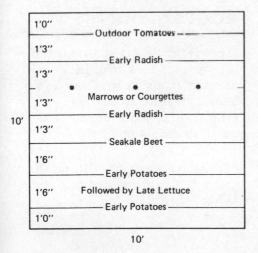

## POTATO GROUP

NOVEMBER TO JANUARY: dig and manure the plot where this group are to go once the parsnips and swedes are out of the way from last year. Don't put any manure under where the tomatoes will be but put any extra manure under the marrows.

FEBRUARY: don't put on any lime – potatoes and tomatoes don't like it.

| | |
|---|---|
| 9" | ———— Dwarf French Beans ———— |
| 1'6" | |
| | ———— Dwarf French Beans ———— |
| 1'3" | |
| | —————— Lettuce —————— |
| 9" | —————— Lettuce —————— |
| 1'0" | |
| | ———— Dwarf Broad Beans ———— |
| 1'0" | |
| | ——— Dwarf Broad Beans ——— |
| 1'9" | |
| | ———— Runner Beans ———— |
| 1'3" | |
| | ———— Runner Beans ———— |
| 9" | |

*(left edge: 10')*

## LEGUMES GROUP

NOVEMBER: dig and manure the whole plot where you are going to plant this group. Put plenty of manure where the runner beans will be.

FEBRUARY: lime the plot, if necessary, to achieve a pH reaction of 6.5.

| | |
|---|---|
| 1'0" | |
| | —————— Leeks —————— |
| 1'0" | |
| | —————— Leeks —————— |
| 1'0" | |
| 6" | —————— Onions —————— |
| 6" | —————— Onions —————— |
| | —————— Onions —————— |
| 1'3" | |
| | ———— Kohl Rabi ———— |
| 1'3" | |
| | ———— Kohl Rabi ———— |
| 1'3" | |
| | ———— Summer Cabbage ———— |
| 1'3" | Followed by Winter Radish |
| | ——— Spring Onions ——— |
| 1'0" | Followed by Savoy Cabbage |

*(left edge: 10')*

## ONIONS & BRASSICAS

NOVEMBER: dig and manure the whole plot where these are to go.

FEBRUARY: lime the ground to achieve a pH reaction of 6.5–7.0.

| | |
|---|---|
| 1'0" | |
| | —————— Turnips —————— |
| 1'0" | Followed by Spinach or Lettuce |
| | —————— Turnips —————— |
| 1'0" | |
| | —————— Parsnips —————— |
| 1'0" | |
| | —————— Parsnips —————— |
| 1'0" | |
| | —————— Carrots —————— |
| 1'0" | |
| | —————— Carrots —————— |
| 1'0" | |
| | ———— Early Beetroot ———— |
| 1'0" | |
| | ———— Main Beetroot ———— |
| 1'0" | |
| | ———— Early Lettuce ———— |
| 1'0" | Followed by Sugar Loaf Chicory |

*(left edge: 10')*

10'

## ROOTS GROUP

NOVEMBER TO FEBRUARY: dig the plot ready for this group as soon as it's clear of any leeks and cabbages from last year. Don't add any manure as it may make the roots misshapen.

FEBRUARY: only lime the ground if the pH reaction has fallen below 6.0.

# ROTATION AND CROPPING SYSTEM FOR THE SMALL MASTER PLAN

Treat the garden year as starting in November. You need four plots, each 10 ft wide. Label them A, B, C and D and sow the plant groups as shown opposite making sure the rows of vegetables run north to south. Keep exactly to the spacings shown on the plans.

## Year 1

| Plot A | Plot B | Plot C | Plot D |
|--------|--------|--------|--------|
| Potato Group | Legumes Group | Onions and Brassicas | Roots Group |

PLOT A: if you sow the radishes in March or early April they will be out of the way by the time the marrows need plenty of room. The potatoes are kept well away from the tomatoes to prevent the spread of disease. When you have dug up the potatoes sow some lettuce in their place.

PLOT B: the runner beans have been put beside a path so that they are easy to look after and to pick. If the broad beans are out of the way by late July, preferably mid July, you can sow some more French beans in their place.

PLOT C: you can have either summer cabbage or winter cabbage (Savoy) or a row of both as shown on the plan. Pull just enough spring onions to make room for each Savoy plant and then pull the rest as you need them. Sow winter radish as soon as you have used the summer cabbage.

PLOT D: if the turnips have been used by July sow some spinach or lettuce in their place.

## Year 2

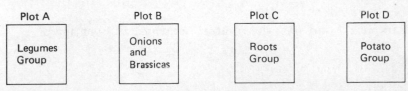

| Plot A | Plot B | Plot C | Plot D |
|--------|--------|--------|--------|
| Legumes Group | Onions and Brassicas | Roots Group | Potato Group |

The same plots are still called A, B, C and D but the plant groups move along one plot as shown. The rows must still run north to south.

PLOT A: if in your own layout the move puts the runner beans between two adjoining plots then turn the whole plan over, as it were, so that they are growing alongside a path and are easy to look after. Don't do this with the other groups.

PLOT C: when you come to dig this plot at the start of the garden year in November it may still contain some leeks and Savoy cabbages from last year. Dig where you can but don't disturb their roots. Complete the digging once they are out of the way. You will still be able to sow this year's seeds in plenty of time.

### Year 3

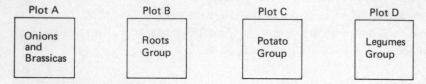

| Plot A | Plot B | Plot C | Plot D |
| --- | --- | --- | --- |
| Onions and Brassicas | Roots Group | Potato Group | Legumes Group |

The same plots are still called A, B, C and D. The plant groups move along once again.

### Year 4

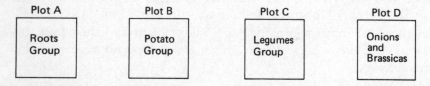

| Plot A | Plot B | Plot C | Plot D |
| --- | --- | --- | --- |
| Roots Group | Potato Group | Legumes Group | Onions and Brassicas |

The plots are still called A, B, C and D. The plant groups move along again.

### Year 5

Go back to Year 1 and start the rotation sequence all over again.

# THE SMALL MASTER PLAN:
## Total Layout for 'Long' Gardens: Year 1

Garden running East to West

Garden running North to South

### Plot A
Potato Group: dig and manure in November to January; no lime.

**East to West (Plot A):**
- 1'0" — Outdoor Tomatoes —
- 1'3" — Early Radish —
- 1'3" — Marrows or Courgettes
- 1'3" — Early Radish —
- 1'3" — Seakale Beet —
- 1'6" — Early Potatoes —
- 1'6" Followed by Late Lettuce
- — Early Potatoes —
- 1'0"

**North to South (Plot A):**
- 1'0" Outdoor Tomatoes
- 1'3" Early Radish
- 1'3" Marrows or Courgettes
- 1'3" Early Radish
- 1'3" Seakale Beet
- 1'6" Early Potatoes
- 1'6" Followed by Late Lettuce
- 1'0" Early Potatoes

10'

### Plot B
Legumes Group: dig and manure in November; lime in February to achieve pH reaction of 6.5.

**East to West (Plot B):**
- 9" — Dwarf French Beans —
- 1'6" — Dwarf French Beans —
- 1'3" — Lettuce —
- 9" — Lettuce —
- 1'0" — Dwarf Broad Beans —
- 1'0" — Dwarf Broad Beans —
- 1'9" — Runner Beans —
- 1'3" — Runner Beans —
- 9"

**North to South (Plot B):**
- 9" Dwarf French Beans
- 1'6" Dwarf French Beans
- 1'3" Lettuce
- 9" Lettuce
- 1'0" Dwarf Broad Beans
- 1'0" Dwarf Broad Beans
- 1'9" Runner Beans
- 1'3" Runner Beans
- 9"

10'

### Plot C
Onions & Brassicas: dig and manure in November; lime in February to achieve pH reaction of 6.5–7.0.

**East to West (Plot C):**
- 1'0" — Leeks —
- 1'0" — Leeks —
- 1'0" — Onions —
- 6" — Onions —
- 6" — Onions —
- 1'3" — Kohl Rabi —
- 1'3" — Kohl Rabi —
- 1'3" — Summer Cabbage —
- 1'3" Followed by Winter Radish
- — Spring Onions —
- 1'0" Followed by Savoy Cabbage

**North to South (Plot C):**
- 1'0" Leeks
- 1'0" Leeks
- 1'0" Onions
- 6" Onions
- 6" Onions
- 1'3" Kohl Rabi
- 1'3" Kohl Rabi
- 1'3" Summer Cabbage
- 1'3" Followed by Winter Radish / Spring Onions
- 1'0" Followed by Savoy Cabbage

10'

### Plot D
Roots Group: dig in November to February when clear of crops; no manure; only lime in February if pH reaction is below 6.0.

**East to West (Plot D):**
- 1'0" — Turnips —
- 1'0" Followed by Spinach or Lettuce
- — Turnips —
- 1'0" — Parsnips —
- 1'0" — Parsnips —
- 1'0" — Carrots —
- 1'0" — Carrots —
- 1'0" — Early Beetroot —
- 1'0" — Main Beetroot —
- 1'0" — Early Lettuce —
- 1'0" Followed by Sugar Loaf Chicory

**North to South (Plot D):**
- 1'0" Turnips
- 1'0" Followed by Spinach or Lettuce / Turnips
- 1'0" Parsnips
- 1'0" Parsnips
- 1'0" Carrots
- 1'0" Carrots
- 1'0" Early Beetroot
- 1'0" Main Beetroot
- 1'0" Early Lettuce
- 1'0" Followed by Sugar Loaf Chicory

10'

10'

N

N

61

# THE SMALL MASTER PLAN:
## Total Layout for 'Long' Gardens: Year 2

Garden running East to West

Garden running North to South

### A

| | |
|---|---|
| 9" | —————Runner Beans————— |
| 1'3" | —————Runner Beans————— |
| 1'9" | |
| 1'0" | ————Dwarf Broad Beans———— |
| 1'0" | ————Dwarf Broad Beans———— |
| 9" | —————————Lettuce————————— |
| 1'3" | —————————Lettuce————————— |
| 1'6" | ———Dwarf French Beans——— |
| 9" | ———Dwarf French Beans——— |

10'

**Plot A**
Legumes Group: dig and manure in November; lime in February to achieve pH reaction of 6.5.

Garden running North to South — A

Dwarf French Beans — 9"
Dwarf French Beans — 1'6"
Lettuce — 1'3"
Lettuce — 9"
Dwarf Broad Beans — 1'0"
Dwarf Broad Beans — 1'0"
Runner Beans — 1'9"
Runner Beans — 1'3"
9"

10'

### B

| | |
|---|---|
| 1'0" | ————————Leeks———————— |
| 1'0" | ————————Leeks———————— |
| 1'0" | ———————Onions——————— |
| 6" | ———————Onions——————— |
| 6" | ———————Onions——————— |
| 1'3" | ——————Kohl Rabi—————— |
| 1'3" | ——————Kohl Rabi—————— |
| 1'3" | ————Summer Cabbage———— |
| 1'3" | Followed by Winter Radish |
| 1'0" | Spring Onions / Followed by Savoy Cabbage |

10'

**Plot B**
Onions & Brassicas: dig and manure in November; lime in February to achieve pH reaction of 6.5–7.0.

Leeks — 1'0"
Leeks — 1'0"
Onions — 1'0"
Onions — 6"
Onions — 6"
Kohl Rabi — 1'3"
Kohl Rabi — 1'3"
Summer Cabbage — 1'3"
Followed by Winter Radish Spring Onions — 1'3"
Followed by Savoy Cabbage — 1'0"

10'

### C

| | |
|---|---|
| 1'0" | ———————Turnips——————— |
| 1'0" | Followed by Spinach or Lettuce Turnips |
| 1'0" | ——————Parsnips—————— |
| 1'0" | ——————Parsnips—————— |
| 1'0" | ——————Carrots—————— |
| 1'0" | ——————Carrots—————— |
| 1'0" | ———Early Beetroot——— |
| 1'0" | ———Main Beetroot——— |
| 1'0" | ———Early Lettuce——— |
| 1'0" | Followed by Sugar Loaf Chicory |

10'

**Plot C**
Roots Group: dig in November to February when clear of crops; no manure; only lime in February if pH reaction is below 6.0.

Turnips — 1'0"
Followed by Spinach or Lettuce Turnips — 1'0"
Parsnips — 1'0"
Parsnips — 1'0"
Carrots — 1'0"
Carrots — 1'0"
Early Beetroot — 1'0"
Main Beetroot — 1'0"
Early Lettuce — 1'0"
Followed by Sugar Loaf Chicory — 1'0"

10'

### D

| | |
|---|---|
| 1'0" | ————Outdoor Tomatoes———— |
| 1'3" | ——————Early Radish—————— |
| 1'3" | • • • |
| 1'3" | Marrows or Courgettes |
| 1'3" | ——————Early Radish—————— |
| 1'6" | ——————Seakale Beet—————— |
| 1'6" | ——————Early Potatoes—————— |
| 1'0" | Followed by Late Lettuce Early Potatoes |

10'

**Plot D**
Potato Group: dig and manure in November to January; no lime.

Outdoor Tomatoes — 1'0"
Early Radish — 1'3"
Marrows or Courgettes — 1'3"
Early Radish — 1'3"
Seakale Beet — 1'3"
Early Potatoes — 1'6"
Followed by Late Lettuce — 1'6"
Early Potatoes — 1'0"

10'

N →

# THE SMALL MASTER PLAN:
## Total Layout for 'Long' Gardens: Year 3

Garden running East to West | Garden running North to South

### Plot A
Onions & Brassicas: dig and manure in November; lime in February to achieve pH reaction of 6.5–7.0.

**A (East to West)**

| Size | Crop |
|------|------|
| 1'0" | Leeks |
| 1'0" | Leeks |
| 1'0" | Onions |
| 6" | Onions |
| 6" | Onions |
| 1'3" | Kohl Rabi |
| 1'3" | Kohl Rabi |
| 1'3" | Summer Cabbage |
| 1'3" | Followed by Winter Radish / Spring Onions |
| 1'0" | Followed by Savoy Cabbage |

**A (North to South)**

| 1'0" | 1'0" | 1'0" | 6" | 6" | 1'3" | 1'3" | 1'3" | 1'3" | 1'0" |
|------|------|------|-----|-----|------|------|------|------|------|
| Leeks | Leeks | Onions | Onions | Onions | Kohl Rabi | Kohl Rabi | Summer Cabbage | Followed by Winter Radish / Spring Onions | Followed by Savoy Cabbage |

### Plot B
Roots Group: dig in November to February when clear of crops; no manure; only lime in February if pH reaction is below 6.0.

**B (East to West)**

| Size | Crop |
|------|------|
| 1'0" | Turnips |
| 1'0" | Followed by Spinach or Lettuce |
| 1'0" | Turnips |
| 1'0" | Parsnips |
| 1'0" | Parsnips |
| 1'0" | Carrots |
| 1'0" | Carrots |
| 1'0" | Early Beetroot |
| 1'0" | Main Beetroot |
| 1'0" | Early Lettuce |
| 1'0" | Followed by Sugar Loaf Chicory |

**B (North to South)**

| 1'0" | 1'0" | 1'0" | 1'0" | 1'0" | 1'0" | 1'0" | 1'0" | 1'0" | 1'0" | 1'0" |
|------|------|------|------|------|------|------|------|------|------|------|
| Turnips | Followed by Spinach or Lettuce | Turnips | Parsnips | Parsnips | Carrots | Carrots | Early Beetroot | Main Beetroot | Early Lettuce | Followed by Sugar Loaf Chicory |

### Plot C
Potato Group: dig and manure in November to January; no lime.

**C (East to West)**

| Size | Crop |
|------|------|
| 1'0" | Outdoor Tomatoes |
| 1'3" | Early Radish |
| 1'3" | Marrows or Courgettes |
| 1'3" | Early Radish |
| 1'3" | Seakale Beet |
| 1'6" | Early Potatoes |
| 1'6" | Followed by Late Lettuce / Early Potatoes |
| 1'0" | |

**C (North to South)**

| 1'0" | 1'3" | 1'3" | 1'3" | 1'3" | 1'6" | 1'6" | 1'0" |
|------|------|------|------|------|------|------|------|
| Outdoor Tomatoes | Early Radish | Marrows or Courgettes | Early Radish | Seakale Beet | Early Potatoes | Followed by Late Lettuce | Early Potatoes |

### Plot D
Legumes Group: dig and manure in November; lime in February to achieve pH reaction of 6.5.

**D (East to West)**

| Size | Crop |
|------|------|
| 9" | Dwarf French Beans |
| 1'6" | Dwarf French Beans |
| 1'3" | Lettuce |
| 9" | Lettuce |
| 1'0" | Dwarf Broad Beans |
| 1'0" | Dwarf Broad Beans |
| 1'9" | Runner Beans |
| 1'3" | Runner Beans |
| 9" | |

**D (North to South)**

| 9" | 1'6" | 1'3" | 9" | 1'0" | 1'0" | 1'9" | 1'3" | 9" |
|-----|------|------|-----|------|------|------|------|-----|
| Dwarf French Beans | Dwarf French Beans | Lettuce | Lettuce | Dwarf Broad Beans | Dwarf Broad Beans | Runner Beans | Runner Beans | |

10' | 10'

N

# THE SMALL MASTER PLAN:
## Total Layout for 'Long' Gardens: Year 4

Garden running East to West          Garden running North to South

**A**

| 1'0" | Turnips |
|---|---|
| 1'0" | Followed by Spinach or Lettuce |
| | Turnips |
| 1'0" | Parsnips |
| 1'0" | Parsnips |
| 1'0" | Carrots |
| 1'0" | Carrots |
| 1'0" | Early Beetroot |
| 1'0" | Main Beetroot |
| 1'0" | Early Lettuce |
| 1'0" | Followed by Sugar Loaf Chicory |

10'

**Plot A**
Roots Group: dig in November to February when clear of crops; no manure; only lime in February if pH reaction is below 6.0.

**A**

Turnips — 1'0"
Followed by Spinach or Lettuce — 1'0"
Turnips
Parsnips — 1'0"
Parsnips — 1'0"
Carrots — 1'0"
Carrots — 1'0"
Early Beetroot — 1'0"
Main Beetroot — 1'0"
Early Lettuce — 1'0"
Followed by Sugar Loaf Chicory — 1'0"

10'

**B**

| 1'0" | Outdoor Tomatoes |
|---|---|
| 1'3" | Early Radish |
| 1'3" | |
| 1'3" | Marrows or Courgettes |
| 1'3" | Early Radish |
| 1'3" | Seakale Beet |
| 1'6" | Early Potatoes |
| 1'6" | Followed by Late Lettuce |
| 1'0" | Early Potatoes |

10'

**Plot B**
Potato Group: dig and manure in November to January; no lime.

**B**

Outdoor Tomatoes — 1'0"
Early Radish — 1'3"
— 1'3"
Marrows or Courgettes — 1'3"
Early Radish — 1'3"
Seakale Beet — 1'3"
Early Potatoes — 1'6"
Followed by Late Lettuce — 1'6"
Early Potatoes — 1'0"

10'

**C**

| 9" | Runner Beans |
|---|---|
| 1'3" | Runner Beans |
| 1'9" | |
| 1'0" | Dwarf Broad Beans |
| 1'0" | Dwarf Broad Beans |
| 9" | Lettuce |
| 1'3" | Lettuce |
| 1'6" | Dwarf French Beans |
| 9" | Dwarf French Beans |

10'

**Plot C**
Legumes Group: dig and manure in November; lime in February to achieve pH reaction of 6.5.

**C**

Dwarf French Beans — 9"
Dwarf French Beans — 1'6"
Lettuce — 1'3"
Lettuce — 9"
Dwarf Broad Beans — 1'0"
Dwarf Broad Beans — 1'0"
Runner Beans — 1'9"
Runner Beans — 1'3"
— 9"

10'

**D**

| 1'0" | Leeks |
|---|---|
| 1'0" | Leeks |
| 1'0" | Onions |
| 6" | Onions |
| 6" | Onions |
| 1'3" | Kohl Rabi |
| 1'3" | Kohl Rabi |
| 1'3" | Summer Cabbage |
| 1'3" | Followed by Winter Radish |
| | Spring Onions |
| 1'0" | Followed by Savoy Cabbage |

10'

**Plot D**
Onions & Brassicas: dig and manure in November; lime in February to achieve pH reaction of 6.5–7.0.

**D**

Leeks — 1'0"
Leeks — 1'0"
Onions — 1'0"
Onions — 6"
Onions — 6"
Kohl Rabi — 1'3"
Kohl Rabi — 1'3"
Summer Cabbage — 1'3"
Followed by Winter Radish — 1'3"
Spring Onions
Followed by Savoy Cabbage — 1'0"

10'

10'

N

# THE SMALL MASTER PLAN:
## Total Layout for a 'Square' Garden: Year 1

**A**

| | |
|---|---|
| 1'0" | Outdoor Tomatoes |
| 1'3" | Early Radish |
| 1'3" | • • • |
| 1'3" | Marrows or Courgettes |
| | Early Radish |
| 1'3" | Seakale Beet |
| 1'6" | Early Potatoes |
| 1'6" | Followed by Late Lettuce |
| | Early Potatoes |
| 1'0" | |

10'

**B**

| | |
|---|---|
| 9" | Runner Beans |
| 1'3" | Runner Beans |
| 1'9" | Dwarf Broad Beans |
| 1'0" | Dwarf Broad Beans |
| 1'0" | Lettuce |
| 9" | Lettuce |
| 1'3" | Dwarf French Beans |
| 1'6" | Dwarf French Beans |
| 9" | |

10'

10'

**D**

| | |
|---|---|
| 1'0" | Turnips |
| 1'0" | Followed by Spinach or Lettuce |
| | Turnips |
| 1'0" | Parsnips |
| 1'0" | Parsnips |
| 1'0" | Carrots |
| 1'0" | Carrots |
| 1'0" | Early Beetroot |
| 1'0" | Main Beetroot |
| 1'0" | Early Lettuce |
| 1'0" | Followed by Sugar Loaf Chicory |

**C**

| | |
|---|---|
| 1'0" | Leeks |
| 1'0" | Leeks |
| 1'0" | Onions |
| 6" | Onions |
| 6" | Onions |
| 1'3" | Kohl Rabi |
| 1'3" | Kohl Rabi |
| 1'3" | Summer Cabbage |
| 1'3" | Followed by Winter Radish |
| | Spring Onions |
| 1'0" | Followed by Savoy Cabbage |

10'

## Plot A
Potato Group: dig and manure in November to January; no lime.

## Plot D
Roots Group: dig in November to February when clear of crops; no manure; only lime in February if pH reaction is below 6.0.

## Plot B
Legumes Group: dig and manure in November; lime in February to achieve pH reaction of 6.5.

## Plot C
Onions & Brassicas: dig and manure in November; lime in February to achieve pH reaction of 6.5–7.0.

**Plot A**
Legumes Group: dig and manure in November; lime in February to achieve pH reaction of 6.5.

**Plot B**
Onions & Brassicas: dig and manure in November; lime in February to achieve pH reaction of 6.5–7.0.

**Plot D**
Potato Group: dig and manure in November to January; no lime.

**Plot C**
Roots Group: dig in November to February when clear of crops; no manure; only lime in February if pH reaction is below 6.0.

# THE SMALL MASTER PLAN:
## Total Layout for a 'Square' Garden: Year 3

A

| | |
|---|---|
| 1'0'' | —————— Leeks —————— |
| 1'0'' | —————— Leeks —————— |
| 1'0'' | —————— Onions —————— |
| 6'' | —————— Onions —————— |
| 6'' | —————— Onions —————— |
| 1'3'' | —————— Kohl Rabi —————— |
| 1'3'' | —————— Kohl Rabi —————— |
| 1'3'' | Summer Cabbage |
| 1'3'' | Followed by Winter Radish |
| | Spring Onions |
| 1'0'' | Followed by Savoy Cabbage |

10'

B

| | |
|---|---|
| 1'0'' | —————— Turnips —————— |
| 1'0'' | Followed by Spinach or Lettuce |
| | Turnips |
| 1'0'' | —————— Parsnips —————— |
| 1'0'' | —————— Parsnips —————— |
| 1'0'' | —————— Carrots —————— |
| 1'0'' | —————— Carrots —————— |
| 1'0'' | —————— Early Beetroot —————— |
| 1'0'' | —————— Main Beetroot —————— |
| 1'0'' | Early Lettuce |
| 1'0'' | Followed by Sugar Loaf Chicory |

10'

D

| | |
|---|---|
| 9'' | —————— Dwarf French Beans —————— |
| 1'6'' | —————— Dwarf French Beans —————— |
| 1'3'' | —————— Lettuce —————— |
| 9'' | —————— Lettuce —————— |
| 1'0'' | —————— Dwarf Broad Beans —————— |
| 1'0'' | —————— Dwarf Broad Beans —————— |
| 1'9'' | —————— Runner Beans —————— |
| 1'3'' | —————— Runner Beans —————— |
| 9'' | |

10'

C

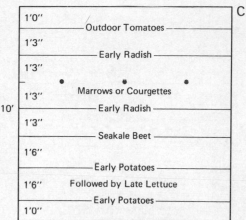

| | |
|---|---|
| 1'0'' | —————— Outdoor Tomatoes —————— |
| 1'3'' | —————— Early Radish —————— |
| 1'3'' | |
| 1'3'' | Marrows or Courgettes |
| 1'3'' | —————— Early Radish —————— |
| 1'3'' | —————— Seakale Beet —————— |
| 1'6'' | —————— Early Potatoes —————— |
| 1'6'' | Followed by Late Lettuce |
| | Early Potatoes |
| 1'0'' | |

## Plot A
Onions & Brassicas: dig and manure in November; lime in February to achieve pH reaction of 6.5–7.0.

## Plot B
Roots Group: dig in November to February when clear of crops; no manure; only lime in February if pH reaction is below 6.0.

## Plot D
Legumes Group: dig and manure in November; lime in February to achieve pH reaction of 6.5.

## Plot C
Potato Group: dig and manure in November to January; no lime.

# THE SMALL MASTER PLAN:
## Total Layout for a 'Square' Garden: Year 4

**A**

| | |
|---|---|
| 1'0" | |
| | Turnips |
| 1'0" | Followed by Spinach or Lettuce |
| | Turnips |
| 1'0" | |
| | Parsnips |
| 1'0" | |
| | Parsnips |
| 1'0" | |
| | Carrots |
| 1'0" | |
| | Carrots |
| 1'0" | |
| | Early Beetroot |
| 1'0" | |
| | Main Beetroot |
| 1'0" | |
| | Early Lettuce |
| 1'0" | Followed by Sugar Loaf Chicory |

10'

**B**

| | |
|---|---|
| 1'0" | Outdoor Tomatoes |
| 1'3" | |
| | Early Radish |
| 1'3" | |
| 1'3" | • Marrows or Courgettes • • |
| | Early Radish |
| 1'3" | |
| | Seakale Beet |
| 1'6" | |
| | Early Potatoes |
| 1'6" | Followed by Late Lettuce |
| | Early Potatoes |
| 1'0" | |

10'

10'

**D**

| | |
|---|---|
| 1'0" | |
| | Leeks |
| 1'0" | |
| | Leeks |
| 1'0" | |
| 6" | Onions |
| 6" | Onions |
| | Onions |
| 1'3" | |
| | Kohl Rabi |
| 1'3" | |
| | Kohl Rabi |
| 1'3" | |
| | Summer Cabbage |
| 1'3" | Followed by Winter Radish |
| | Spring Onions |
| 1'0" | Followed by Savoy Cabbage |

**C**

| | |
|---|---|
| 9" | Dwarf French Beans |
| 1'6" | |
| | Dwarf French Beans |
| 1'3" | |
| | Lettuce |
| 9" | |
| | Lettuce |
| 1'0" | Dwarf Broad Beans |
| 1'0" | Dwarf Broad Beans |
| 1'9" | |
| | Runner Beans |
| 1'3" | |
| | Runner Beans |
| 9" | |

10'

N

## Plot A
Roots Group: dig in November to February when clear of crops; no manure; only lime in February if pH reaction is below 6.0.

## Plot D
Onions & Brassicas: dig and manure in November; lime in February to achieve pH reaction of 6.5–7.0.

## Plot B
Potato Group: dig and manure in November to January; no lime.

## Plot C
Legumes Group: dig and manure in November; lime in February to achieve pH reaction of 6.5.

**SMALL MASTER PLAN ROTATION SEQUENCE**

Months starting with November

N D J F M A M J J A S O N D J F M A M J J A S O N D J F M A M J J A S O N D J F M A M J J A S O N D

Width of plot 10'

1' 2' 3' 4' 5' 6' 7' 8' 9' 10'

Dig and manure — No Lime needed

Tomatoes
Radish
Marrow
Radish
Seakale Beet
Spinach or Lettuce
Early Potatoes
Early Potatoes

Dig and manure — Lime if necessary

French Beans
Lettuce
Lettuce
Lettuce
Dwarf Broad Beans or
Perhaps French Beans
Runner Beans

Dig and manure — Lime — Sp Onion

Leeks
Onions
Kohl Rabi
Summer Cabbage
Winter Radish
Savoy
Sp. Onion
Savoy

Dig — Probably no Lime needed — Dig — Dig

Turnip
Spinach or Lettuce
Parsnip
Carrot
Early Beetroot
Main Beetroot
Early Lettuce
Sugar Loaf Chicory

= Plant    = Harvest

| | Year 1 | Plot A | Year 1 | Pot B | Year 1 | Plot C | Year 1 | Plot D |
|---|---|---|---|---|---|---|---|---|
| | Year 2 | Plot D | Year 2 | Plot A | Year 2 | Plot B | Year 2 | Plot C |
| | Year 3 | Plot C | Year 3 | Plot D | Year 3 | Plot A | Year 3 | Plot B |
| | Year 4 | Plot B | Year 4 | Plot C | Year 4 | Plot D | Year 4 | Plot A |

69

## WHAT SEEDS TO ORDER FOR THE SMALL MASTER PLAN

The following is given as a general guide as the amount of seed in a packet can vary, as also can the size of onion sets and seed potatoes. Always check what it says on the seed packets. You will also find helpful advice in seed catalogues.

### Seeds usually sold by the packet

If you are reasonably careful with seed one small packet of each of these should be enough to sow the Small Master Plan twice over. Perhaps you could share them with a friend.

Beetroot – early (Boltardy)  
Beetroot – maincrop  
Cabbage – Savoy  
Cabbage – summer  
Carrot  
Chicory – sugar loaf  
Kohl rabi  
Leeks  
Lettuce – early  
Lettuce – maincrop  

Marrows or courgettes  
Onions – spring  
Parsnip  
Radish – early  
Radish – winter  
Seakale beet  
Spinach (optional)  
Tomato – outdoor  
Turnip  

### Seeds usually sold by volume or weight

Broad beans – dwarf One packet or $\frac{1}{4}$ pint  
French beans – dwarf One packet or $\frac{1}{4}$ pint  
Runner beans     One packet or $\frac{1}{4}$ pint  
Onion sets      $\frac{1}{2}$ lb: this should give over 70 sets to be planted 4–6 in. apart.  
Early potatoes    3–4 lb: you will need 20 potatoes planted 1 ft apart.

### Plants

You may wish to obtain plants of the following instead of raising them from seed:

| | | | |
|---|---|---|---|
| Beans – French | 26 plants | Leeks | 40 plants |
| Beans – runner | 26 plants | Marrow or courgette | 3 plants |
| Cabbage – Savoy | 6 plants | Tomatoes – outdoor | 6 plants |
| Cabbage – summer | 10 plants | | |

**Alternatives**

If you want to grow any of the 'alternatives' listed on page 74 one small packet of any of the following will be more than enough:

| | |
|---|---|
| Capsicum (sweet peppers) | Endive |
| Cauliflower | Haricot beans |
| Chinese cabbage | Melons – cataloupe |
| Corn salad | Salsify |
| Cucumber – outdoor or ridge | Scorzonera |
| Curly kale (borecole) | Spinach or spinach beet |

GARLIC: one small 'clove' is used for each plant. You get about eight garlic cloves to the oz.

JERUSALEM ARTICHOKES: these are grown from tubers. Ten tubers (enough for one 10 ft row) would weigh about 1 lb, depending on size.

See the 'Sowing and Harvesting Guide' on page 83.

# 6. The Little Plots

If you have just one small vegetable plot, say 15 ft by 15 ft or 10 ft by 10 ft, then grow only one group of vegetables each year. This will keep your soil healthy and give you good crops. Make sure the rows of vegetables run north to south.

## ONE PLOT 15 FT BY 15 FT

Read the information on 'The Medium Master Plan', starting on page 42.

In the first year grow these veg-etables from the Potato Group.

In the second year grow these vegetables from the Legumes Group.

In the fourth year grow these vegetables from the Roots Group.

In the third year grow these vegetables from the Onions & Brassicas Group.

In the FIFTH year go back to the Potato Group and begin again.
  See page 55 for guidance on the quantities of seeds to order.

## ONE PLOT 10 FT BY 10 FT

Read the information on 'The Small Master Plan', starting on page 57.

In the first year grow these vegetables from the Potato Group.

In the second year grow these
vegetables from the Legumes
Group.

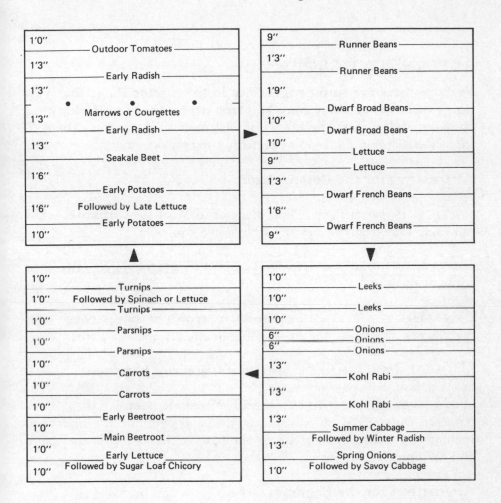

In the fourth year grow these
vegetables from the Roots
Group.

In the third year grow these
vegetables from the Onions &
Brassicas Group.

In the FIFTH year go back to the Potato Group and begin again.
See page 70 for guidance on the quantities of seeds to order.

# 7. The Master Plans and Your Own Garden

## ALTERNATIVE CROPS

**Perhaps there are some vegetables in the Master Plans that you don't care for, or there may be some others that you're longing to grow.** Select from the following alternatives. If you keep them to the places suggested it won't upset the rotation system.

### Alternatives for the Potato Group

CAPSICUMS (sweet peppers): in place of some of the **tomatoes** – but put them under tall cloches if you live in a cool area.

CUCUMBERS (outdoor or ridge): instead of **marrows** or instead of some of them.

CANTALOUPE MELONS: in place of **marrows** or **sweet corn** – but use cloches or a frame unless you live in a really sheltered area.

JERUSALEM ARTICHOKES: instead of **maincrop potatoes**.

SPINACH or SPINACH BEET: instead of **seakale beet**.
You can miss out sweet corn altogether and continue the marrows, melons or cucumbers right across the plot, or vice versa in the Large and Medium Master Plans.

### Alternatives for the Legumes Group (peas and beans)
The plans have been designed to give you a supply of peas or beans right through from June to the first frosts, but because they are all members of the same family you can grow more of one type of pea or bean in place of another.

HARICOT BEANS: in place of any of the **peas** or **beans**.

74

MORE FRENCH BEANS: instead of the **celery** or vice versa, or instead of **runner beans**.

CELERIAC: instead of the **celery**.

MORE EARLY LETTUCE: instead of the **parsley** – or vice versa.

## Alternatives for the onions and brassicas

GARLIC: instead of some of the **shallots, onions** or **leeks**.
You can grow more of any of these in place of the others.

CAULIFLOWERS (summer heading): in place of **calabrese** or **summer cabbage**.

CAULIFLOWERS (autumn or winter heading): instead of **Brussels sprouts** or **purple sprouting broccoli** or **Savoy.**

KALE (curly): instead of **Brussels sprouts** or **purple sprouting broccoli** or **Savoy.**

CHINESE CABBAGE: instead of **kohl rabi**.

ANY OTHER BRASSICA: in fact any type of brassica can be grown instead of the brassicas shown in this group as long as there is enough space for the type you want.
    Don't extend the brassicas into the 'onion' area.

CORN SALAD (lamb's lettuce): this can be grown instead of any other crop in this group.

## Alternatives for the Roots Group

ENDIVE: instead of **sugar loaf chicory**.

SALSIFY or SCORZONERA: instead of any of the crops in this group.

MORE BEETROOT, CARROTS, or PARSNIPS: instead of the **swedes** or **turnips** or instead of each other. But you must not grow more swedes or turnips – these must be restricted to the area shown.

## FITTING A PLAN TO YOUR GARDEN

It's highly unlikely that one of the Master Plans will exactly fit your garden as it is. If you don't wish to change your garden to suit one of the plans then you can probably change one of the plans to suit your garden.

Before deciding on the most appropriate move take a trip round your plot with a tape-measure. Make a simple but accurate plan on squared paper of a bird's eye view of the space you have available and then note on the plan which direction is north – so that you run the rows as near north-south as possible. Divide the spaces into four roughly equal plots, label them A, B, C and D and then decide which Master Plan is the nearest fit.

If your plots are wider than the plan you can add some rows of vegetables, and if they are narrower you can miss some out.

Let's have a look at a couple of sample plots and see how this can be done. We must, of course, stick to the rotation system and only add

**Example**

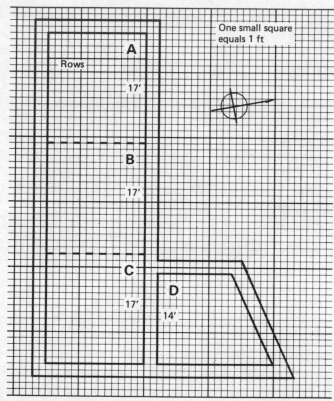

varieties from the appropriate plant groups. (See page 15 for 'Plant Groups' and page 74 for 'Alternative Crops'.)

The first garden is not symmetrical but it divides fairly easily into four roughly equal areas – three of which at 17 ft wide are just a little wider than the Medium Master Plan and one at 14 ft just a little narrower. So we could use the Medium Master Plan with the following changes.

**First year**

**Plot A**   Add 1 row of potatoes   +2 ft

**Plot B**   Add 1 row of French beans and more celery   +1 ft 3 in.
             1 row of lettuce   +9 in.

**Plot C**   Add 1 row of leeks   +1 ft
             1 row of shallots   +1 ft

**Plot D**   Delete 1 row of carrots   −1 ft

There are, of course, quite a number of different changes that could be made instead and these are only suggestions.

**Example**

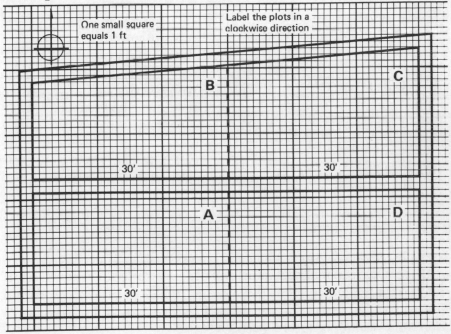

This vegetable garden is a large one. It's fairly symmetrical but has one sloping boundary. With the rows running north to south this gives four plots each 30 ft wide. The Medium Master Plan would fit in twice but I think most people would use the Large Master Plan and then add to it. Something like this:

**Large Master Plan plus.**

PLOT B

| | |
|---|---:|
| 1 row of runners 5 ft from first row – use space between for another row of dwarf broad beans | 5' 0" |
| 2 rows of French beans and more celery | 3' 0" |
| 1 row haricot beans | 1' 6" |
| | 9' 6" |

PLOT C

| | |
|---|---:|
| 2 rows leeks | 2' 0" |
| 1 row shallots | 1' 0" |
| 1 row Savoy (and radish) | 2' 0" |
| 1 row sprouts (and kohl rabi) | 2' 6" |
| 1 row purple sprouting broccoli | 2' 6" |
| | 10' 0" |

PLOT A

| | |
|---|---:|
| 2 rows maincrop potatoes | 4' 0" |
| 1 row early potatoes | 1' 9" |
| 1 row sweetcorn and marrows | 1' 9" |
| 1 row seakale beet | 1' 9" |
| | 9' 6" |

PLOT D
(*Alternatives page 74)

| | |
|---|---:|
| 1 row swedes | 1' 6" |
| 2 rows parsnips | 2' 0" |
| 2 rows carrots | 2' 0" |
| 2 rows salsify* | 2' 0" |
| 1 row scorzonera* | 1' 0" |
| 1 row sugar loaf chicory | 1' 0" |
| | 9' 6" |

**Now measure your own garden and then tailor-make your own plan.**

## KEEP A RECORD

A simple record of what is sown and harvested each year is a great help when it comes to making decisions and ordering seeds for future years. If you make a few notes about the weather, which varieties do well and which give problems, you can have a garden biography that makes interesting reading in future years.

There are two very simple record systems that together will give you the information for this biography.

## 1. The seed packets

Don't use them as markers for the rows, and **don't throw them away.**
Directly you sow a row of seeds write the date of sowing on the packet. If
you sow another row later on record that date too. Make a note about the
weather conditions at the time on the packet also. In August or September, when you have sown all your seeds, slit along one side and the
bottom of each packet, open the packets out and staple them together at
the top left hand corner (in two lots if necessary) or keep them in a big
envelope. These packets now give you information on the seed merchant, the variety, the cost, cultural instructions, the dates of sowing and
what the weather was like.

## 2. Date and weight book

This is a simple 8 by 5 in. notebook which you keep in the kitchen and in
which you jot down everything that is harvested from the garden. Use
the left hand pages for dates, weights and varieties and the right hand
pages for any comments you feel inspired to make. It could read like this:

| DATE | | VALUE | |
|------|------|-------|------|
| | | | First two weeks of July wet and windy with only 2 hot sunny days |
| 7/7 | 1 Cucumber Green House Topnotch | | Good but small. Not warm enough |
| 7/7 | 3 lb Peas. Little Marvel | | Excellent. Grow next year |
| 8/7 | Big bunch of young carrots Chantenay | | - - - |
| 9/7 | " " . AUTUMN KING | | Very big potatoes - almost too big for earlies |
| 9/7 | 2 lbs Potatoes Arran Pilot | | CRISP AND DELICIOUS |
| 9/7 | Radishes ICICLE Big bunch | | Good |
| 9/7 | 1 lb Courgettes GREEN BUSH | | Still excellent |
| 9/7 | 2 lb Peas LITTLE MARVEL | | " |
| 11/7 | 5 lb Pots. ARRAN PILOT " | | Still very big |
| 11/7 | 2½ lb " " | | " |
| 11/7 | 1 lb Courgettes 'Green Bush' | | Big and tender |
| 12/7 | 1½ lb Beetroot BOLTARDY | | still good |
| 13/7 | 2 lb Little Marvel Peas | | ✓ |
| 14/7 | 1 lb Courgettes 'Green Bush' | | This variety all leaves and little fruit Probably the wet weather |
| 14/7 | ¼ " " Tender co True | | Good |
| 14/7 | Bunch young carrots Scarlet horn | | ✓✓ |
| 16/7 | 2 lbs Little Marvel Peas | | O.K. getting bigger. |
| 16/7 | 2 cucumbers Topnotch ('Green house) | | One of them woody. The rest excellent. |
| 16/7 | 2 lb Kohl Rabi | | |

I've put a column for 'value' as I like to record what the vegetables would
have cost if bought in the shops that day. You might like to do the same.

EXPENDITURE: reserve some pages at the back of the book for recording what you spend on seeds, manure, fertilisers, seed-trays, pots, etc., so that you can compare this with the value of the crops harvested.

## Average expectations

You may simply want to compare your results with what could normally be expected. It's not easy to say what is 'normal' as so much depends on the fertility of the soil, where the plots are sited and, of course, the weather. A long hot summer can literally double the yield of some crops and halve the yield of others. I think the following can be regarded as good yields so if you do better you've done very well.

The list doesn't include 'exotic' plants like melons where it's not easy to give a norm and it is not sensible to include crops like parsley, radish or spring onion where it is quality and not weight that's most important.

| Vegetable | Good crop from a 20 ft row | Your own results | | | |
| --- | --- | --- | --- | --- | --- |
| | | Year 1 | Year 2 | Year 3 | Year 4 |
| Artichoke, Jerusalem | 25 lb | | | | |
| Beans, broad tall | 20 ,, | | | | |
| Beans, broad dwarf | 15 ,, | | | | |
| Beans, French dwarf | 20 ,, | | | | |
| Beans, runner | 40 ,, | | | | |
| Beetroot | 25 ,, | | | | |
| Broccoli, calabrese | 10 ,, | | | | |
| Broccoli, purple sprouting | 25 ,, | | | | |
| Brussels sprouts | 18 ,, | | | | |
| Cabbage, Savoy | 35 ,, | | | | |
| Cabbage, summer | 30 ,, | | | | |
| Carrots | 15 ,, | | | | |
| Cauliflowers | 10 heads | | | | |
| Celeriac | 20 lb | | | | |
| Celery | 20 heads | | | | |
| Chicory, sugar loaf | 20 ,, | | | | |
| Chinese cabbage | 18 ,, | | | | |
| Curly kale | 25 lb | | | | |
| Endive | 15 heads | | | | |
| Kohl rabi | 20 lb | | | | |
| Leeks | 15 ,, | | | | |
| Lettuce | 25–50 heads | | | | |
| Onions | 15 lb | | | | |
| Parsnip | 28 ,, | | | | |

| Vegetable | Good crop from a 20 ft row | Your own results | | | |
|---|---|---|---|---|---|
| | | Year 1 | Year 2 | Year 3 | Year 4 |
| Peas, dwarf | 25 lb | | | | |
| Potatoes, early | 35 ,, | | | | |
| Potatoes, maincrop | 50 ,, | | | | |
| Salsify | 10 ,, | | | | |
| Scorzonera | 10 ,, | | | | |
| Seakale beet | 30 ,, | | | | |
| Shallots | 12 ,, | | | | |
| Swedes | 30 ,, | | | | |
| Spinach | 15 ,, | | | | |
| Spinach beet | 30 ,, | | | | |
| Turnips | 15 ,, | | | | |
| Winter radish | 20 ,, | | | | |
| | *Good crop from each plant* | | | | |
| Courgette, tender young ones | 18 lb | | | | |
| Cucumber, greenhouse | 20 fruit | | | | |
| Cucumber, outdoor | 10 ,, | | | | |
| Marrow, medium to large | 10 ,, | | | | |
| Tomato, greenhouse | 6 lb | | | | |
| Tomato, outdoor | 3 ,, | | | | |

**Analyse the results**

You can go one step further. Use the information from the seed packets and the 'Date and Weight' book to make an 'at a glance' biography of the vegetable garden. Add your own comments on the weather or make it more scientific by keeping a record of the daily amounts of rain and sunshine – which are published by some newspapers.

**Note:** subsequent pages will start and finish with later months as the later maturing crops get recorded.

WEATHER RECORD 19...

| DATE | APRIL RAIN INS | APRIL SUN HRS | MAY RAIN INS | MAY SUN HRS | JUNE RAIN INS | JUNE SUN HRS |
|---|---|---|---|---|---|---|
| 1 | — | 6.6 | .040 | 1.3 | .109 | 8.2 |
| 2 | .253 | 1.6 | | | | |
| 3 | .268 | 0.5 | — | 4.4 | .059 | 7.1 |
| 4 | .025 | 6.5 | .198 | 1.7 | .201 | 6.3 |
| 5 | .137 | 3.5 | .020 | 3.1 | | |
| 6 | .095 | 10. | .050 | | | |

LARGE MASTER PLAN
3 PLOTS 20' x 20'
1 PLOT 20' x 19'

Q = QUANTITY
V = VALUE

| YEAR 19... | RAIN INS. | SUN HRS. | RHUBARB SOWN Q | V | RADISH SAXERRE 7 MAR 9 APRIL Q | V | RADISH ICICLE 9 APRIL 17 MAY Q | V | LETTUCE TOM THUMB 18 MAR IN FRAME Q | V | LETTUCE LIT. GEM. 9 APRIL 9 JULY Q | V | SPINACH BEET 9 APR Q | V | COURGETTE GREEN BUSH 17 APRIL P/O 27/5 Q | V | COURGETTE TENDER+TRUE 17 APRIL P/O 27/5 Q | V |
|---|---|---|---|---|---|---|---|---|---|---|---|---|---|---|---|---|---|---|
| MARCH | 1.88 | 125 | | | | | | | | | | | | | | | | |
| APRIL | 1.76 | 87 | 4 lb | | | | | | | | | | | | | | | |
| MAY | 1.30 | 197 | — | | 4 lots | | | | 52 | | 25 | | 7 lb | | 1 lb | | 1 lb | |
| JUNE | 1.49 | 140 | 13 lb | | 6 lots | | 7 lots | | | | 22 | | 5 lb | | 9 lb | | 1 lb | |
| JULY | 5.29 | 158 | | | | | 6 lots | | | | — | | 6 lb | | 15 lb | | 12 lb | |
| AUG | 1.27 | 93 | | | | | | | | | 36 | | | | 8 lb | | 7 lb | |
| SEPT | 1.08 | 136 | | | | | | | | | | | | | 4 lb | | 4 lb | |
| OCT | 2.42 | 88 | | | | | | | | | | | | | | | | |
| TOTALS | | | 17 lbs | | 10 lots | | 13 lots | | 52 | | 83 | | 18 lb | | 37 lb | | 25 lb | |
| COMMENTS | A late Spring followed by a dull wet Summer | | Good quality. 10 lb frozen for winter use | | V. Good quality | | Excellent | | Good | | Good as ever | | OK. Pulled up end of August. Parsnips over-shadowing it. | | Plus 2 big Marrow Good Q. in spite of the wet summer. Compact plants | | Plus 2 big Marrows Early fruit rotted off in rain. Plants grew very large & covered other crops. G. Qual. fruit | |

## Profit and loss

You can now work out how much you spent on the vegetable garden and the value of the crops you produced. You will need to assess the cost of:

CAPITAL ITEMS: tools, greenhouse, frame, wheelbarrow, hose pipe, paving slabs, etc. I suggest you cost these over ten years. I know some of them will last longer but you will have earned no interest on the money you spent on them – so it will be about right.

SEMI-CAPITAL ITEMS: bamboo canes, cloches, seed-trays, plant pots, nets, etc. Cost these over five years.

ANNUAL COSTS: these will, of course, include seeds, plants, manures, composts, cotton, twine, pesticides, etc.
You can now compare your total annual costs with the value of the crops produced in one year.

You won't be a millionaire. In fact I reckon you'll have spent up to half the value of your crops in producing them. But what we can't put a value on is the taste, the freshness, the ability to grow the varieties we want and pick them when we want – and the sense of achievement. You may reckon it's money very well spent.

## THE SOWING AND HARVESTING GUIDE

This shows you the months in which seeds may be sown and the crops harvested, but it should only be used as a general guide. Sowing times will vary depending on where you live and the state of the weather and the soil. Far better to wait another week or even another fortnight than to put your seed to bed in cold wet conditions.

Most vegetables are sown where they are to grow and then the young plants progressively thinned until they are the right distance apart. But others, like brassicas and leeks, are started in a 'seed bed', a small spare plot where seeds are sown in short rows and then the best plants selected for putting out in their final positions when they are large enough to handle. If you haven't room for a seed bed then just use the normal planting out positions for your nursery rows.

Progressively thin the seedlings of cabbage, broccoli, kale and sprouts to 2–3 in. apart, protect them from the birds and slugs and plant them out when they're 4–6 in. tall. With leeks sow the seed thinly, just three to the inch, and there will be no need to thin them. Then choose the best plants from your 6 ft row for planting out. To be on the safe side you may wish to grow a 9 ft row for the Large Master Plan.

Sow the other vegetables straight into their growing positions. To get earlier crops the 'frost shy' ones can be started under glass, or perhaps in the house if you've got a wide south facing window sill, and then planted out when all danger of frost is past. You'll find detailed information on each type of vegetable in the chapter on 'Culture of Individual Crops'.

To save yourself the trouble you may wish to buy plants from a local nursery. The 'Sowing and Harvesting Guide' tells you how many plants you need, but the ideal distances between plants will vary depending on the variety grown so do check with the nursery or read the notes on the seed packet before you decide on the final distance apart.

And before you sow any seeds turn to page 119 and read the chapter on 'Seed Sowing'.

# THE SOWING AND HARVESTING GUIDE

| Start these in a seed bed | Length of row in seed bed | Large Plan | Med. Plan | Small Plan | Final distance between plants in inches | Depth of drill in inches | F = Freeze  S = Store  P = Pickle |
|---|---|---|---|---|---|---|---|
| Broccoli  Calabrese | 3' | 10 | 7 | | 24 | ½ | F |
| Broccoli P. Sprouting | 3' | 10 | 7 | | 24 | ½ | F |
| Brussel Sprouts | 3' | 8 | | | 30 | ½ | F |
| Cabbage  Savoy | 6' | 26 | 10 | 6 | 18-24 | ½ | |
| Cabbage  Summer | 6' | 20 | 30 | 10 | 12-18 | ½ | |
| Cauliflower Australian | 4' | | | | 18 | ¾ | |
| Cauliflower  Winter | 3' | | | | 24 | ¾ | |
| Kale  Curly | 4' | | | | 18 | ¾ | F |
| Leeks | 6' | 120 | 60 | 40 | 6-9 | ½ | |

Sow these where they are to grow

| | | | | | Final distance between plants in inches | Depth of drill in inches | F = Freeze  S = Store  P = Pickle |
|---|---|---|---|---|---|---|---|
| Beans  Dwarf Broad | | | | | 9 | 2 | F |
| Beans  Dwarf French | | | | | 9 | 2 | F |
| Beans  Haricot | | | | | 9 | 2 | S |
| Beans  Runner | | | | | 9-12 | 2 | For salt |
| Beans  Tall Broad | | | | | 6-9 | 2 | F |
| Beetroot  Early  Boltardy | | | | | 4-6 | ½ | S |
| Beetroot  Main Crop | | | | | 6 | ½ | S |
| Carrot | | | | | 3-6 | ¼ | S |
| Celery  Self Blanching or American Green | | | | | 9 | ¼ | |
| Chicory  Sugar Loaf | | | | | 10 | ½ | |
| Chinese Cabbage | | | | | 12 | ½ | |
| Corn Salad | | | | | 3-4 | ½ | For salt |
| Cucumber  Outdoor | | | | | 24 | ¾ | |
| Endive | | | | | 12-15 | ½ | |
| Garlic | | | | | 9 | 1 | S |
| Jerusalem Artichoke | | | | | 12 | 6 | S |
| Kohl Rabi | | | | | 6 | ½ | F |
| Lettuce  Various varieties | | | | | 4-9 | ½ | |

| These can be sown under glass for earlier crops | J F M A M J J A S O N D J F M A | Row spacing | Plant spacing | Notes |
|---|---|---|---|---|
| Parsnip | | 6-9 | 1 | S |
| Peas | | 2-3 | 2 | F |
| Potatoes  Early | | 12 | 5-6 | |
| Potatoes  Maincrop | | 18 | 5-6 | S |
| Radish  Various | | 1-2 | ½ | |
| Radish  Winter | | 6-8 | ½ | |
| Salsify | | 6-8 | 1 | S |
| Scorzonera | | | 1 | S |
| Seakale Beet | | 12 | ½ | F |
| Shallots (Sets) | | 6-9 | 1 | S or P |
| Spinach | | 8-12 | 1 | F |
| Spinach Beet | | 12-15 | 1 | F |
| Spring Onion | | 1-2 | ¼ | |
| Swede | | 9-12 | ½ | |
| Sweet Corn | | 12-18 | 1 | F |
| Turnip | | 4-6 | ½ | F |

| These can be sown under glass for earlier crops | No. of plants needed Large Plan | Med. Plan | Small Plan | J F M A M J J A S O N D J F M A | | | |
|---|---|---|---|---|---|---|---|
| Beans  Dwarf French | 54 | 24 | 26 | | 9 | 2 | F |
| Beans  Runner | 52 | 40 | 26 | | 9-12 | 2 | F or salt |
| Capsicum  Sweet Peppers | | | | | 15-18 | ½ | |
| Cauliflower  Summer | | | | | 24 | ¾ | |
| Celeriac | | | | | 12 | ¼ | S |
| Celery  Self Blanching | 40 | 28 | | | 9 | ¼ | |
| Cucumber  Outdoor | | | | | 24 | ¾ | |
| Marrow or Courgette | 6 | 6 | 3 | | 24 | ¾ | S. F. |
| Melon  Cantaloupe | | | | | 36 | ¾ | |
| Sweet Corn | 24 | 15 | | | 12-18 | 1 | F |
| Tomatoes  Outdoor | 13 | 10 | 6 | | 18-24 | ¼ | F Puree |

█████ = Sow     ——— = Plant out     ▒▒▒ = Harvest

# 8. The Soil

The precious topsoil in which our vegetables are grown is rarely more than 2 ft deep and is often only 1 ft deep. Think of that in comparison to the two thousand million square miles of the total surface of the earth. It makes the dust on the mantlepiece seem positively thick by comparison.

The earth's crust is in layers and when excavations are made, such as cuttings for roads or mining, we can see these layers clearly. That thin dark layer on the surface is the topsoil. It has usually been formed over thousands of years from weathered rock which has broken down into sands and powders. Mixed up with it are the organic remains of plants and animal life; and living in it is a host of organisms from earth worms down to bacteria, all of them affecting its structure and ability to grow plants. Underneath is the subsoil, which has fewer organic remains and fewer living organisms in it than the topsoil, and is lighter in colour, and below that is the underlying rock.

*What are known as sedentary soils and sedentary subsoils lie on top of parent rock of the same basic material.*

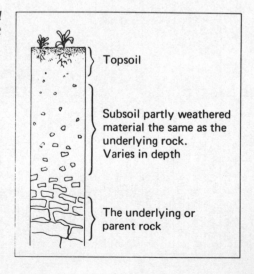

Topsoil

Subsoil partly weathered material the same as the underlying rock. Varies in depth

The underlying or parent rock

*Other soils bear no relation to the underlying rock. They are called transported soils and that doesn't mean brought in by the builder's lorry. There are four types of transported soils. Those deposited by glaciers millions of years ago; aeolian soils which have been moved by the wind; colluvial soils which have slipped down a slope to give a deep soil at the base of a hill; and alluvial soils which have been deposited by water — usually river flood plains.*

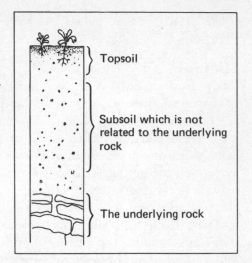

Topsoil

Subsoil which is not related to the underlying rock

The underlying rock

## TOPSOILS

Our gardens have topsoils of many different kinds, and most of us don't have any choice in the matter. We have to do our best with the soil we've got and continually try to improve it. There are hundreds of different types of soil but we can divide them into very approximate kinds according to the amount of sand, silt or clay in them

We could use one of twelve standard terms to describe their texture:

| | | | |
|---|---|---|---|
| Sand | Loam | Silt loam | Silty clay |
| Loamy sand | Sandy clay loam | Silty clay loam | Sand clay |
| Sandy loam | Clay loam | Silt | Clay |

We might also have to add the description 'gravelly' or describe them as peaty or chalky.

The way we cultivate our plots will depend partly on the basic type of soil we have.

### Sandy soils

These are nice and easy to work and are usually well drained. This is useful in winter and in very wet weather because if plants are waterlogged they will die just as surely as if they get no water at all. But sandy soils dry out too quickly in the summer and need large quantities of organic material to help them retain moisture in hot weather — such things as compost, farmyard manure or peat. This organic content also helps to stop the sandy soil blowing away in the wind.

Sand is poor at retaining plant foods: they get washed out. So sandy soils need organic materials and plant nutrients continually replaced in them to produce good crops. Then they'll produce some very fine ones.

### Silt soils

They occur mainly as alluvial soils deposited in river plains and are made up of finer particles than sand. Because of their structure they are prone to 'capping' after heavy rain – this is where the soil particles run together at the surface to form a continuous crust or cap. If this crust dries out it can form a barrier to stop seedlings coming up and water and air getting down. To prevent capping at seed sowing time leave a fairly coarse seed bed and incorporate organic matter to keep the soil open and to stabilize its structure.

Apart from this, silt soils are excellent for the vegetable garden. They are usually deep and fertile with a high available water capacity and a good natural reserve of nutrients.

### Clay soils

The problems of clay are well known. It's heavy and difficult to work. It sticks to your boots and to your spade and trying to get a fine seed bed in it can be very frustrating. A very clayey vegetable garden that is badly drained is virtually impossible to work in the wetter months and crops can die from the waterlogging. If we walk on the soil when it's wet it can 'pan down' and form a hard layer like cement.

So what do we do with clay soils? They should be rough dug in the autumn, and preferably left in ridges to expose the greatest possible surface of the soil to the rain, wind, snow and frost. In the spring keep off the soil till it has dried out and it will then crumble down to a reasonable tilth.

Clay soils can be improved by the addition of compost, strawy farmyard manure, leaf mould, wool shoddy or other organic material. Spent hops are also useful but you need a lot of them. The same goes for peat.

One great advantage of clay soils is that plant nutrients don't easily wash out of them. And lime has a very good effect on clay. It breaks it down and makes it less sticky.

So with a clay soil you need to do your winter digging early, incorporate plenty of organic stuff, leave the soil rough and lime it in the early spring. It will then repay you with some excellent crops.

### Peaty soils

These tend to occur in areas that have been waterlogged over thousands of years and the peat has been formed by the continual growth and decay of aquatic plants. The peat can be up to 30 ft deep so it forms the subsoil as well as the topsoil. Large areas of Lincolnshire have such soils.

Provided they are properly drained these peaty soils are easy to work and don't need bulky organic manures added to them. They are usually short of potash and phosphates and the acid state of the soil has to be counterbalanced with lime. Skilfully managed they produce very good horticultural crops.

### Loamy soil

The ideal kind of soil: a mixture of sand, clay and plenty of organic matter that produces a good dark crumbly soil that is easy to dig, easy to hoe and makes a fine seed bed. It retains moisture in hot weather but does not become waterlogged in wet weather. It doesn't pan down. Loamy soils supply plants with the right balance of air and water, they retain nutrients and grow almost all crops very well indeed.

**As gardeners our aim must be to turn our garden soil into a loamy one and keep it that way.**

(N.B. When turf is stacked upside down in a large pile and allowed to rot down the resultant crumbly soil is also called 'loam'. It makes a good basis for potting composts.)

## SUBSOILS

The layer under the topsoil is usually called the subsoil. It can be based on sand, clay or chalk or a mixture of them. It is important horticulturally and many plants send roots down into this layer where they may find some plant nutrients and moisture.

### Chalk

If the subsoil is chalk then you will get very good drainage. This is usually an advantage, although in very dry summers the drainage can be too good and the plants can suffer as a result. The chalk brought to the surface during digging will prevent the topsoil becoming acid and may save you having to apply lime. However, be careful not to bring large quantities of chalk to the surface otherwise you'll spoil the structure of your topsoil and make it unpleasant to work in.

A chalk subsoil may, of course, make your soil too alkaline. If tests show this is so then add every possible kind of organic manure you can get. Compost, peat, animal manures, sewage, hops and shoddy should all be used for winter manuring, and organic mulches should be used in summer. While the use of sawdust is not normally recommended, as it can extract nitrogen from the soil during its rotting process, on a very alkaline soil it is worth using as a summer mulch up to $\frac{1}{2}$ in. deep. Spread it on the surface between the rows of crops and dig it in during the winter. But don't use sawdust unless the soil really is very alkaline and it is the only thing you can get.

Hoof and horn is a good slow release nitrogen fertiliser to use just before you spread the sawdust.

Chalk soils will probably not give you very good crops of potatoes and tomatoes but they can give good crops of other vegetables including salads, brassicas and the pea and bean family.

## Clay

If your subsoil is clay then you may well have a drainage problem. In very badly waterlogged soils this may mean having land drains put in. Plants don't like to be waterlogged; they also don't like to be cold – and a wet soil is usually a cold one.

Drainage is certainly improved by double digging or 'bastard trenching' as it is called. (Bastard trenching is explained in the chapter on 'Digging'.) It is sometimes worth digging a drain-trench or culvert right across the garden from the highest to the lowest point, perhaps leading to a ditch. The trench should be about 2 ft wide and 2 ft deep. A 5 or 6 in. layer of old bricks, rubble or large clinker should be placed in the bottom. On top of this put a 2 in. layer of small clinker and then if you have any turfs place them upside down on the small clinker before filling in the trench again. Make sure the subsoil goes back as the subsoil and the topsoil stays on the top.

## Sand

If you have sand as a subsoil then you will get very good drainage, but this may be too good in dry weather. Plenty of organic material in the topsoil is the only answer and you will need to water the plants more often than with other subsoils.

In general the golden rule with subsoils is to leave them where they are. Don't bring them to the surface. As many of you know only too well, building sites are sometimes left with the subsoil on the surface and it takes a lot of humus over many years to convert it into a reasonable topsoil.

# 9. Digging

There is a school of thought that says: 'Don't bother to dig at all. After you've sown your seeds put well-rotted manure or compost on the surface of the soil and let the worms and the weather take the plant foods down.'

If you have a very light sandy soil then I think there is quite a lot of sense in this method. Sandy soils tend to leach out their nutrients all too readily and you could well get better value from your manure or compost if you use it this way instead of digging it in. It will also act as a mulch to conserve moisture and stop these light sandy soils from drying out so quickly or blowing away.

But it does seem that the medium and heavy soils derive great benefit from the traditional autumn or winter dig. Why is this?

1. It helps drainage – stops plants getting waterlogged, and well-drained soil is warmer.
2. It enables us to incorporate organic material, such as compost or farmyard manure, at the depth in the soil that we need it.
3. It ensures that air gets mixed up with the soil – plant roots need oxygen.
4. It allows water to travel more freely through the soil towards the plant roots.
5. We can leave the soil 'rough dug' so that the winter weather will improve its condition and make it workable when the spring comes round.
6. It also gives us a chance to clean up the garden; to dig up those old potatoes that got left in the soil by chance and to clean the weeds off the surface and dig them in – although perhaps those weeds shouldn't have been there in the first place.

What method of digging should we use? There are ways of digging that cultivate the soil to a depth of 3 ft but I don't propose that we go to that extent. Broadly speaking we have three choices: *single digging, simple trenching* or *double digging,* usually called *bastard trenching.*

## SINGLE DIGGING

This consists of pushing in the spade or fork, digging up the 'spit', turning it over and putting it back where it came from. With a heavy or clay soil it is certainly better than doing nothing as it does let the winter weather break down the top layer of soil.

Gardeners often do this single digging in summer after they have cleared off one crop and want to plant another in the same place. Don't do it if the weather is at all dry: it's a certain way of losing soil moisture. Better by far to clean up the top inch or so of the soil with a hoe and rake and plant the next crop without any digging.

There are several mechanical diggers on the market which make light work of single digging, but single digging is not as good as trenching.

## SIMPLE TRENCHING

A trench, about 10 in. deep and 1 ft 6 in. wide is taken out at one end of the area to be dug. The earth is taken to the other end and used to fill in the last trench at the end of the dig. Simple trenching enables manure to be incorporated in each trench as the plot is dug; the operation is the same as bastard trenching except that the trench does not have to be so wide as the subsoil is not turned over.

## BASTARD TRENCHING

The soil is dug two spits deep – about 20 in. in all – but the soil layers stay where they are – the topsoil at the top and the subsoil at the bottom. This digging should be done in the autumn or early winter and the surface soil should be left in rough clods for the frost to deal with. Use a full size garden spade, not a fork.

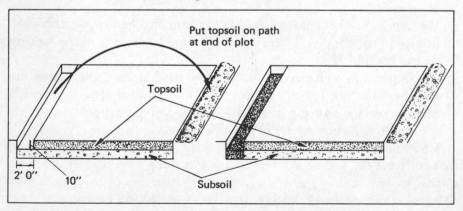

Put topsoil on path at end of plot

Topsoil

2' 0"    10"

Subsoil

**Step one**

Take out a trench 2 ft wide and 10 in. deep at one end of the plot and put this topsoil at the other end of the plot. (10 in. is the depth of a full size garden spade.)

**Step two**

Step down into the trench and, working your way backwards along the trench, dig over the subsoil to the full depth of the spade.

**Step three**

Skim off any weeds from the surface of the topsoil near the trench and place these in the bottom of the trench. Don't do this with tap-rooted weeds like dandelion – put those on the bonfire. Now spread manure or compost in the bottom of the trench over the dug subsoil. (The manure should have been placed ready in small heaps on the plot before starting to dig, so that you know how much you can spare for each trench.)

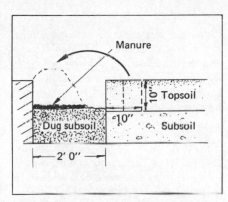 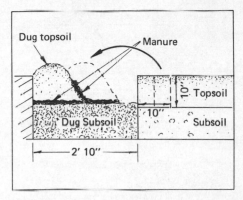

**Step four**

Dig the next 10 by 10 in. spit of topsoil and turn it over on to the dug subsoil. Throw the soil forward so that you keep an open trench all the time and leave it as rough clods.

Keep the spade upright so that you dig to its full depth and do handle that 10 in. wide spit as two 5 in. slices rather than risk straining your back.

When you get to the end of the row straighten up, take time to admire your handiwork and then repeat the operation.

**Step five**

Step down into the new trench. Dig over the subsoil.

Spread manure in the trench and on the sloping side so that it is distributed throughout the depth of the top spit but with none being left on the surface of the plot. Then place the next 10 by 10 in. spit of topsoil on the manure. Throw the soil forward and keep an open trench. Leave the soil rough.

Continue like this to the end of the plot then fill in the last trench with the heap of topsoil that you took out of the first trench.

## DIGGING FOR THE MASTER PLANS

If your vegetable garden is laid out as in the Master Plans, with two plots adjacent, you should not, strictly speaking, move any of the soil from one plot into the other plot or the benefits of crop rotation will be partly lost. You can avoid this and also save yourself having to cart that trenchful of soil from one end of the plot right to the other.

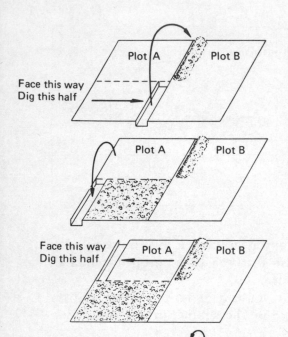

*If you are doing simple trenching, take out a trench 10 in. deep and 18 in. wide half way across Plot A and stack this soil on Plot B in the position shown. Dig this half of Plot A in the way previously described.*

*When you get to the end of this half of Plot A fill in the trench (which should still be 10 in. deep and 18 in. wide) with soil from the other half of Plot A as shown.*

*Now dig the second half of Plot A.*

*And fill in the last trench with the soil that has been stacked on Plot B. That completes the digging of Plot A.*

*Dig Plot B in the same way. Take out a trench in the position shown and stack the soil on the path ready to fill in the last trench.*

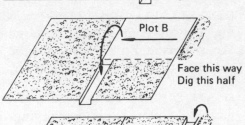

*Dig the first half of Plot B and fill in the trench from the other half of Plot B.*

*Dig the second half of Plot B and fill in the final trench with the soil that was stacked on the path.*
**All the soil from Plot A is still in Plot A and all the soil from Plot B is still in Plot B.**

You can save yourself some work by digging in a fan shaped pattern as there will then be no need to move soil to fill in the 'halfway' trench. However it is much more difficult to keep the plot level and get an even distribution of compost if you dig in this way.

I dig in a pattern which is a compromise between the orthodox method and the fan shaped one. It still needs care to keep the soil level but certainly saves some time and effort. However, I would only recommend either of these systems if you are an experienced digger and have a good eye for levels.

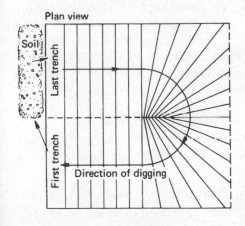

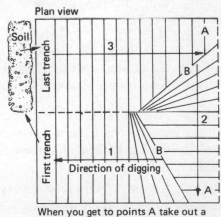

When you get to points A take out a trench and put the soil in the gutters B.

## SOME THOUGHTS ON DIGGING

The robin and the blackbird will certainly join you in your digging and cast a critical eye over your work, so show them that you know a thing or two.

DECIDE ON YOUR SOWING PLAN before you start to dig. Put marking sticks in your plots to show where the hungry feeders like runner beans, peas and marrows are to be sown and put in extra manure or compost in those places as you dig.

SHARE OUT YOUR MANURE in convenient small heaps on the surface of the plots ready for digging in. Some people like to scatter the manure all over the plot before they start, but if the weather is wet it sticks to your boots and makes a right mess. I suggest you put the manure straight from the heaps into the trenches. If you are using well-rotted compost it won't stick to your boots in the same way.

DON'T DIG WHEN THE SOIL IS VERY WET. You won't do the soil much good and with that water in it you'll be lifting a lot more weight as you dig.

DO TAKE YOUR TIME when digging. A steady slow pace will enable you to keep digging the whole day long, especially if you straighten up and take a short rest at the end of every row.

KEEP YOUR SPADE CLEAN. Have a scraper with you when you are digging. Keep your spade bright and shiny – it'll slide through the soil so much easier. Rub it over with an oily rag every time you put it away. Hang the rag up where the spade is kept so that you don't forget.

GET YOUR BETTER HALF TO BUY YOU A STAINLESS STEEL SPADE. They are expensive but if you can afford one they do help to turn digging into a pleasurable exercise rather than a chore.

WEAR A GOOD PAIR OF BOOTS with a good thick sole. If you wear shoes your foot is liable to get sore where you press it on the spade and if you dig with wellingtons on the spade may cut through them and spoil them.

HAVE PAVING SLABS FOR PATHS if you can. It's like having a permanent ruler round your plots – it tells you the width of your spits and where to put your marking sticks.

# 10. Water in the Soil and Garden Tools

An odd heading, but there is a close association between the two.

Most vegetables are at least 90 per cent water. There is a continual flow of water through them taken up by the roots and transpired from the leaves by the energy of the sun. A mature lettuce will transpire more than half its own weight every sunny day. This water enables the plants to stand erect and keep their shape and it brings up dissolved nutrients from the soil. If plants don't have a ready supply of water available at their roots they won't grow to their full size and will tend to run to seed early. They won't taste as good and in an extreme water shortage they will die.

Water is also flowing and transpiring at the same rate through any weeds in the garden and on a sunny day bare patches of damp soil will also lose water by 'evaporation', but it will be only a fraction of the water lost through the plants and weeds.

So our aim must be to keep down the weeds and reduce the evaporation of water from the soil. The best way of doing this is by using the Dutch hoe.

## THE DUTCH HOE

This is probably the most important tool in the garden after the spade. It is used for hoeing between the plants. Carefully walk backwards between your rows of crops pushing the hoe forward in front of you as you go to cut off any weeds from their roots and to turn the top half inch of soil into a loose dust. Try not to cut off your crops. By walking backwards you will not tread on the areas you have hoed.

The fine loose soil is called a 'dust mulch' and will reduce the evaporation of water from the bare soil. Be very careful to confine the mulch to the shallowest depth that you can. If you bring damp soil up to the surface it will lose its moisture and the net result will be water wastage and not water conservation. Deep hoeing would also damage

97

the roots of your crops, which can spread quite a long way from the plants.

When the weather is dry do this dutch hoeing at least once every fortnight, whether the soil looks as if it needs it or not. In this way you'll kill off the weed seedlings before they appear and you'll maintain the dust mulch. It takes very little time to do and in the long run it's so much easier than 'weeding'.

## THE LINE, THE DRAW HOE AND THE STICK

You can make a garden line with a length of cord and two sticks but it's worth treating yourself to the luxury of a proper metal reel.

Stretch the line across the plot where you want to make a seed drill and push the sticks in the soil at either end to anchor it. Use the draw hoe for taking out the drill. Stand with your back foot on the line to stop it moving and, keeping the blade of the hoe against the line, gently but firmly pull the hoe towards you.

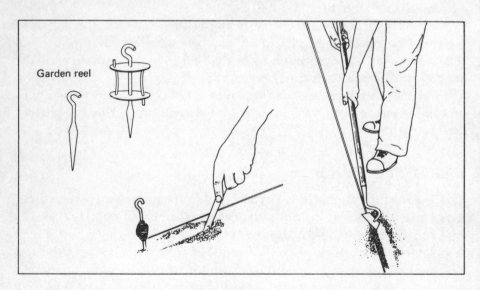

Garden reel

You can make a very good drill without a hoe just by drawing a thick piece of stick through the soil. I use a piece of broom handle about 3 ft long.

The draw hoe can also be used for taking out deeper drills for peas and for earthing up potatoes, although I prefer to use a spade.

## THE RAKE

Get yourself a good modern rake with a light metal handle rather than a heavy wooden one. Use it for raking down the soil into a fine tilth for making those seed drills at sowing time, and for clearing up leaves and other debris in the autumn.

## THE CULTIVATOR

If you've got some soil that's gone solid where you've been walking on the garden beside a row of peas or beans and you want to loosen it up for the next crop use a garden tool called a cultivator. It's got three or more vicious looking hooked tines on it and you use it with a chopping action to cultivate the top couple of inches of soil ready for the next crop. A very useful tool, and much better than using a fork which brings too much damp soil to the surface with consequent water loss.

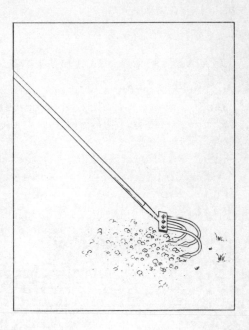

## THE TROWEL AND THE DIBBER

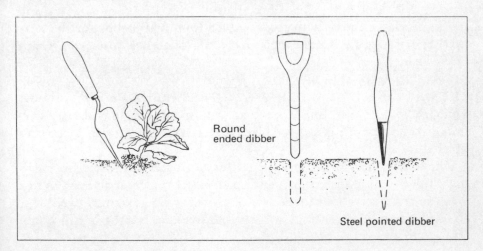

Round ended dibber

Steel pointed dibber

The trowel enables you to transplant seedlings without damaging their roots, although an old tablespoon will serve almost as well for this purpose.

The dibber is used for making holes – say for leeks. Mine is a handle that broke off a spade. I pointed and smoothed the end and then cut grooves round it at 3 in. spacings so that I know how deep a hole I'm 'dibbing'.

## THE SPADE AND THE FORK

Buy the best you can afford. They do come with different length handles so get one that suits your height. For the vegetable garden they need to be full-sized ones with the blade or prongs 10–11 in. deep.

There is a special kind of fork with flat prongs that is used for digging up potatoes – but it's not absolutely necessary as the ordinary digging fork will do this job quite well.

## THE WHEELBARROW

This is a necessity in anything but the very smallest garden. It will be used to carry soil, paving slabs, bricks, sand, cement, concrete, garden refuse, manure, compost, plants, lawn mowings and a lot else. It needs to be strong, light, easy to push, manoeuvrable and leakproof.

The wheelbarrows of old were beautifully made wooden ones with wooden wheels but you needed to be pretty strong to push them empty, let alone full. There are many kinds of wheelbarrows and trucks available today with from one to four wheels but for the normal vegetable grower and gardener the choice comes down to perhaps one of two.

THE GALVANIZED GARDENER'S WHEELBARROW (not the heavier builder's one) with one wheel at the front and a tubular steel framework supporting a galvanized sheet-steel body with a capacity of $2\frac{1}{2}$–4 cwt.

The load is distributed between your arms and the wheel so pushing a full barrow can be hard work. But it has the great advantage that you can maltreat a well-made one to an incredible extent. I even light small bonfires in mine (not to be recommended) and it's still going strong after twenty years.

THE BALLBARROW is an ingeniously designed wheelbarrow with a large plastic ball for the front wheel, a lightweight but strong plastic body and a carrying capacity of 2½–3 cwt. There's also an extension that may be fitted to it.

Among its advantages are lightness of weight, good manoeuvrability and a design that puts the load above the wheel when you are pushing it, so there is less strain on your arms.

## THE GARDEN SPRAY

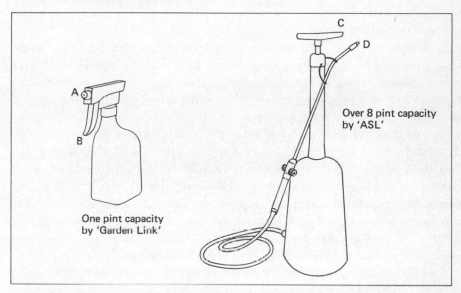

Very necessary if you wish to apply insecticides. You'll find it useful if you have two sprays – a small one and a large one as in the diagram. Both are worked by air pressure and are made of plastic. The small one sprays through the nozzle 'A' as you pump the handle 'B'. The large one is pumped up first with the handle 'C' and then sprays through the adjustable nozzle 'D' which can be controlled by an on/off tap.

## WATER FROM THE HOSE, THE WATERING CAN AND THE BUTT

By far the best water for your garden is rain – the gentle persistent kind that is slowly but surely absorbed by the soil until it is holding a plentiful supply of water for the plant roots at any depth, but with good drainage so that the soil is never waterlogged as this would exclude air which the roots also need.

We may sometimes grumble that we have too much rain, but in most summers we need to apply water artificially to help young plants to survive and to encourage the maximum growth of established plants. Under normal summer temperatures 1 sq. yd of vegetation will transpire nearly half a gallon of water every day. If just the top inch of soil is wetted it can be temporarily useful for small seedlings but the water will soon be used up and won't reach the deeper rooted plants. In fact shallow watering can encourage some plants to send out roots near the surface and the plants will not survive unless the surface soil continues to be supplied with water.

Our aim must be to copy that persistent gentle rain and the easiest way is with a hose and sprinkler. Make sure that the sprinkler applies a fine shower of small water droplets evenly distributed over the area being watered. Large droplets of water tend to break down the surface soil into a mud and create a crust or 'pan' which causes subsequent water to run off and not penetrate the soil. Sudden heavy rain can have the same effect. If this does happen let the soil almost dry out and then use a hoe or cultivator to break up the crust again. Don't cultivate any deeper than the thickness of the crust. When you're using the sprinkler leave it on long enough in each area to ensure that the soil is watered in depth. Dig a small test hole with a trowel half an hour after you've turned off the hose to check how far the water has gone down. It will often show that more is needed.

Use the watering can for young seedlings or small plants but make sure the water penetrates right down to their roots. Plastic watering cans are lighter to carry than the metal ones and some have long spouts which makes it easier to water individual plants. Make sure you get a strong one.

Plants need warmth as well as moisture and if you water them in the evening this will lower the temperature of the soil for the whole night. If you have the choice it's better to water earlier in the day so that the soil has a chance to warm up again by nightfall.

Watering can be a chore. There can be a temptation not to bother, so make it as easy for yourself as you can. Have a hose permanently laid from a tap to the vegetable garden. Run it along the bottom of the fence or under the hedge so that it's not unsightly. Make sure you have enough hose to reach to the furthest part of the vegetable garden without having to manoeuvre it across your crops.

Have a water butt or water tank near the vegetable plot. If it can't be fed with rain water from a roof then keep it topped up with the hose. Keep a watering can near it so that you don't have to make a special journey to the house every time you need a can of water. The water from the butt will have been warmed by the sun – an added advantage.

Water butts can be expensive. A builders' mechant may charge less for a domestic water tank, or a strong dustbin will do the job quite well if it's sunk into the soil to give it more support. Keep the lid on to stop leaves blowing into it or algae forming in the water. (If you have young children open water tanks can be very dangerous. Make sure any tanks are well above the ground so that they are not easy to fall into, and that they have secure lids.)

**We live in a pleasant temperate climate, ideal for growing so many vegetable crops. We can increase the yield of those crops dramatically by making sure they don't suffer from a shortage of water in the summer months.**

# 11. Manure, Compost, Fertilisers and Lime

## THE FLOGGED PLOT – THE WORN-OUT SOIL

Tens of thousands of town gardens and some country ones as well have got thin disease-ridden soil in which good vegetables will not grow. One of the reasons for this is the attempt to grow the same crops year after year – the same tired old runner beans down the end of the garden with some sickly cabbage as their bedfellows. Proper crop rotation will take us part of the way in solving this problem, but only part of the way. For those plots are not only pest and disease ridden, they are starved.

Many years ago, when the houses were put up, those gardens produced excellent vegetables. But some people had the mistaken idea that growing vegetables was a way of getting something for nothing, something on the cheap. Many of the tenants were hard up, and one can't blame them, but some of the better-off also treated their gardens in the same way. They continually took from them and put nothing back; and in vegetable growing that just won't work.

Under poor soil conditions plants will become sickly and easily succumb to pests and diseases, just like we do. If plants are growing well then they have the robustness to shrug off many attacks. It doesn't matter if a couple of leaves get nibbled away when there are plenty more coming along to take their place. **So we need to get our soil in the right condition.**

Unfortunately we can't do this by just sprinkling on some artificial fertiliser. Large areas of America, India, South Africa and other countries were ruined as crop-producing areas by doing just that. The artificials stimulated plant growth but the humus content of the soil slowly but surely disappeared leaving the earth thin and at the mercy of the wind. It blew away.

The thin earth in many British back gardens has not blown away but it's a poor thing in which to try to grow crops. It is lacking in humus as well as plant nutrients. To put matters right these gardens need to have more organic matter put back into them each year than is taken out by the crops until, in a few years, the soil is once again a rich loamy earth instead of something more like thin sand or hard clay.

In uncultivated areas nature continuously replaces the humus content of soil by the natural cycle of the growth and decay of all animal and plant life. Even where the ground is cropped by grazing herds they leave their dung behind to replace what they have taken as food. Soils must have organic matter continually put back into them. If that is done then fertilisers can play a part as a tonic or booster. The humus from organic matter also darkens the soil which helps it to absorb and retain the warmth from the sun which further helps the plants to grow.

One popular and much advertised organic material is peat. It is useful in supplying humus to the soil but if it is used by itself it won't supply the enzymes, balanced minerals and foods for the millions of bacteria and fungi that should be living and working in the soil to keep it in the right condition for growing healthy crops. For that you must use fully balanced organic material such as compost or farmyard manure.

## FARMYARD OR STABLE MANURE

Farmyard manure usually means cow manure mixed up with straw, although it may contain some pig or poultry manure. Horse or stable manure is usually sold separately.

Good manure is expensive and sometimes difficult to obtain. It can vary greatly in the amount of plant foods it contains, depending on the way the animals have been kept and where the manure has been stored. Animal urine is a very valuable ingredient of manure, owing to its high mineral content, but a lot of this can be washed out by the rain if the manure is stacked in the open. Farmyard manure usually contains more plant nutrients than horse manure, provided that it's got plenty of straw in it and has been stacked under cover. But don't refuse any horse manure you can get hold of.

Buying manure 'by the bag' is expensive. It's best to get a load from a manure merchant or farmer, although farmers are now coming round to putting the manure back on their own land.

If your soil is thin and worn out then there is a lot of organic content to be put back into it. If your total plots measure, say, 40 ft by 40 ft, you may decide to invest some money in at least one ton of manure to give your soil a good meal to start it off on the road to recovery. But that is just like giving a hungry boy a good breakfast. The continual basic supply of food for your soil must be compost.

## THE COMPOST HEAP

Compost is a rather confusing word. It can describe the growing medium we use in seed trays and pots or it can mean the crumbly dark brown well-rotted material from the compost heap. We're talking about the latter.

We must continually put back in the soil as much organic material as we take out when we remove the crops – it's impossible to exaggerate the importance of this. If your soil is thin then for several years you must put in more organic content than you take out so that you gradually redress the balance and restore the soil to its proper condition. After that you must put back as much as you take out each year.

It's essential to have at least one compost heap, and preferably two or three, and continually gather all possible vegetable refuse from the garden and the kitchen. It must never be thrown away in the dustbin. Suitable materials for turning into compost are potato and vegetable peelings, crushed egg shells, orange peel and banana skins, any fruit that's going rotten, pea pods, lettuce leaves – in fact every single scrap of vegetable waste from the house. You can add feathers from old pillows and eiderdowns but take them to the compost heap and wet them before you tear them open or you'll have feathers everywhere. Cotton flock takes a long time to rot down but can be added in small quantities. Don't use any man-made materials.

Make it easy for yourself and your family to do this collection. In the kitchen near the sink have a 'compost colander' into which every scrap of suitable kitchen waste is put. Outside the back door have a large compost bucket with a lid on it and empty the colander into this every day. Empty the bucket on to the compost heap when it's full. If your neighbours can't be bothered to make their own compost then supply them with a compost bucket and empty it for them on to your compost heap.

From the garden collect all dead plants and flowers, grass cuttings, hedge clippings that aren't woody, weeds, the parts of the vegetable plants you don't eat and any organic manure from poultry, pigeons, guinea pigs or rabbits. Include the bashed-up stumps of cabbages but not the roots – burn those. Make sure lawn mowings are layered in with other materials. Don't include badly diseased material, oils or fats and don't try to compost sawdust or woody material. The heap will also be able to decompose up to 10 per cent of its own volume of ordinary newspaper if this is torn up small, soaked in water and well mixed in. Don't add glossy paper or coloured paper.

Compost heaps need:

1. A mixed diet: heaps made solely from one material like lawn mowings will almost certainly fail.
2. Moisture.
3. Air.
4. Shelter to help them heat up.
5. An activator: this is an organic source of nitrogen to feed the bacteria in the heap and is sprinkled on every 6–8 in. layer. Good activators are dried blood, fishmeal, hoof and horn, seaweed meal, dried sewage sludge. The occasional layer of animal manure makes a good activator. You can also buy proprietary inorganic activators, but I prefer the organic ones.

### Better than nothing compost

If you haven't time to make some compost bins put your vegetable matter in a 3 ft square heap on the soil in a corner of the garden. Keep the top of the heap flat so that you build it up in layers. Try to make it of a mixture of materials and water them if they are dry. Don't add tree leaves – rot these separately.

Sprinkle some activator over each 6–9 in. layer and keep the heap covered with matting or sacking – something that will keep the heat in but let the gases out. When it is 3 ft high start another heap.

Turn each heap when it is rotted, making sure the outer material goes to the centre of the heap. Then leave it to rot again.

Use any well-rotted heaps to dig in as autumn manure. Don't use the compost as a mulch, it will contain too many weed seeds.

### Good compost

Good compost is made in compost bins which keep in the warmth and help the compost to heat up to about 60°C. This ensures rapid and thorough decomposition and cooks any weed seeds. The traditional and possibly the best one is made from wooden planks. But new wood is expensive so build them with whatever material you can get – bricks, concrete blocks, breeze blocks, railway sleepers, corrugated iron sheets or bales of straw if you live in the country. The box should have three fixed sides and a front of loose boards which can be taken out when you wish to shovel out the compost. The base should be

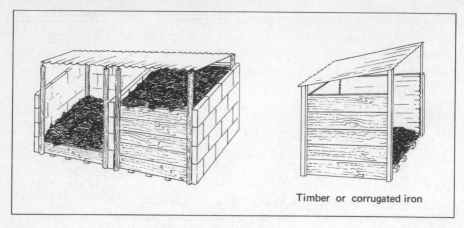

Timber or corrugated iron

well–spaced loose boards, or a sheet of strong weldmesh, sitting on rows of bricks on the soil so that there is a continual supply of air from underneath. The bin should measure 3 ft by 3 ft and be up to 3 ft high, with a roof of corrugated iron 1 ft above the top of the compost.

The best system is to have two or three boxes side by side. They'll help to keep each other warm and moist and it means you can have compost loads in different stages of development.

## The Godfrey box

You can build a compost box fit for a king if you have a supply of rustic poles about 3 in. in diameter and up to 7 ft long. It's easy to make, good to look at and will produce top quality compost. For a double box with total outer measurements of 6 ft long by 4 ft 3 in. wide you will need:

RUSTIC POLES:

| | |
|---|---|
| Uprights: | 10 at 5 ft 6 in. long. |
| | 3 at 6 ft long. |
| | 2 at 7 ft long. |
| Back rails: | 12 at 6 ft long. |
| Side rails: | 36 at 4 ft long. |
| Roof support rails: | 2 at 7 ft long. |

FRONT BOARDS: planks of wood about 2 ft 4 in. long to make the fronts which are each 2 ft 4½ in. wide by 3 ft high. The boards are simply dropped in behind the front uprights to retain the compost as the boxes are filled. (As the uprights will be set 2 ft in the ground they

# The Godfrey box

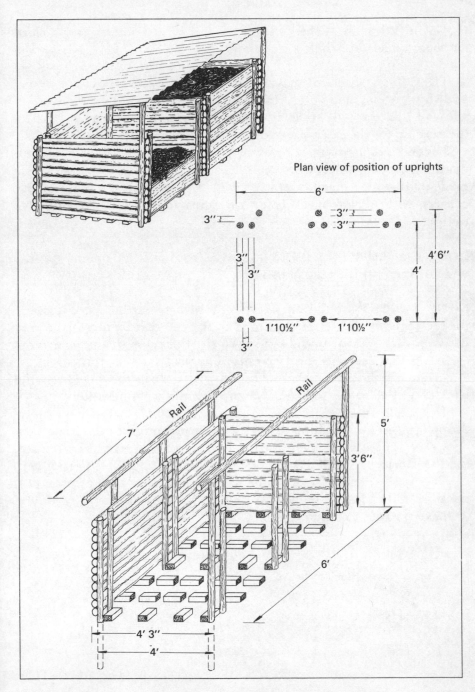

Plan view of position of uprights

6'

3"

3"

3"

3"

3"

4'6"

4'

1'10½"    1'10½"

3"

Rail

Rail

7'

5'

3'6"

6'

4' 3"

4'

should be treated with preservative. It's also preferable to treat the other timbers.)

HOUSEBRICKS: 36 of these. They are laid on the soil to give a clear air space under the whole structure.

WELDMESH: 2 sheets of galvanized weldmesh each about 2 ft 4½ in. wide by 4 ft long laid on top of the bricks to support the compost but allowing air through to it from underneath. It's probably best to measure up for the exact sizes you need when you've built the boxes.

Weldmesh is a strong wire mesh generally used in industry and is made in varying thicknesses and sizes of mesh. A 3 by 1 in. mesh made of 10-gauge metal does very well. You will need to cut out the corners with a pair of pliers or tin snips to fit snugly round the uprights.

CORRUGATED IRON SHEETS: to give a 'roof' 7 ft long and 4 ft 6 in. wide to keep off the rain and snow.

CONSTRUCTION: build on a level site of bare earth. Dig out holes for the uprights and set them firmly in place so that there is just room between each pair of uprights to take the thickness of the poles you are using for back rails and side rails. The plan assumes this is 3 in.

Set out the bricks on the earth. They will keep the side rails and back rails clear of the soil and also support the weldmesh floor.

Now build up the back wall and then the side walls by simply dropping the horizontal poles between the uprights. No nails are necessary. The only things that actually need to be fixed in place are the two horizontal top rails that support the corrugated iron roof and the roof itself. The back rail can be nailed through to the uprights, but the front rail and roof should be fitted so that they can be taken down to make it easier to empty the bins.

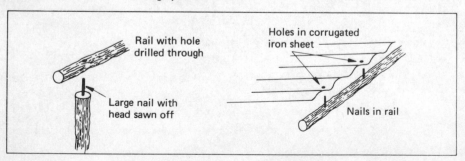

Rail with hole drilled through

Large nail with head sawn off

Holes in corrugated iron sheet

Nails in rail

Put some bricks or other weights on the roof to keep it in place in windy weather. Line the sides of the bins with opened-out cardboard boxes to keep in the heat.

If you need more than two compost boxes you can use the same basic design to make a row of three, or even four boxes – if you can get long enough back rails.

### Filling the compost boxes

Ideally enough mixed material should be accumulated to fill a box and let it compost in one operation: it will reach a higher temperature and be a better end product. But if you can't do this still follow the other rules and you'll end up with pretty good compost.

Make the first layer of coarse stemmy material to keep the air supply at the bottom open. Always spread each layer evenly over the whole area of the box – don't be tempted to just dump it in the middle. If the material is dry, wet each 6–9 in. layer with a couple of gallons of water. Make it moist, not sodden.

Then scatter activator over each layer which will feed the bacteria to make the compost heat up to about 60°C and cook any weed seeds and roots. Have a bit of old matting or sacking to cover the top of the compost to keep warmth and moisture in. You can use plastic sheet or carpet but make a dozen 1 in. diameter air holes in it.

Heaps made in spring and early summer should be ready for the winter dig, and autumn-made heaps by the spring, having reached the stage where they have cooled down, the red worms have moved in and the compost is like dark crumbly Christmas cake. Keep mature compost protected from the rain until you are ready to use it.

## LEAFMOULD

Large quantities of dead leaves from trees and shrubs should be stacked separately to make leafmould. They should not be included in the compost heap as they take two years or more to rot down and will prevent the compost from heating up properly; and it's a shocking waste of good humus-forming material to burn them.

Make a leafmould 'cage' by driving four well-creosoted posts or lengths of angle iron into the ground as uprights and fixing wire netting or weldmesh round them to form the cage. This can be 4 ft square by 4 ft high, or even bigger, and sited in any spare corner.

Into it put all the leaves you can get from your own or neighbours' trees and from the trees in the street, first removing any plastic bags, cigarette packets or twigs. If the leaves are very dry soak them with the hose but otherwise they need no attention at all. Pile them into the cage, tread them down and add more leaves until the cage is filled with a solid mass of leaves.

In about two years the heap will have shrunk to about half its original size and will be ready for digging in as part of the autumn supply of organic material. The leafmould can be mixed in with rotted compost or manure in the November dig. If you use it by itself it will be somewhat short of plant nutrients but it will help to build up the humus content of the soil and will improve its condition. If you have two cages the leaves from consecutive years can be stacked separately.

## MUSHROOM COMPOST

Mushrooms are grown commercially on a mixture of straw, horse manure, dried blood and ground chalk. After the mushrooms have been cropped the resultant spent compost is sold off as a 'manure'.

An occasional load is good for the vegetable garden, especially if you can't get any farmyard manure, but don't use it every year or you may be adding a bit too much chalk to your garden and making it too alkaline. If the mushroom compost has been made with gypsum instead of ground chalk then there's no problem in this respect.

## SEAWEED

If you live by the sea then seaweed is a good source of organic manure. It contains very little phosphorus but otherwise is almost as good as farmyard manure. Either dig it in in the autumn or winter or use it as a top dressing or 'mulch' in the spring and summer.

## WOOL SHODDY

This is a waste product of the woollen trade and to be of any real value it should be free from oil. It is slow in action and may take many years to rot down. It is low in plant nutrients but is a good source of humus to improve the structure of sandy or clay soils. It can be dug in at 1 lb to the square yard.

## FERTILISERS

As we have already seen, soils need humus from decayed organic material to improve their structure and create a proper medium for root development. Plants also need a whole range of nutrients to achieve proper growth. Some are already in the soil, others are added by the manure or compost and yet others by sunlight and air.

Many gardeners find that they can grow good crops without the addition of fertilisers, once they have built up their soil structure with manure or compost and especially if their compost has been well fed with 'activators'. Other gardeners, who do not wish to get too involved in the complexities of plant requirements, dig in plenty of organic material in the autumn and then scatter a general-purpose fertiliser like National Growmore over their plots in the spring, prior to seed sowing.

But soils do vary, and the nutrient requirements of different plants also vary, so other gardeners find it worthwhile to analyse their soils and make good any specific nutrient deficiencies. Soil testing kits can be obtained from seed merchants and garden centres.

## MAJOR PLANT NUTRIENTS AND TRACE ELEMENTS

Plants need carbon, hydrogen and oxygen, which they get from photosynthesis. Green plants use the energy from sunlight to build up complex substances from water and carbon dioxide. So growing our plants right out in the sunshine supplies these.

Plants also need potassium, nitrogen, phosphorus, calcium and magnesium. They may also need traces of copper, zinc, molybdenum, boron and iron: these are referred to as 'trace elements'. Some of these substances occur naturally in the soil, while others are supplied with manure or compost. The three major plant foods are potassium, nitrogen and phosphorus, and it is worth ensuring that your plants are getting their proper requirements of these.

### Potassium

The lighter soils tend to be deficient in potassium or potash, as it is called. There is evidence that plants need satisfactory levels of potassium to help photosynthesis. It is vital for the development of flowers and fruit, so pod-producing or seed-producing vegetables like peas, beans and tomatoes need it. It also helps in disease resistance and is needed by plants that have their 'crop' below ground – like potatoes and carrots.

*113*

SULPHATE OF POTASH is the usual form of potassium used in horti-
culture. Care should be taken to apply only the amount that your soil
needs; rarely more than 1 oz to the square yard and often much less.

WOOD ASHES contain modest traces of potash, about a sixth of that
in sulphate of potash, so put your bonfire ashes on the garden.

## Nitrogen

Nitrogenous fertilisers increase leaf and stem development and are
used particularly for brassicas and other leaf crops. They produce leaf
tissue with large but relatively thin-walled cells; excessive nitrogen
results in what is called 'soft growth', which is more susceptible to
attacks by pests and damage by frosts. Use nitrogen fertilisers as
quick-acting top dressings in the spring but not in the autumn or
winter. Only apply those amounts your soil needs.

SULPHATE OF AMMONIA is a widely used nitrogen fertiliser. Do not
mix it with or apply it at the same time as lime because ammonia may
be produced causing possible scorching of plants. Use at between $\frac{1}{2}$ oz.
and 2 oz. per sq. yd.

HOOF AND HORN is used as a slow-acting nitrogen fertiliser, but it is
usually an expensive one. Use at between 1 oz. and 3 oz. per sq. yd.

FISH MANURE is made from waste fish and if the manufacturers have
removed the oil it is quite quick acting. It is rich in nitrogen and
phosphates but contains little potash, unless this has been added by the
makers. It can be used via the compost heap as an activator or straight
on the soil at between 2 oz. and 4 oz. to the sq. yd.

## Phosphorus

Phosphates encourage good fibrous root formation, which assists
plants to take in nutrients and trace elements from the soil. This gives
them a good start in life and encourages early plant maturity. Phosphates are especially needed by root crops, and help to produce the
steady continuous growth that enables plants to survive attacks by
pests and endure a drought.

SUPERPHOSPHATE is soluble and gets used by the plant immediately.
It should be applied to a soil that has been adequately limed some

weeks previously so that it does not mix with free lime. It may be applied at up to 2 oz. to the sq. yd.

STEAMED BONEMEAL is a slow-acting fertiliser and is very useful for all crops but especially peas and beans that need a steady supply of phosphates throughout the season. It may be used at up to 2 oz. to the sq. yd.

BASIC SLAG is a phosphate fertiliser but it also contains some lime, calcium and small amounts of other nutrients. It is generally used as a base dressing during soil preparation in the winter at the rate of about 4 oz. to the sq. yd and will be of use to the plants in the following spring.

**To sum up**
Bring your soil to the right condition by continually replacing its humus content with compost and manure. This in itself may supply all the needs of your plants but a dressing of a balanced fertiliser, like National Growmore a couple of weeks before seed sowing, is a simple but rather hit and miss way of adding nutrients.

If you want to be more exact either have your soil analysed or buy a soil testing kit to check whether it is short of nitrogen, phosphorus or potash. The kit will also enable you to test whether your soil needs lime.

## LIME

Lime sweetens the soil and corrects acidity. It supplies calcium – a plant nutrient – and on heavy soils it improves the texture and workability. Lime helps to decompose organic matter in the soil and it releases plant foods that might otherwise be 'locked up' and unavailable to the plants.

Soils are either alkaline, neutral or acid and a pH scale is used to express this. Plants have different pH preferences but most vegetables do best in a soil with a pH reaction of 6.5, which is just below neutral. But a soil does not stay at the same pH level. The calcium content can be leached out by the rain, it can be lost by crop removal, by the use of some fertilisers like sulphate of ammonia or by atmospheric pollution which adds acid to the soil. The continual addition of organic manures so necessary for our plants also tends to make the soil less alkaline. To correct this loss of calcium from the soil we have to add lime.

Lime should be sprinkled on the surface in January or February so that the rain washes it into the soil. It should not be dug in or mixed with manure or fertiliser, and should never be applied as a matter of routine but only when tests show that it is needed to bring the soil up to the pH levels shown on the Master Plans. On a chalk soil or some clay ones it may be that no lime is needed at all.

Liming materials are not absolutely pure and as luck would have it some useful traces of elements like manganese, zinc and molybdenum are added to the soil in the lime.

There are several types of lime but the two most commonly used by gardeners are ground limestone or chalk (calcium carbonate) or hydrated lime (calcium hydroxide). The amount to apply will depend on how acid the soil is, the pH level that is needed and the texture of the soil. Clay soils need more lime than sandy ones to bring them to the pH level required but they will then hold that pH level for longer than the sandy ones, where the lime tends to get washed out.

The Master Plans are designed so that lime can be added to reach pH 6.5 for the legumes crop the first year and then a little more added to that plot the following year to reach pH 6.5–7.0 for the onions and brassicas. In most soils no lime will be needed in the following two years as pH 6.0 is needed for the roots crop in year three and pH 5.5 for the potato group in year four.

But a great deal will depend on your own particular soil. There are so many types of soil throughout the country, that only trial and error and a yearly test of your plots will tell you how much lime to add to each one. The following amounts can be taken as a guide.

If you use ground limestone . . . the amount per square yard is

|  | On sandy soils | On loam soils | On clay soils |
| --- | --- | --- | --- |
| To raise pH by 0.5 | 120 grams or 4 oz | 150 grams or 5 oz | 200 grams or 7 oz |
| To raise pH by 1.0 | 300 grams or 11 oz | 350 grams or 12 oz | 450 grams or 15 oz |
| To raise pH by 1.5 | 500 grams or 18 oz | 550 grams or 20 oz | 700 grams or 24 oz |

If you use hydrated lime . . . the amount per square yard is

|  | On sandy soils | On loam soils | On clay soils |
| --- | --- | --- | --- |
| To raise pH by 0.5 | 80 grams or 3 oz | 100 grams or 4 oz | 150 grams or 5 oz |
| To raise pH by 1.0 | 200 grams or 7 oz | 230 grams or 8 oz | 300 grams or 11 oz |
| To raise pH by 1.5 | 330 grams or 12 oz | 370 grams or 13 oz | 500 grams or 18 oz |

So if you have a clay soil and need to raise the pH from 6.0 to 6.5 then sprinkle either 5 oz of hydrated lime or 7 oz of ground limestone per sq. yd.

## Application
As you don't want the lime to end up in your neighbour's garden choose a still day and a dry one. If the surface of the soil is frozen, so much the better as this will avoid it being trodden down.

Walk backwards scattering the lime with a trowel or small hand shovel from a bucket so that any slight wind that there is blows the lime away from you. If you weigh the amount that the trowel or shovel holds it's easy to apply the right quantity to each square yard. The lime should be applied as evenly as possible and it's easier to do this if you cover a strip one yard wide at a time. Use a garden line to mark each strip or simply put some stones a yard apart on the paths as guide marks.

## Lime needs of different plants
Most vegetables prefer a soil with a pH reaction of about 6.5, just below neutral, but some like a more acid soil.

| | | |
|---|---|---|
| *Slightly more acid* | Asparagus pea | 6.0–6.5 |
| | Aubergine | 6.0–6.5 |
| | Melons | 6.0 |
| | Peas | 6.0–6.5 |
| | Peppers | 6.0 |
| | Pumpkin/Squash | 6.0 |
| | Radishes | 6.0 |
| | Seakale | 6.0–6.5 |
| | Swedes | 6.0–6.5 |
| | Sweet corn | 6.0–6.5 |
| | Sweet peppers | 6.0 |
| | Turnips | 6.0–6.5 |
| *More acid still* | Marrows | 5.5 |
| | Potatoes | 5.5 |
| | Tomatoes | 5.5 |
| | Vegetable spaghetti | 5.5 |
| | *All other vegetables* | 6.5 |

As the pH reaction rises or falls beyond the figures given then you get an increasingly less satisfactory result if all the other factors are satisfactory.

The Master Plans take account of these pH requirements, using some slight compromises in view of all the other things that have to be taken into account in a mixed vegetable plot.

**Warning.** Hydrated lime is often considered quite safe to handle but it should be used with care as it can cause dermatitis. It should be kept away from the eyes and should not be inhaled. Wear rubber gloves when handling it and wash thoroughly afterwards. In fact, it is sensible to do this when using any fertilisers or insecticides.

# 12. Seed Sowing

What a pleasure and a pain this can be. After the hard work of digging and liming and patiently waiting for the warmer weather to arrive one fine day in spring we open a seed packet and bending down to scatter the seeds evenly and carefully along the row, half the contents come out in one go. They're the same colour as the soil so we can't pick them up again and they're all mixed up with the wet earth anyway. The pleasure has slightly turned to pain. Let's see if we can keep most of the pleasure and avoid some of the pain.

SEE YOUR SEEDS: a little lime or talcum powder shaken up in the packet with the darker seeds will make them easier to see against the soil.

STATE OF THE SOIL: don't try to sow seeds when the soil is damp and sticky. Wait till the wind and the sun have made the ground dry and crumbly so that the earth doesn't stick to your boots and you can draw the drills in comfort.

Seeds won't germinate properly in cold wet soil anyway, and you can ruin its structure by walking on it when it's wet. If you wait for the right weather nature will almost certainly balance up to bring your crops to maturity at the right time.

## PREPARE THE MARKERS

It can be very frustrating when you get to the end of the plot when you're sowing seeds to find that you haven't got room for the last row because you've allowed an inch too much for each of the others. So prepare your seed markers in advance and put them *all* in their allotted places before you sow any seeds. This will ensure that you've made no mistakes and have got the right distances for each row.

Small plastic labels tend to get buried in the soil so use 'firewood sticks' about 10 in. long and ½ in. square as markers. Chop them up from old wooden boxes or planks. If the wood isn't white then paint it with some emulsion before cutting it up so that you have a light surface on which to write the vegetable names – in pencil or biro. Put one stick at the end of each row and, having sown the seeds, stretch a single strand of black cotton between them about an inch above the soil to deter the birds from scratching around where the seeds are.

Turn the markers inwards on the rows you haven't sown and then turn the names outwards when the seeds have been put in so that you know where you've sown.

You'll need 100 sticks for the Middle Master Plan and about 130 for the Large Master Plan, so that's a job for any wet week-end in winter once you've decided what to sow.

Some people use the seed packets to mark the rows but this isn't a good idea as the packets look untidy and can get blown about by the wind. In any case they've usually got useful information on them which you may need to refer to. Write the date of sowing and any other comments on the packets and keep them as reminders of what did well when you're ordering the seed for next year.

## PREPARE THE GROUND

By seed sowing time the top few inches of your soil should have been weathered down to a crumbly structure by the frost and the wind.

On a day when the soil is dry and in the right condition so that it doesn't stick to your boots spread any fertilisers that you're going to use in the same way that you previously spread the lime. Rake the soil backwards and forwards until the fertilisers are well mixed in the top inch or so and the soil is level. Remove any large stones. Firm the soil by shuffling across it with boots or wellingtons on until it's all trodden down. Now rake it again until its a fine tilth and no particle of soil is larger than a pea and most are smaller than a grain of wheat. You now have a good seed bed.

If you did this when the soil was too wet you would ruin its structure and turn it into a hard pan, **so do wait until it's dry and crumbly.** Sowing times will, of course, vary depending on which part of the country you live in, which way your garden faces and the type of soil you have as well as whether the spring is a late or early one.

The timing of operations in this book is based on 'average' conditions in a fairly sheltered part of the Midlands on a good loamy soil. If you live in a cold area, or have a cold heavy soil, or the spring is late you may have to sow and plant later. If you live in a warm sheltered area and have a good warm soil then it may well be safe to sow up to several weeks earlier. You must be guided by local conditions and by experience.

## TAKING OUT THE DRILLS

The basic aim in all seed sowing is the same: to make a hole or take out a drill, put in the seed, cover with soil and gently firm it down again so that the soil is in contact with the seeds. The method varies according to the size of the seed.

### The standard drill

This is used for most seeds. Peg out a line to mark the position of the row and take out the drill using a stick, a draw hoe or the angle of a rake. Small seeds need shallow drills about ¼ in. deep, others ½ in., and some deeper still. Always check the instructions on the seed packet. If you plant seeds too deeply they may not come up.

| Depth ¼ in. | ½ in. | ¾ in. | 1 in. |
|---|---|---|---|
| Carrot | Beetroot | Cauliflower | Parsnip |
| Celeriac | Broccoli | Cucumber | Salsify |
| Celery | Brussels sprouts | Curly kale | Scorzonera |
| Onion seed | Cabbage | Marrow | Spinach |
| Tomato | Capsicum | Melon | Spinach beet |
| | Chicory | | Sweet corn |
| | Chinese cabbage | | |
| | Corn salad | | |
| | Endive | | |
| | Kohl Rabi | | |
| | Leeks | | |
| | Lettuce | | |
| | Parsley | | |
| | Radish | | |
| | Seakale beet | | |
| | Swede | | |
| | Turnip | | |

'Station sowing' is recommended for sweet corn and beetroot to save wasting seed. See page 125.

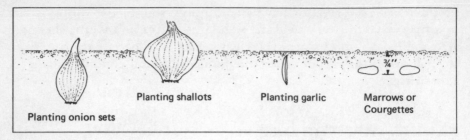

Planting shallots

Planting garlic

Marrows or Courgettes

Planting onion sets

## Planting onion sets

Take out a 1 in. deep drill using a line as a guide. Place the sets 4–6 in. apart in the drill. Replace the earth leaving the tips of the sets showing, firming the earth round each set.

## Planting shallots

Use an old dessertspoon or trowel to scoop out small holes about 1 in. deep and 9 in. apart. Place each shallot in its hole and pull the soil up round it but don't press it into the ground as this makes it harder for the roots to go down. Use a line to make sure the row is straight.

## Planting garlic

Plant the little cloves just below the surface. Use an old spoon and put them 9 in. apart.

## The potato drill

This is a large version of the standard drill and you can take it out with the draw hoe or dig it out with a spade.

## The pea or bean drill

A flat bottomed drill rather like a very shallow trench, taken out with

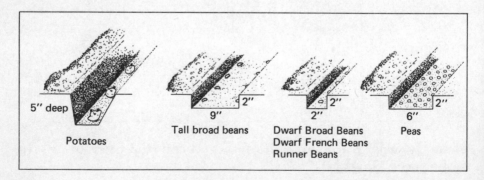

5″ deep

Potatoes

9″ 2″

Tall broad beans

2″ 2″

Dwarf Broad Beans
Dwarf French Beans
Runner Beans

6″ 2″

Peas

a draw hoe or by 'skimming' with a spade, and of course a line to make sure it's straight.

Pea and bean seeds make a tasty meal for mice and many a gardener has been mystified by the poor germination of the seeds when these unwelcome visitors have had them. Some old prickly holly leaves or small pieces of gorse scattered along the drill before you replace the soil will make things uncomfortable for them and keep them off.

## Marrows, courgettes, outdoor cucumbers and outdoor melons

If you wish to sow these in the open take out a hole where each plant is to be – about 6 in. square and 3 or 4 in. deep – and fill it with compost or good soil. Plant two seeds in each such 'station' on their edges and about ¾ in. deep. If both the seedlings come up remove the poorer one.

## SOWING THE SEED

Now slow down, take a deep breath and relax. If you take your time in sowing your seeds and do it properly you can save a lot of time later on. Think about the crop you're going to sow and how far apart the plants will be when they've grown.

A lot of time is wasted in having to thin 'hedges' of seedlings that have been sown too closely; and because the roots of the seedlings get all tangled up together, thinning them can disturb the plants that are left. So try to sow your seeds so that you have very little thinning to do. With radish, for example, the plants should end up about 1 in. apart, so sow just two seeds to the inch or even just one. There is no point in sowing more when the seedlings will have to be pulled up and thrown away. Sow lettuce seeds at the same spacings, two to the inch, then continually thin the seedlings as they grow so that they are always just clear of each other until they are at their correct spacings. Transplant the early thinnings if you have empty spaces and eat the later ones.

With carrots there is another good reason for sowing them thinly. If you touch them early in the season the pungent carroty smell this creates will attract the carrot fly. It will lay its eggs near the seedlings and the maggots will eat into the carrots. You can control them with insecticides but a better plan is to sow the seeds very thinly, again just two seeds to the inch and then leave the plants strictly alone until July. Don't touch them at all. You can then start thinning the carrots and use those thinnings as edible young carrots – about as thick as your little finger. Delicious. With reasonable luck your crop will be free of maggots.

So the golden rule is **take the trouble to sow thinly.** It will save you time in the long run and give you better crops.

With the large seeds, like peas and beans, plant at the spacings recommended on the packets but put in a few spares at the end of the row for transplanting into any gaps.

After sowing the seeds pull the soil back over the drill with the rake and then using the flat back of the rake gently firm the soil down over the seeds.

### Sowing in mid summer
If the soil is very dry take out the drill, water along the bottom with a trickle from a can or a jug, sow the seeds, cover them with dry earth and don't be tempted to water them again until they come up.

### Holding the packet
It's all very well saying 'sow thinly', but how do you stop the seeds all staying at the back of the packet or coming out in one fell swoop? Open the packet with a knife or scissors so that you have a straight edge at the end and not a torn one. Open out the packet and make a crease about an inch long in the middle of one side. Hold the packet between the thumb and big finger and tap it on the edge with the first finger. The seeds will roll down towards the opening but the crease will force them to 'queue up' and just a few will come out at one time. After a bit of practice it is possible to get them to drop out one at a

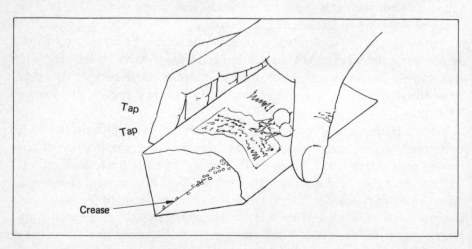

time. It's a question of tap, tap, tap, and if too many seeds start to come forward tilt the packet back and start again.

If the seeds are fairly large ones then you may find it easier to put a few in the palm of one hand and sow them singly with the other.

## Station sowing

This system takes the theory one stage further. Instead of sowing the seeds all along the row and thinning them later on, three seeds are sown at 'stations' the same distance apart that you want the final plants. So, with parsnips that are normally thinned to 9 in. apart, three seeds are sown every 9 in. and then thinned down to one per station. In practice it's usual to sow at half this distance, called half stations, to allow for the slugs seeing the seedlings before you do, and then ultimately thin them to the final distance.

# 13. Culture of Individual Crops

Some gardeners go for yield, some for flavour and others for looks. It depends on whether the crops are destined for the show bench or the kitchen and the seed catalogues contain enough varieties to please almost all of us.

If, amidst a bewildering choice, you are not sure which varieties to order one safe method is to choose those that have received an award from the Royal Horticultural Society. Each year the Society invites entries for trials of different vegetables (and flowers). Entries are received from seed firms and raisers and the appropriate seed sent for trial. The crops are assessed at various stages of growth by a panel of experts. Only those that are outstanding from habit of growth, disease resistance, colour and uniformity will receive an award. Those awards are:

| | |
|---|---|
| First Class Certificate | Vegetables of great excellence |
| Award of Merit | Vegetables which are meritorious |
| Highly Commended | Vegetables which are noteworthy |
| Commended | Vegetables which are noteworthy |

So the letters A.M. RHS 1978 after the name of a variety on a packet or in a catalogue would mean it got an Award of Merit in the Society's trials in that year. Any of the awards is a recommendation of a good variety. The Society is limited in the number of trials it can carry out each year so some other varieties on sale will also be excellent but may be relatively new to the market or have not been assessed by the Society.

The varieties recommended in the following pages are believed to be reliable and obtainable and many of them have received awards from the Society. There is also some advice on growing them, but it isn't possible to give infallible guidance on growing crops as so much depends on the soil we have, the weather we get and the part of the country we live in. We all have to adjust our sowing and growing programme to our own local situation but I think you should find the information useful and I trust reliable.

May I suggest two simple rules to start with:
1. Have a look in your neighbours' gardens. It's always worth knowing what grows well locally and what doesn't.
2. Always read what it says on the seed packet. Perhaps the variety you have chosen needs some slightly different treatment, so follow the advice of the firm who put the seed in the packet.

## ARTICHOKE, GLOBE

There are two kinds of artichokes commonly grown in gardens, the globe and the Jerusalem. They are nothing like each other to look at although they are both members of the plant family *Compositae*. The globe artichoke is grown for the fleshy scales of the globe-shaped flower heads which are cooked and eaten with a sauce.

These plants are perennial with the tops dying down each winter. Although they are decorative enough for the odd plant to be grown in the flower border they should really be given their own bed. They need plenty of room in a sunny situation and should be planted 3 ft apart in rows which are 4 ft apart. So a space 8 ft by 19 ft would accommodate a dozen plants.

They can be raised from seed or propagated by suckers from existing plants.

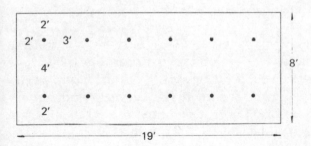

### Seed sowing
The seeds should be sown outdoors in March and April ½ in. deep in drills 1 ft apart and the plants thinned to 6 in. apart. They should then be moved to their permanent beds in the following spring, being planted the same depth as in the seed bed.

127

## Plants

You may either obtain these from a nursery or take suckers from existing strong plants when they are about 9 in. high. Use a sharp knife and cut off each sucker with some roots attached to it. You can do this in November, potting up each sucker and putting the pots in a cold frame or cold greenhouse for the winter to give them protection from frosts. They are then ready to plant out the following spring. Or you can just take off well-rooted suckers from existing plants in April and plant these straight away in their new positions, about 4 in. deep, but you'll need to keep them well watered until they are growing freely.

## Cultivation

The plants are gross feeders so dig in plenty of compost or manure during the autumn or winter before planting – a barrow load to each 10 sq. yd. The same quantity should be forked into the ground between the rows each spring. If the soil is acid apply lime in February or March to bring the pH reaction to 6.5.

The plants should be kept well watered in dry summers but they must not be waterlogged in winter or they may die off.

Cut down the tops together with the large leaves in the autumn but leave the central smaller leaves at the bottom of the plant to protect the crown from frost. In areas where severe frosts may be expected soil or straw may be heaped over the rows in the winter and then removed in early spring.

Keep the beds hoed and clear of weeds and keep a look out for slugs which are very partial to the new young shoots.

## Harvesting

Don't allow any flower heads to develop the first year, but they may be gathered freely from the second year onwards. Cut the heads when they are plump but still young and tender. If you cut them with about 6 in. of stalk on they can be stood in water until you need them. Cut the central heads first and then the laterals will produce a second crop.

## Summary

Obtain plants from a nursery or take suckers from existing plants in November or in April. Set out in rows 4 ft apart with the plants 3 ft apart in the rows. The soil should be well manured and have a pH reaction of about 6.5. Protect the plants from severe frosts in winter. Harvest the heads from the second year after planting.

**Recommended varieties**

Camus de Grande Bretagne: an excellent variety but the plants are prickly.

Green Globe which is free of prickles.


## ARTICHOKE, JERUSALEM

Quite a different vegetable from the globe artichoke (although they are both members of the family *Compositae*), as the edible part is the tuber, which grows underground like potatoes. It is related to the sunflower and it is thought that the name Jerusalem is a corruption of 'girasole', the Italian name for sunflower.

The tubers have a somewhat earthy taste which appeals to some people but not to others. The plant is a strong grower with the tops reaching 6–10 ft tall. It may be planted in the place of maincrop potatoes but ideally it should be planted on its own away from other crops.


**Planting**

The plants are propagated from tubers saved from the previous year's crop and should be a little smaller than a hen's egg. Large tubers may be cut in half at planting time as long as each piece has some 'eyes'. They are planted in late March or early April in rows 2 ft 6 in. apart with the tubers 1 ft apart in the rows and 6 in. deep, or they may be replanted in November at the time of lifting the crop.


**Cultivation**

They will grow in most soils but will do best when grown in rich soil in an open situation. The plants do not like to be waterlogged and too much manure may make the tubers taste coarse.

Hoe regularly and, when the young plants are through the soil, earth them up like potatoes.


**Harvesting**

The tubers may be left in the soil as they will stand a certain amount of frost, in which case the tops may be cut down to within about a foot of the ground and placed on top of the plants as some protection. Alternatively, the plants may be dug up and the tubers stored in sand.


**Summary**

Set small tubers 6 in. deep and 1 ft apart in rows 2 ft 6 in. apart, preferably in their own bed. Leave in the ground and dig as required or lift the whole crop in November and store in sand.

## Varieties

Jerusalem artichokes are not easy to obtain and it will be a case of getting what you can.

## ASPARAGUS

A member of the lily family *(Liliaceae)* and related to the onion. Since Greek and Roman times the young shoots have been highly prized as a vegetable. Asparagus is native to Britain and other parts of northern Europe and so it is not difficult to grow. It is a perennial crop that needs its own individual bed and, if properly planted and tended, the asparagus bed may remain productive for ten to fifteen years or even longer.

Asparagus will grow in most soils as long as they are well drained and have been completely cleared of perennial weeds. It grows best in a medium to light deep rich sandy loam. You can grow your own plants from seed or obtain one-year-old plants from some seedsmen or nurseries.

### Seed sowing

In March or early April when the soil is warm sow the seeds thinly in drills 1½ in. deep and 1 ft apart. The seeds are slow to germinate but soaking in water for twenty-four hours before sowing will help them along. Thin the plants to 4–6 in. and, apart from weeding them and keeping them watered in very dry weather, leave them to grow until the following March or April when they are transplanted to their permanent site.

### Plants

If you haven't grown your own plants then order them in February at the very latest so that you get them in time. Some seedsmen stipulate a minimum of twenty-five plants or so if you order by post. As soon as they arrive open the package and if the soil is too wet for planting them out, put them in a shallow trench and cover the roots with 6 in. of soil until you are ready for them. Don't let the roots dry out.

### Preparing the bed

If you intend to have a very large asparagus bed the rows should be

4–5 ft apart with the plants 1 ft 3 in. apart in the rows. You can carry out a more modest scheme by having a bed 6 ft wide with two rows of plants 3 ft apart and 1 ft 6 in. in from the sides of the bed; twenty-four plants spaced 1 ft 3 in. apart in these two rows will fill a bed 6 ft wide by just over 16 ft long.

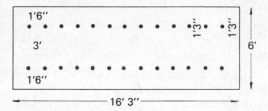

Dig over the plot in the autumn or early winter before planting, incorporating manure or garden compost. It is best if you bastard trench the plot (see chapter on 'Digging'). Leave the ground rough for the winter frosts to break it down.

In February apply lime, if necessary, to get a pH reaction of 6.5–7.0. Rake the ground level in March when the soil is dry.

### Planting

Carry out the planting in March or early April when the soil has warmed up. You can set out the plants individually by making a hole for each one 5 in. deep with a trowel and large enough to take the roots spread out fanwise to their full length round the plants. The crown of the plant should be 3 in. below ground level and then the soil replaced. Plant 1 ft 3 in. apart.

But a better system is to take out a trench for each row 1 ft wide, 8 in. deep at the sides and 5 in. deep in the middle. You may find this easier to do by taking out the whole trench 8 in. deep and then replacing fine soil to a depth of 3 in. in the centre of the trench. Spread out the roots of each plant and then cover with more fine soil 3 in. deep over the crowns. Gradually fill the trench with soil as the plants grow during the first season.

### Harvesting

You must needs be patient. Don't cut any shoots from the plants for the first two years. In the third year harvest the shoots for just six weeks and then in subsequent years for eight weeks. Cut all sizes of shoots at each gathering. The spears are ready to be cut when they show as dark green shoots about 2 in. long above the ground and as thick as your finger. Don't leave them until they are very much longer than this or they won't be succulent and tender. Use a long sharp knife and cut the spears 3 in. below ground level, being careful not to injure younger shoots coming through in the same place. Then cease cutting, leave the stems and foliage to grow freely and resist the temptation to cut them for floral displays.

## Cultivation
Keep the bed hoed and clear of weeds. Cut down the plants when the foliage changes colour in the autumn before the ripe berries from the plants drop on the soil. In the autumn or early winter top dress with compost or manure, or, if you live by the seaside, with seaweed. In February or March, when the soil has started to warm up, mound up soil over the rows to a depth of about 3 in. and if you didn't use seaweed as a top mulch sprinkle 3 oz of common salt per sq. yd.

## Summary
Set one-year-old plants 1 ft 3 in. apart in a deep rich soil with the crowns buried 3 in. deep after carefully spreading out the roots. Don't gather a harvest until the third year and then only for six weeks. Cut down the tops in autumn and earth up the rows in early spring. Harvest for eight weeks from the fourth year. Keep clear of weeds and give an autumn mulch of compost, manure or seaweed.

## Recommended varieties
Martha Washington from seed.
Connover's Colossal from seed or as plants.
Royal Pedigree as plants.

## AUBERGINE (Egg Plant)

A member of the potato family *(Solanaceae)* to which the nightshade, the tomato and the sweet pepper also belong. It probably came from southern Asia where, since remote antiquity, it has been cultivated for its egg-shaped fruits and used as a vegetable. It is a handsome plant and is best grown under glass in pots although in very sheltered districts the pots may be put outside in the summer months.

## Seed sowing and cultivation
The seeds germinate slowly. Sow them under glass at 15–20°C (60–70°F) in a pan of moist seed compost from January to March.

When the seedlings have their first pair of true seed leaves pot them up into 2½ or 3 in. pots. Then when they are 6–9 in. high pot them on into 6 or 7 in. pots and maintain humid conditions. Occasionally syringe the plants with tepid water, especially at flowering time. When the fruits are swelling feed them every week with a liquid fertiliser.

### Harvesting
The fruit are ripe for picking when they are of a smooth oval appearance with highly polished skins. They may be sliced and fried in butter or stuffed with minced meat, onions and seasoning and baked.

### Recommended varieties
Moneymaker.
Long Purple.
Slim Jim.

## BROAD BEANS

One of the earliest green vegetables, broad beans are delicious if they are picked when young and tender but let them get big and tough and they are one of the dullest of vegetables. Those from a shop are often in the latter category and if you want them at their best you must grow your own.

Broad beans come in two types. Tall ones which grow about 3 ft tall and dwarf ones which are bushy in habit and only grow to about 1 ft 3 in. They may be either white or green seeded – no difference in taste but some people consider the green ones more attractive on the dinner plate.

### Seed sowing
November sowings may be made in sheltered districts and if the winter is mild and not too wet these autumn sowings can produce early crops. But they are normally sown from the middle of February to the end of April, with the dwarf ones being sown up to June. Choose a dry day when soil conditions are right. Nothing will be gained by sowing them in cold wet soil.

TALL ONES: sow these 2 in. deep in a double row with 9 in. between the two lines of the row and the seeds 6–9 in. apart.

DWARF ONES: sow these in single rows with 1 ft between the rows and 9 in. between the plants.

With both types sow a few spare seeds at the end of each row to transplant into any gaps when they are about 2 in. tall.

## Cultivation

Broad beans need a deeply dug, well-manured soil that has a pH reaction of about 6.5. Blackfly can be a nuisance but strong growing plants in a good soil can put up with blackfly much better than poor weak plants. Use the Dutch hoe between the rows and keep them clear of weeds. As they grow the tall varieties will need enclosing with a support of sticks and string to prevent them being blown over in wet windy weather. The dwarf ones do not need any support.

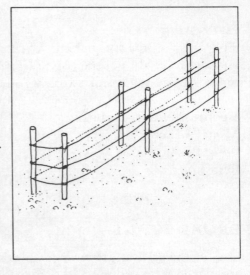

**As soon as the plants carry plenty of flowers pick out the growing tops to deter attack by blackfly.** It's in the tender tips that this pest usually first appears.

## Harvesting

The pods will swell up first and then the beans will grow to fill the pods. Pick them when the individual beans are no bigger than your thumbnail and eat them or freeze them on the same day. As soon as the crop is finished cut down the plants and put them on the compost heap. Leave the roots in the ground as the root nodules will enrich the soil.

## Summary

TALL VARIETIES: sow in November or February to April in a 9 in. double row 2 in. deep with the seeds 6–9 in. apart. Support them as they grow.

DWARF ONES: sow in November (under cloches if you have them) or February to June in single rows with 9 in. between the plants and 1 ft between the rows. Pick both varieties when they are young.

## Recommended varieties

TALL ONES – NOVEMBER SOWN: Aquadulce.

TALL ONES–SPRING SOWN: Windsor; Masterpiece Green Longpod; Dreadnought.

DWARF: the Sutton.

## DWARF FRENCH BEANS

The French bean can be sown a bit earlier than its cousin the runner and can be picked earlier too.

### Seed sowing

From mid April to mid July sow the seeds 2 in. deep and 3 in. apart in single rows with 1 ft 6 in. between the rows. Thin the plants to 9 in. apart when they are a couple of inches tall. You can transplant to fill in any gaps if you take plenty of soil with the plants and water them in. French beans can also be brought on earlier in boxes or pots under glass in the same way as runners, or they may be started a month earlier under cloches.

### Cultivation

A deeply dug rich soil with a pH reaction of about 6.5 will produce good crops. Keep them clear of weeds and as the plants grow give them some support. The simplest way to do this is with a few house bricks, some long canes or poles and a few short sticks. Or the plants may be supported individually by being tied to short sticks or propped up with twiggy sticks. If you don't give them some support they tend to flop over and the beans get muddy and eaten by slugs.

**Harvesting**
Pick the beans continuously when they are young and pencil thin and use them either sliced or whole.

**Recommended varieties**
There are a number of varieties to choose from, most of them good for freezing and some that can be left to ripen on the plants and used as haricots.

NORMAL VARIETIES: the Prince; Sprite (stringless); Tendergreen (stringless).

FOR DRYING: Chevrier Vert.

## HARICOT BEANS

The small pods are delicious when cooked whole while they are still young and green, or they may be allowed to ripen on the plants to produce the small white haricot beans for winter use.

**Cultivation**
Sow and cultivate in exactly the same way as dwarf French beans but for the best results sow them early, at the beginning of April, under cloches. This gives the pods time to develop and mature by the end of August or early September.

**Harvesting**
When the pods have turned brown on the plants pull up the whole plant and hang upside down in a shed to dry. When the pods are perfectly dry and yellow the simplest way to extract the beans is to put the plants in a sack or wrap them loosely in a cloth and beat them with a stick to thresh out the beans. Spread the seeds on paper to complete the drying process before storing them in a dry frost-proof place.

**Recommended variety**
Purley King (sometimes called Comtesse de Chambord).

# RUNNER BEANS

Quite rightly a king among vegetables, especially if picked when young and succulent and eaten on the same day. Not only an excellent vegetable but a handsome plant as well, growing 9 ft or more tall on good deep well-manured soil.

## Seed sowing

Runner beans will not germinate unless the soil is warm, and as a sharp frost will easily kill the young plants don't sow them until mid May in the open or April under glass or cloches. Sow a double row 2 in. deep with 1 ft 3 in. between the two lines forming the row and the seeds 9–12 in. apart. Sow some spare beans at the end of the row for transplanting into any gaps when they are a couple of inches tall. If you grow more than one double row leave a space of 5 ft between but use the space for an early maturing crop like dwarf broad beans.

## Plants

One way to get the longest growing season and hence the biggest crop is to bring on plants in a greenhouse or a frame or even indoors; anywhere that is frost proof and light but not over warm. Either use $2\frac{1}{2}$ or 3 in. pots and grow one bean in each pot, or get some wooden 'grape boxes' from the greengrocer (usually 1 ft wide and 1 ft 6 in. long and at least 4 in. deep). Each box will grow about thirty-five plants.

Sow the beans at the end of April in potting compost, and cover with plastic film or a plastic bag which must be removed directly the plants come through. Keep them in the light. Harden them off at the end of May and plant them out the first week in June. Buy plants from a garden centre if you don't want to grow your own.

## Fail safe method

As a fail safe method sow seeds *between* the poles in mid May and put out the plants *beside* the poles at the end of May or early June. If a late frost gets the plants you will still have the seeds to come up and if there are no late frosts your plants will be well away to an early start and you can discard the ones from the seeds when they do come up.

## Cultivation

Runner beans must have a deeply dug soil with plenty of compost or manure in it and a pH reaction of 6.5. If your ground is not well

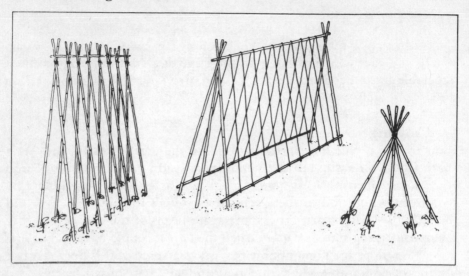

manured then dig out a trench 1 ft deep a few weeks before sowing with at least a 3 in. layer of compost or manure at the bottom of it. Replace the soil and sow at the normal time when the soil has settled.

The traditional way to grow runners is up a support framework of poles which can be 7 ft to 9 or even 10 ft tall, although you'll then need a pair of steps to pick the beans. It is easiest to build the framework before putting in the seeds, with a double row of poles 1 ft 3 in.–1 ft 6 in. apart and 9 in.–1 ft between each pole (so that a bean may be sown at each one). To get the sturdiest structure push the poles into the ground in an upright position, then pull each opposing pair together near the top, cross them over and lay another pole in the V formed. Tie together with string.

Or if you can't get a large number of poles, strands of string may be used stretched from poles running along the top and the bottom of a support structure.

If you haven't room for a row of runners put up a small wigwam of poles, perhaps in the flower garden, and train the beans up them. They can look quite attractive, but do vary the position from year to year.

**Watering**

It is often said that spraying the plants with soft water in the evening helps the flowers to set in dry weather. This is doubtful but it is certainly true that large mature runner beans transpire a lot of moisture from their leaves and need to be kept well watered; and if you do that watering with a hose you'll knock off a lot of the blackfly. But do it in the daytime so that the soil has a chance to warm up again by nightfall. Put a mulch of compost over the roots if you can spare some.

### Harvesting
Pick the beans when they are young and will easily snap in half when doubled over. Make sure every mature bean is picked as this will encourage the small ones to develop. Eat or freeze them on the same day.

At the end of the crop cut off the plants at ground level, put the tops on the compost heap, leave the roots in the soil to enrich it and carefully store the poles in the dry for next year.

### Summary
Runner beans are hungry feeders so plant them in deep, well-manured soil or dig out a trench where they are to grow and put manure at the bottom. Erect a framework of poles and then sow the seeds in late May 2 in. deep and one at each pole. Or sow them under glass in April and put out the plants the first week in June when the danger of frost has passed. Pick the beans as soon as they are ready and use them the same day.

### Recommended varieties
Enorma.
Achievement.
Prizewinner.
Streamline.

## BEETROOT

Modern varieties of beetroot are deep red, small and tender and are delicious as a hot vegetable as well as for salads. If you want a change of colour you can grow golden ones as well.

### Seed sowing
There are early varieties such as Boltardy which can be sown from mid March to the end of April, and main varieties which are sown from the end of April right through to July.

Sow them ½ in. deep in rows 12 in. apart. Beet seeds are different from most in that each one is a seed 'cluster' that will produce three or four seedlings. 'Half Station' sowing suits them best (see page 125).

Put in one seed every 2 in., thin the seedlings down to one when they come up and do the final thinning to 4 or 6 in. apart when they are the size of walnuts, so that the thinnings can be used as baby beet. Don't let them get any bigger than this before thinning or you'll inhibit the growth of those left in; and don't sow the main varieties before the end of April or they are likely to try to go to seed rather than produce good roots.

## Cultivation

Beetroot need a deeply dug fertile soil but with no new manure or compost: one that has been well manured for a previous crop is ideal.

Protect your beetroot seedlings from both slugs and birds or they may disappear overnight. Keep them clear of weeds and well watered in dry weather.

## Harvesting

If you grow both an early and a maincrop variety you can pull beetroot when you need them right through from early July till October. They are a crop that mature over a long period so just keep pulling the biggest as they come along. If you are using the Large Master Plan you should also have some to store in sand for the winter as well (see 'Storing Your Crops').

## Summary

Grow an early and a maincrop variety. Sow the early ones in April and the maincrop in May ½ in. deep in rows 1 ft apart. Pull them from July onwards as you need them and store the rest in sand for the winter.

## Recommended varieties

EARLY: Boltardy.

MAINCROP: Globe; Cheltenham Green Top (long).

## BROCCOLI–CALABRESE

An Italian variety of sprouting broccoli that has become very popular in the last few years and rightly so. It produces a central green head that should be cut in August, and green side shoots in September and October.

## Seed sowing

Sow ½ in. deep in a seed bed row about 3 ft long in late April or May. Thin the seedlings to 2–3 in. apart and put out the best plants in their final positions in June or early July, leaving 2 ft between each plant. Yes, they do need that amount of space.

Water the plants well a few hours before moving them. Use a trowel so that you keep plenty of soil on the roots. Plant them slightly deeper than they were previously growing and firm them with the foot after planting. Always hold by the leaves so that you don't damage the stem.

## Cultivation

Calabrese is a brassica and needs a deeply dug fertile soil with a pH reaction of 6.5. It will not grow well in acid soils. If your soil is good the plants will grow well and become rather top heavy so it's worth supporting each one with a stout cane or stick. Tie the plant loosely to it. Keep the ground hoed and clear of weeds.

## Harvesting

In August cut out the central head to use first and then cut the side shoots as they develop. Cut these with 4 or 5 in. of stem and cook and serve them like asparagus, or as a normal green vegetable. Continually keep these 'spears' cut so that they don't open out as flowers. More spears will then develop from the leaf axils (the place where the leaf joins the stem). Pull up the plant when it has finished yielding. Bash up the top and put it on the compost. Cut off the root and put it on the bonfire or in the dustbin.

## Summary

An excellent vegetable. Sow seed ½ in. deep in late April or May and set out the best plants in June 2 ft apart. Plant firmly. Use the central head as soon as it has developed in early August and then cut the side shoots as they come along with about 4 in. of stem. Support the plant with a stake.

## Recommended varieties

Express Corona.
Corvet.
Green Duke.

# SPROUTING BROCCOLI

A marvellous vegetable that stands the winter and is ready for use the following March when there is little else available in the vegetable garden.

### Seed sowing

In late April or May sow the seeds ½ in. deep in a 3 ft long seed bed row, just two seeds to the inch. Thin the young seedlings to 2–3 in. apart and in June plant them out 2 ft apart. Water the young plants first, move them with plenty of soil on them, firm them in and water again. Protect from the birds and slugs.

### Cultivation

Sprouting broccoli need a deeply dug fertile soil with a pH reaction of 6.5 – almost neutral. Keep them clear of weeds and water when the weather is dry and they will grow into very large plants that will each need supporting with a really stout stake against the winter snow and gales. Give them added anchorage by piling more soil round the base of the stems as they grow and treading it firmly down.

The pigeons love it, so if you want to keep those broccoli spears for yourself you may well have to protect them with nets.

### Harvesting

Start cutting the spears with about 4 in. of stem as soon as they develop and more will come along. Quite when this will be will depend on the weather. When the plant has finished yielding, dig it up, bash up the top and put it on the compost and put the root on the bonfire or in the dustbin.

### Summary

Sow the seed thinly ½ in. deep in late April or May. Thin early and transplant in June. Plant firmly and support each plant with a stake. Protect from the birds and cut the spears in early spring the next year.

### Recommended variety

Broccoli-Purple Sprouting.

# BRUSSELS SPROUTS

Quite where this well-known variant of the brassica family originated isn't known, but records indicate that it was sold in Belgium as early as 1213, so it has been with us a long time and is a favourite British vegetable.

### Seed sowing
Sow the seed thinly in March or early April in a 3 ft long row ½ in. deep. Thin them early to 2–3 in. apart, protect from slugs and birds and plant out by May or early June 2 ft 6 in. apart, no closer. Tread the soil down firmly round the plants, support each one with a stake and you should get some good firm sprouts for your Christmas dinner.

### Cultivation
But if you want good sprouts you'll have to plant them in good soil. The ground should be deeply dug and heavily manured and it should be almost neutral with a pH reaction of 6.5. Sprouts need plenty of space and a long season of growth. Keep them well watered in the early stages if the weather is dry and keep them clear of weeds.

### Harvesting
Pick them from the bottom upwards as they mature, taking some from each plant and leaving the small ones higher up the stems to develop. Use them the day you pick them. Ten minutes cooking is enough and with a dab of butter they're delicious. Finally cut the top off the plant and use that. Dig up the plants, put the bashed-up top on the compost and the root in the dustbin or on the fire.

### Summary
Brussels sprouts need a long season of growth so plant the seed in March or early April ½ in. deep. Thin early and plant out in May 2 ft 6 in. apart. Support each plant. Pick the sprouts from the bottom up as they mature.

### Recommended varieties
Peer Gynt (October).
Bedford Winter Harvest (October–December).
Citadel (December onwards).

## CABBAGE

Childhood memories of overboiled cabbage that had to be eaten was enough to put a lot of people off this vegetable for life. But it's a most useful plant; there are dozens of varieties and it is very much back in favour.

The Master Plans suggest Savoys for use in mid winter and summer cabbage like Greyhound or Hispi, which you can plant closer together, for use in summer. They will be out of the way to give the Brussels sprouts and broccoli plenty of room to develop.

### Seed sowing and plants

SUMMER CABBAGE: get these sown first, as soon as the weather is suitable, in late March or April. Sow the seed ½ in. deep in a 6 ft row and you will get plenty of plants from which to choose the best ones to put in their final positions in May or June. Thin the seedlings early to produce good plants. Water the plants well a few hours before you lift them and try to get them up and into their new homes with plenty of soil round their roots. Firm them in well after planting.

SAVOYS: treat the same way as summer cabbage but don't sow them until late April or May and plant out in late June or July with up to 2 ft between each plant. They'll look very isolated to start with but they do need that room.

### Cultivation

All cabbages like a rich soil with plenty of manure in it. Being brassicas they like it to be almost neutral with a pH reaction of 6.5. A dressing of lime will also help to control club root. Keep the soil well hoed and clear of weeds and keep the plants watered if the weather is dry – particularly when they are young.

Birds seem to take a delight in pecking at newly planted out brassicas even if they've left them alone in the seed bed. So some protection may well be necessary when the plants are young, or even when they are older if you're troubled with pigeons.

### Harvesting

Cut the cabbages when they are ready with a very short stem to leave a good stump in the soil. The stumps will often then produce a secondary growth of young 'greens'. When you've taken this second harvest do make sure the roots and stumps are burnt or go in the dustbin. Any leaves may, of course, go on the compost.

## Summary

Sow seed thinly ½ in. deep in a 6 ft long row. Sow summer cabbage in March or April and Savoys in late April or May. Thin them early and put out the plants in May/June (summer ones) and June/July (Savoys). Plant firmly and keep watered and free from weeds. Cut when ready and use the stumps to produce a few greens before disposing of them.

## Recommended varieties

A small selection from a great number of good ones.

SUMMER AND AUTUMN HEADING: Greyhound; Golden Acre Progress; Hispi.

WINTER HEADING: January King; Ormskirk Rearguard.

## CAPSICUM (Sweet peppers)

There are several types of capsicums which are used as either decorative plants or for their edible fruits which are called chillies or peppers. The 'sweet pepper' is becoming increasingly popular and can be used either as green peppers or allowed to ripen on the plant and turn red. Plants may be obtained from nurseries in late May and June or they may be grown from seed.

## Seed

They are easy to grow from seed. Sow under glass in pots of compost about ½ in. deep during March at a temperature of 15–18°C (59–64°F). The cooler part of the airing cupboard will do quite well as long as the pot is covered with plastic film until the seed has germinated. Inspect daily to check. As soon as they have germinated bring into full light, prick out individually when large enough to handle into 2½ or 3 in. pots and place on a south-facing window sill away from draughts or in a greenhouse.

## Cultivation

Harden off the plants in a cold greenhouse or cold frame before planting out in June when all danger of frosts has passed. They may then be grown outdoors in a sunny sheltered place against a south wall, or in a cold greenhouse, or potted on into larger pots and grown indoors on a window sill that has plenty of light and no draughts. They do well in growing bags.

## Harvesting
Each plant will produce many fruits over several months. Carefully pick them off as soon as they are large enough to use green or allow them to stay on the plants and turn red.

## Recommended varieties
Early Prolific.
New Ace.
Worldbeater.
Twiggy.

# CARROTS

If they didn't exist I think we would have to invent them – they are such attractive plants. Carrots were introduced into British agriculture from the Low Countries in the seventeenth century and have been a firm favourite ever since – especially with children, who are so often attracted to the idea of growing them and so often disappointed with the results. The rules for growing carrots are simple but essential.

## Seed sowing
Sow them from March onwards at no more than two seeds to the inch in ¼ in. deep drills of fine soil in rows 1 ft apart. The seeds are difficult to see against the soil so make them stand out by shaking them up in the packet with a little dry lime or talcum powder.

Grow an early and a late variety and you'll have a long season of use.

After sowing firm the soil gently with the back of the rake, put a strand of black cotton over each row to deter the sparrows from having dust baths in the fine soil and leave them alone, apart from carefully hoeing between the rows every two weeks. Don't touch them at all until the first week in July. If you do handle them the smell from the young roots and leaves may attract the carrot fly which will lay its eggs near them and the resultant larvae will make a right mess of your carrots with maggots in nearly every root.

## Cultivation
Carrots need deep cultivation, with the soil broken up, so that their roots go down straight and true. No new manure should be dug in or the carrots will send out lots of roots in search of it and you'll end up with a tangle of knitting instead of a good straight root. Carrots suc-

ceed best on land that has been deeply dug and manured for previous crops. That is one reason why, in the Master Plans, they follow the brassicas.

### Harvesting

In July thin the young plants to 3 in. apart and a few weeks later to 6 in. apart. If they are difficult to pull out ease each one up with an old dining fork so as not to disturb the ones that are left in. Firm the soil back in place, don't leave any thinnings lying about and resist touching the carrots until you next need to pull some. Use the thinnings to eat. They'll be about as big as your little finger and a delightful dish.

Before the winter frosts appear in late October or early November dig up the big mature carrots and store them in sand or dry earth. (See 'Storing Your Crops'.)

### Summary

Carrots need a deeply dug fertile soil with no new manure. Sow them $\frac{1}{4}$ in. deep at two seeds to the inch and leave them strictly alone until the first week in July. Then progressively thin to 6 in. apart using the thinnings to eat. Don't leave any thinnings lying about. Store the fully grown carrots in sand before the winter frosts spoil them.

### Recommended varieties

EARLY: Nantes Champion Scarlet Horn; Amsterdam Forcing.

MAINCROP: Chantenay Red Cored; Autumn King.

## CAULIFLOWER

The well-known member of the cabbage family with a large white head or 'curd'. The difference between cauliflowers and what is called 'heading broccoli' is not at all obvious and I think they are best regarded as three types of cauliflower:

> Early varieties for summer use
> Australian varieties for autumn use
> Winter varieties.

### Seed sowing

The early varieties should be sown under glass in late September to early October or in January/February and, when they are large enough to handle, pricked out into a cold frame or cold greenhouse 4 in. apart each way and then planted out in the garden in March or April.

The Australian and winter varieties are sown in a prepared seed bed in the open in late April or early May. The seed should be sown $\frac{1}{2}$ to $\frac{3}{4}$ in. deep.

## Plants
These may also be obtained from a nursery, if you don't want to grow your own, but you may have to take pot luck on varieties. Plant out the early varieties in March and April and the Australian and winter types in June and July. Most varieties need plenty of room – up to 2 ft each way between plants – but as there are so many varieties do check what it says on the seed packet.

## Cultivation
Cauliflowers need a rich soil that contains plenty of compost or manure and, unless you garden on chalk or limestone, the soil will almost certainly need liming to give a pH reaction of 6.5. Put out the plants before they get too big, watering them well first and transplanting them with as much soil round the roots as possible. Set them just a little deeper than they were before so that they are well anchored and then firm the soil round each plant with your foot.

Keep down any weeds with the Dutch hoe and give the plants copious waterings in dry weather.

## Harvesting
They are best cut directly the curds have reached mature size. If you have more than you need at one time, protect them from the sun and weather by breaking one or two of the inner leaves over them until they are required.

## Recommended varieties

EARLY: All the Year Round; Mechelse; Snowball.

AUTUMN (AUSTRALIAN): Boomerang; Canberra.

WINTER: St George; Angers No. 1 and No. 2.
Winter varieties may be killed by severe frosts and in cold or exposed districts it's best to grow purple sprouting broccoli instead.

# CELERIAC

Sometimes known as turnip rooted celery it grows rather like a turnip and tastes like the rooty heart of celery. It may be eaten raw or used in soups and casseroles.

## Propagation
The seeds and plants should be raised and planted out in exactly the same way as self-blanching celery except that they need to be planted out 1 ft apart either way instead of 9 in.

## Cultivation
They need this extra room because they are very hungry feeders. To get good plants they must be grown on a heavily manured soil and need to be given copious amounts of water in dry weather. As the root balls start to swell remove any side growths and from August onwards remove the outer ring of leaves every two weeks to help the bulbs to swell.

## Harvesting
A couple of weeks before lifting pull the soil up over the bulbs to help to blanch them. If you live in the south of England you can leave the roots outside during the winter, digging them as you want them but protecting them with straw or sacking from very severe frosts. Otherwise they may be dug up and stored in sand in the same way as carrots.

## Recommended varieties
Globus.
Marble Ball.

# CELERY

Celery is related to the carrot. Both are members of the plant group *Umbelliferae*.

The traditional white celery is grown in trenches some 18 in. deep on soil with a high humus content, and it is best kept well watered. The trenches are filled in to blanch the plants as they develop. The individual plants may be wrapped in paper to prevent the earth getting between the stalks. Some gardeners say this spoils the flavour and they don't mind the extra chore of washing out the soil from between the stalks when it's ready to use.

'Self blanching' and 'American green' celery are much easier to deal with and don't need trenches. They are grown in a block with the plants approximately 9 in. apart in both directions.

## Seed sowing

The seeds may be sown in open ground ¼ in. deep in April or May but, as the seed is very fine, it really is best started in seed trays under glass or on a windowsill.

In March or April fill a small seed tray or a 5 in. flower pot with potting compost (the peat-based kind). Press it down so that the tray or pot is three-quarters full, water with a fine rose and leave it for a few minutes to drain off. Scatter the seeds thinly over the whole area and sift some more compost over them so that they are just covered. Slip the whole tray into a plastic bag to retain the moisture and cover with a sheet of brown paper to exclude the light. Keep the seed at room temperature 15–17°C (60–65°F). If they don't come up within a week put them in a colder place (say 10°C) for a few days and then back to 15°C again. Directly they come up remove the paper and plastic bag and put the seed tray near the light – a south-facing windowsill will do.

## Growing on the seedlings

Prick the seedlings out a couple of weeks later. First well water your seedlings in their container, then fill a plastic seed tray (9 by 14 in.) with potting compost. Smooth it out and press it down so that it is ¼ in. lower than the top of the tray. Take an ordinary pencil and, pushing it straight in, make fifteen evenly spaced holes in the compost.

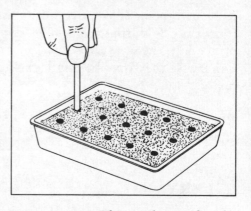

You'll need three trays for the Large Master Plan and two for the Middle Plan. Using the pencil or a spoon handle ease out the little plantlets from their container, keeping the roots intact and holding them by the leaves and not by the stem – rather like the difference between holding you by the hair or round the throat: the former might be painful but it won't kill you, whereas the latter might well do so. The same applies to the seedlings. Drop the roots well down into the holes you've made and firm them in. When you've filled the tray with plants put it back in the light for another couple of weeks making sure that it doesn't dry out but is not waterlogged.

Then transfer the trays to a cold frame or put them under cloches in the garden for the plants to harden off. Or put the trays in the garden by day and bring them in at night or if there is a frost.

## Planting out
You may of course wish to get plants from a nursery instead of growing your own. In either case the young plants should be put out in their final positions in May. They need to be planted 9 in. apart each way. Rake the soil level and then scratch lines on the surface 9 in. apart in both directions where the plants have to go.

Having previously watered them tap the sides of the seed trays firmly against the path and then tap the end of the tray in the same way. Tip out the compost and plants in one complete block.

Break it up carefully, keeping as much root intact for each plant as you can. Plant them where the lines cross and water them in well.

## Cultivation
Celery is a very hungry feeder indeed and it is a waste of time trying to grow it in poor soil. The ground must be bastard trenched and enriched with plenty of farmyard manure or well-rotted compost. The plants must be kept well watered whenever the weather is dry and failure to do this will encourage the plants to send up a central stem and go to seed.

## Harvesting
Self-blanching or American green are excellent varieties of celery when well grown. They will not, however, survive hard frosts and are ready for use from August onwards.

## Summary
It's best to sow the seeds under glass in March or April. Sow thinly and just cover with sifted compost. Keep at 15–17°C (60–65°F) but vary the temperature to get the seed to germinate. Transplant into large seed trays when big enough to handle – just fifteen plants to a tray. Plant out to their final positions in rich soil in May, 9 in. apart in each direction, to form a block of plants. Keep well watered and use from August onwards.

## Recommended varieties
American green.
Golden self blanching.

## CHICORY (Sugar Loaf)

This is a close relative of the plant that supplies the chicory root used as an additive to coffee and the blanched chicory that you can buy as a winter salad food. But sugar loaf chicory doesn't have to be blanched. It is a plant that is not yet very well known in Britain but it produces solid crunchy heads like well-grown cos lettuce that will stand in the garden in fresh condition over a long period and will keep well in the fridge.

### Seed sowing
Best results are obtained from a June or July sowing, $\frac{1}{2}$ in. deep in rows 1 ft apart. Progressively thin the plants to a final distance of 10–12 in.

### Cultivation
They need a reasonably fertile ground – one that has been manured for a previous crop is suitable – so they fit in well with the Roots Group. Keep the ground hoed and free from weeds.

### Harvesting
The plants will start to become usable by the end of October. They will stand a certain amount of frost and, in sheltered districts, if the weather is mild, they can stay in the garden all winter, especially if you can protect them with cloches. The heads can also be cut and stored in a cellar, the shed or the fridge for many weeks. When you come to use them take off the outside leaves and use the crisp solid heads as you would lettuce.

### Recommended varieties
Sugar Loaf (Pain de Sucre).
Winter Fare.

## CHINESE CABBAGE

A salad plant that is becoming very popular and is often sold in the shops as 'Chinese Leaves'. It can in fact be cooked like cabbage or eaten raw like lettuce (or cook the outer leaves and eat the inner ones).

### Seed sowing
In July sow in the open ground $\frac{1}{2}$ in. deep in rows 1 ft 6 in. apart.

Thin the plants to 1 ft apart as soon as they are large enough to handle. It is not worth trying to transplant the seedlings – they will rarely do well.

**Cultivation**
They need a good rich soil with a pH reaction of 6.5 and it is most essential that the soil is kept moist at all times. If the plants receive a check during the growing season they may not develop normally.

**Harvesting**
They need about three months to develop so they should be ready for use in October and November.

**Recommended varieties**
Sampan.
Pe-Tsai.

# CORN SALAD or LAMB'S LETTUCE

A useful substitute for lettuce, popular on the continent, which is ready for use from Christmas onwards.

**Seed sowing**
Sow in mid August to the end of September $\frac{1}{2}$ in. deep in drills 6 in. apart. Thin the plants to 6 in. apart as soon as they are large enough to handle. (It may also be sown in spring for summer and autumn use.)

**Cultivation**
Any normal well-cultivated soil will produce reasonable plants. In winter protect the plants with straw, bracken or cloches.

**Harvesting**
You can either gather the leaves one at a time from the plants or pull up the whole plant. They need to be well washed as they are low growing and get splashed with soil.

**Recommended varieties**
Large-leaved English.
Large-leaved Italian.

*153*

# CUCUMBER – GREENHOUSE VARIETIES

Greenhouse cucumbers are generally superior to outdoor ones. Although ideally they require a more humid and shaded atmosphere than tomatoes, most people manage to grow them together in the same greenhouse. If you do grow both use the side beds for tomatoes and the end of the greenhouse away from the door for cucumbers.

## Seed sowing

For a heated greenhouse sow the seeds singly in $2\frac{1}{2}$ or 3 in. pots in a temperature of 17°C (65°F) from February to May, placing the seed on edge about $\frac{3}{4}$ in. deep. If your greenhouse is unheated raise the plants indoors in the same way as outdoor cucumbers, or buy plants.

## Planting out

This can be done as soon as the plants have produced four to six leaves, or in an unheated greenhouse in the latter part of May. Plant them in raised mounds of compost 6 in. high or plant them in 10–12 in. pots. Large plastic buckets with holes made in the bottom (or the bottom cut out) do very well, too. Plant deeply: the seed leaves should almost touch the soil.

## Cultivation

A good growing compost can be made up by mixing equal parts of well-rotted manure and John Innes No. 3.

If you are growing cucumbers in a large area you can pinch out the growing tip of each plant to allow four side shoots to develop and then train these in. If you are growing up the end wall of a small greenhouse have two plants about 3 ft apart and allow them to grow with a central stem. Cut off all tendrils and male flowers as they appear. The female flower has a small elongated cucumber behind the petals, the male flower is on a short stalk. Pollination would make the cucumbers taste bitter.

Cucumbers will develop on side shoots growing out from the main stem and from the leaf axils of the main stem itself. Pinch out the latter from the bottom 2 ft or so of the plant and allow just one cucumber to develop on each side shoot – stopping this at two leaves past the cucumber. If the plant grows well you may allow more cucumbers to develop.

Support the plant with a framework of canes. Allow it to grow to the top of the far wall and then along the apex of the roof.

## Watering
Cucumbers need more water than tomatoes: this may mean watering twice a day in very hot weather, and syringing the plants as well.

## Harvesting
If you keep the cucumbers picked more will develop. Pick them while the flesh is still firm and before any seeds have formed.

## Summary
For a heated greenhouse sow the seed singly on edge in small pots at a temperature of 17°C (65°F) from February to May. For an unheated greenhouse raise the plants indoors and plant out at the end of May. Grow in large pots or on mounds of good compost. Either pick out the growing tip to allow four side shoots to develop or grow up a central main stem. Remove male flowers. Pick before seeds develop in the cucumbers.

## Recommended varieties
Telegraph.
Femspot (all female).
Bittex.

## CUCUMBER – OUTDOOR

The 'ridge' or outdoor cucumber used to be a short fat thing with hairy spines, but a number of very good varieties are now available. There are yellow ones shaped like apples, gherkins for pickling and slender green ones like greenhouse varieties.

## Seed sowing
Sow the seed outdoors in mid May ¾ in. deep in a little pocket of compost or good soil on well-manured ground and cover with a cloche. Put in two or three seeds at each 'station' and then thin down to the best plant.

But if you can start your plants in a greenhouse, in a frame, or indoors you'll get an earlier crop. Sow two seeds in a 3 in. pot of potting compost in mid April and cover with plastic film or put into a plastic bag to keep in the moisture. Keep at a minimum temperature of 17°C (65°F) – the cooler part of the airing cupboard is ideal – and inspect them daily. Directly they are up place the pot in the greenhouse or on a south-facing windowsill in a warm room, thinning the plants down to the best one if they both come up. As they develop into big plants keep them well watered and you may have to support them with a thin cane.

Or get plants from a nursery if you don't want to grow your own.

## Planting
Plant outdoors at the end of May or early June with at least 2 ft between each plant. Protect from any late frosts.

## Cultivation
Outdoor cucumbers need land that has been heavily manured. They will grow quite well on normally cultivated land but they will do better still if they have a deep layer of manure, about 6 in. below the surface. Take out a trench 6 in. deep and 1 ft 6 in. wide. Fill it with compost or manure and replace the soil to form a mound. Plant the cucumbers on top of the mound, 2 ft or more apart. When seven leaves have formed pinch out the growing tip of the plant to encourage side shoots and more cucumbers. The female flowers have an embryo cucumber just behind the flower while the male ones are on short stalks. With greenhouse varieties it is normal to remove any male flowers as pollination can make the cucumbers taste bitter. If you grow ridge varieties this isn't necessary.

## Harvesting
Keep the cucumbers picked as they develop and this will encourage more to set. Don't leave mature cucumbers on the plants. Closely wrapped in plastic film they will keep in the bottom of the fridge for up to a couple of weeks.

## Summary
Start them under glass in mid April in pots or sow them directly into the ground in mid May ¾ in. deep. Or buy plants. Put out the plants at the end of May or early June, preferably on a mound of soil with a good layer of manure 6 in. below the surface. Keep the cucumbers continually picked to get a long cropping season.

## Recommended varieties
Nadir.
Burpee Hybrid.
Burpless Tasty Green.

## CURLY KALE or BORECOLE

A very useful winter vegetable which withstands the hardest weather; considered by some to be the best winter green vegetable.

### Seed sowing
Sow the seeds ¾ in. deep in a short row in a prepared seed bed in April or May and thin the seedlings to 3 or 4 in. apart as soon as you can handle them.

### Plants
Set them out 2 ft apart each way in their final positions during June and July and firm them in really well.

### Cultivation
Like all brassicas kale does best in a rich well-cultivated soil that has a pH reaction of 6.5. Keep the young plants well watered in dry weather until they are established and keep the ground hoed and clear of weeds at all times. Kale can produce some pretty big plants so if you are growing a large variety it's worth supporting each plant with a stout stake to stop it being blown about by the winter winds.

### Harvesting
Let them grow freely and build up good big plants before you start to pick from them. Early in the new year take out the central head and this will encourage side shoots to develop. The leaves and shoots are then picked as required and others come along to take their place.

### Recommended varieties
Dwarf Green Curled.
Tall Green Curled.
Pentland Brig.

## ENDIVE

A useful salad as it is easy to grow and ready for use in autumn and winter when lettuce are scarce. The slight touch of bitterness, which distinguishes it in taste from lettuce, is pleasantly acceptable. It can also be cooked.

## Seed sowing
It may be sown in a spare corner and then transplanted when 2 or 3 in. high, or it may be sown where it is to grow. Sow the seeds ½ in. deep, just one to the inch, in rows 15 in. apart and thin to 12 to 15 in. apart.

For summer use sow in late March or April but for the more useful autumn and winter crop sow in June and July. If the soil is dry rake just the top inch into a fine tilth, take out the drill, carefully trickle water just along the bottom of it, sow the seed and cover with dry soil. Do not water again until they are up.

## Cultivation
They like a fertile, well-drained soil. Water the growing plants in dry weather and keep them clear of weeds.

## Harvesting
Endive needs to be blanched before use. When nearly full grown and three to four weeks before it is required the leaves may be gathered together and tied with soft string or raffia to exclude the light from the inner leaves – the ones to be eaten. Or a simpler method is to cover a few plants at a time with wooden boxes, large flower pots, or, perhaps better still, with cloches that have been whitewashed. Make sure you close up the ends of the cloche with a piece of wood, slate, or whitewashed glass or plastic. To blanch plants for winter use, lift before severe frosts and replant in boxes of soil which can be put in a shed or cellar.

## Summary
Grow them like lettuce but 12–15 in. apart. Blanch them by covering over to exlude the light a few weeks before you need them. June or July sowings will be ready in autumn and winter.

## Recommended varieties

FOR SUMMER USE: Moss Curled.

FOR AUTUMN OR WINTER USE: Batavian Broad Leaved.

# GARLIC

Garlic is becoming almost as essential in British kitchens to flavour dishes as it is in continental ones.

## Planting

A bulb of garlic is made up of a dozen or more individual sections or 'cloves' and it is these individual cloves that are planted separately to grow into further complete bulbs. In March to May plant the cloves upright with their tips just below the surface, 9 in. between each plant and 1 ft between each row.

## Harvesting

Lift and dry the crop in late summer in the same way as shallots, and store in a dry frost-proof place.

# KOHL RABI

A handsome vegetable widely used on the continent and easy to grow. A member of the brassica family it is like a turnip but has a milder taste and the 'root', which is really a swollen stem, sits above the ground and so is a very clean vegetable to prepare. The outer skin is either purple or green but the flesh is white.

## Seed sowing

Sow the seeds ½ in. deep in drills 15 in. apart in April or May or in succession to mid July and progressively thin the seedlings to 9 in. apart.

## Cultivation

Kohl rabi need to be grown quickly to be at their best and for that they need a fertile soil with a pH reaction of 6.5. Keep them clear of weeds but when hoeing be careful not to draw any earth up to the plants. Let them sit on the surface.

## Harvesting

Use the plants as soon as they are the size of a billiard ball and certainly no bigger than a tennis ball while they are young and tender. If they are at all fibrous you have left them too long in the ground. Peel and cook like a turnip. They will deep freeze very well.

## Recommended varieties

White Vienna.
Purple Vienna.

## LEEKS

Cultivated in ancient Egypt in the time of the Pharaohs and probably brought to England by the Romans, the leek is the emblem of the Welsh and the pride of the Scots who use it in Scotch Broth and Cock-a-Leekie. Much of its popularity is due to its extreme hardiness as well as to its fine flavour.

### Seed sowing

Large exhibition leeks can be obtained by sowing the seed under glass in February in trays of seed compost. When they are an inch high prick them out 1½ in. apart into trays of potting compost. Harden off and plant out in May as described below.

But these early sown leeks will not be as hardy as the later sown ones. It's better to sow the seed outdoors in March or April ½ in. deep, just three seeds to the inch, in a row 6 ft long. Cover with fine soil and firm with the back of the rake.

### Planting out

In June or July when the plants are 6–8 in. high, soak the row prior to lifting and take them up carefully with a fork keeping as much root intact as you can. Cut the tips of the leaves back ½ in. or so with a pair of scissors to restrain the growth of the leaves until the roots are established. Make holes with a dibber 6–9 in. deep, and the same distance apart, and drop a leek into each hole. Fill the hole with water – not with soil. This will wash a little earth round the roots and the hole will give the leek room to develop.

### Cultivation

Leeks need a deeply dug and well-manured soil with a pH reaction of 6.5 which is why they are included with the Onions & Brassicas in the Master Plans. When you are doing the autumn digging make sure the manure is placed deep down where the roots of the leeks will be.

To get longer blanched stems the plants may be earthed up as they grow or cardboard tubes may be dropped over them when they've grown well out of their holes. This blanches them without earth getting between the leaves – but they'll do quite well without either of these measures.

### Harvesting

Leeks may be dug from the garden throughout the winter as long as the soil isn't frozen too hard to get your spade in. It's worth having a few dug up and kept in the bottom of the fridge in case you or the leeks get frozen in. If you want to clear the ground at the end of the winter dig up any remaining ones and heel them in together in any odd corner. Make sure they are covered with soil to their original depth and use them as you want them.

**Summary**
Sow the seed very thinly in March/April $\frac{1}{2}$ in. deep in a short row outdoors. Plant out in June/July, dropping each leek into a 6–9 in. deep hole made with a dibber. Water in. Leave in the ground for the winter and use as required.

**Recommended varieties**
Winter Crop.
Catalina.

# LETTUCE

To some people 'lettuce' is a dreary bit of thin green wet cardboard served in restaurants and hotels; or a big floppy limp thing bought from a shop. To others it's a marvellous summer salad of solid crisp crunchy hearts with the sweet taste of spring.

The problem is many sided. Lettuces don't travel well and they should be eaten the day they are picked – nay, the hour they are picked. Shops want to sell something that looks a lot for your money and restaurants like flat leaves that will be good and lie down on the plates.

The lettuce you grow, provided it is grown quickly in good soil, is a completely different vegetable from the one you buy and the choice of varieties is so wide there's something to suit everyone. Taste is such an individual thing that none of us can say what will taste good to others but I would like to suggest that you include 'Little Gem' among the lettuce you grow. Many people think it's the best flavoured lettuce of all and I agree with them. Choose two or three varieties so that you have a long season of supply.

**Seed sowing**
Sow the seed thinly. Yes I know it's difficult, but it will save you a lot of time trying to thin them out later. Just two seeds to the inch in a

drill ½ in. deep from March onwards, depending on the variety. If you have some cloches they will certainly help to keep the cold winds off the early varieties and bring them on quickly.

Sow half a row at a time once every couple of weeks and then you'll have a long season of supply. Or you can transplant the thinnings from one half row into another half row. The slight check they receive makes them come on later so you've extended your season that way. If you do transplant, water well before you do so, make sure you take up each seedling with plenty of soil round it and water well in. An old tablespoon is a good tool for moving lettuce seedlings.

## Cultivation
Lettuce will only grow well in a soil that is rich in organic material so incorporate plenty of manure or compost in the winter dig. They need it for nourishment and because it helps to retain the moisture in the soil in the summer months. Lettuce like a pH reaction of 6.5. Water well in dry weather.

## Harvesting
Pick as soon as they are ready. Pull up the roots and put them on the compost heap. Use half a row at a time and immediately sow some more seed in the same place, right up to mid August.

## Summary
Lettuce must have good soil. Sow from March to August very thinly ½ in. deep in rows 9 or 12 in. apart. Thin early and hoe between the rows to keep them free of weeds. Sow more seed in the same place as you clear each half row, but sow in a different place next year.

## Recommended varieties
Just a few from many good ones:
Tom Thumb (early); Buttercrunch; Little Gem (cos); Sigmaball; Minetto; Lobjotts Green (cos); Winter Density (cos).

MIXED LETTUCE: quite good for the smaller plots, to extend the season of supply, but when you thin them make sure you leave in different shaped and different sized seedlings – or you might end up with just one variety.

# MARROW

The magic of marrows stays with us from our childhood. Is it because, like their cousin the pumpkin, they might turn into a fairy coach, or is it just their shape and size? Probably the latter, although size is not the thing that impresses today's cook. Really young marrows, about 6 in. long, are becoming more and more appreciated. They are cooked as courgettes with their skins on.

In fact the difference between courgettes and marrows is not at all clear and several varieties of marrows can be picked as courgettes when 6 in. long, picked when 12 in. long at the young marrow stage, or left on the plants to become fully grown. The choice is yours.

### Seed sowing

Sow under glass in mid April. Put two seeds $\frac{3}{4}$ in. deep on their edge in a $2\frac{1}{2}$ or 3 in. pot of compost, cover with plastic film or put in a plastic bag and keep in the dark at a temperature of 17–23°C (65–75°F). Inspect them daily. The airing cupboard is ideal if you haven't a heated greenhouse. Directly the plants are up, remove the plastic and bring into full light either in the greenhouse or on a south-facing windowsill in a warm room. If both seeds come up then thin down to the best one. As the plants develop keep them well watered and pot on into larger pots if necessary. Or get plants from a nursery if you don't want to grow your own.

Seed may also be sown outdoors at a depth of 1 in. from May to June. Put in two or three seeds at each 'station', 2 ft apart in each direction, and thin down to the best plants.

### Planting out

Put out your plants at the end of May or early June, 2 ft apart each way. If your soil is very rich or you decide to grow trailing plants rather than bush ones then put them in 3 ft apart. Protect from late frosts.

### Cultivation

Marrows need deeply dug well-manured soil. You can either incorporate plenty of manure at digging time or you can grow them on a mound of compost with a 6 in. layer of soil on top of the compost, as described under 'Cucumber – Outdoor'.

## Harvesting

If you cut the marrows while they are young the plants will be much more productive and will give you a crop right through from June to October. You can grow a few to full size in the later part of the season. Let them ripen off well on the plant, but cut them before the frosts, and you can keep them till January or February if you hang them up in a net in a dry, airy, frost-proof place. They are then ideal to use as stuffed marrows.

## Summary

Sow seed outdoors in May or June 2–3 ft apart at a depth of 1 in. Or bring them on earlier under glass or indoors. In mid April sow two seeds on their edge ¾ in. deep in each pot and single down to the best plant when they come up. Grow in full light, then plant out in late May or early June in good soil. Protect from late frosts. Pick them while they are at the courgette size and leave a few to grow to mature marrows at the end of the season if you wish.

## Recommended varieties

Green Bush.
Zucchini.
Table Dainty (trailing).

## MELON

I think this is one fruit that should be allowed to slip into a book on vegetable growing, as the cantaloupe type melons may be grown outdoors in the vegetable garden in sheltered areas in place of marrows. They may also, of course, be grown in the greenhouse and if it's heated there is a wider choice of varieties.

## Seed sowing and cultivation

Grow them the same way as outdoor cucumbers or greenhouse cucumbers with the following differences.

1. HEAT: melons need more heat than cucumbers so put a frame or cloches over the outdoor ones and grow the greenhouse ones with a little more warmth. But keep them ventilated.

2. NO SHADE: grow melons in full light with no shade.

3. POLLINATION: the female flowers – the ones with the little embryo melons behind – need to be fertilised with the pollen from the male flowers. When several female flowers are fully open pick a fully open male flower, strip off the petals and gently touch the pollen on to the centre of the female flowers.

4. WATER: keep melons a bit drier than cucumbers and when the fruits start to ripen, you'll see slight cracks near the stalk, give them hardly any water at all.

5. SUPPORT: the larger melons growing in the greenhouse may well need supporting with individual nets to take their weight off the plants. Slip a piece of glass or slate under the outdoor ones to keep them off the ground.

## Recommended varieties

OUTDOORS OR IN A COLD GREENHOUSE: Sweetheart; Ogen; Charantais.

IN A HEATED OR COOL GREENHOUSE: the above or Blenheim Orange; Superlative; Emerald Gem.

## ONION

A plant that has been cultivated from time immemorial and an essential one in almost every kitchen. The main crop of onions may be grown from seed or from sets – small, partly grown onions. Sets are much easier for the amateur to grow but let us deal with seed first.

### January sowing under glass

To produce bigger and earlier crops onion seed may be sown under glass and the seedlings transplanted to their final positions during April. Sow in seed trays of seed compost firmed down and filled to ½ in. from the top. Place the seed ¾ in. apart in each direction all over the tray. Push them just under the surface of the soil and cover with a small amount of sifted compost. Water with tepid water through a fine rose. Cover the trays with a sheet of glass and brown paper and remove these when the seeds come up. Ideally the temperature should be between 12 and 15°C (55 and 60°F).

When the plants are ½ in. tall carefully prick them out into further seed boxes 2 in. apart. Give light waterings from time to time. Transfer to a cold frame at the end of March to harden off and plant out in April.

In a mild winter it is possible to raise the seeds under cloches or a frame instead of a greenhouse.

For these potentially big onions the rows should be 1 ft–1 ft 3 in. apart with 6–9 in. between the plants. Water the boxes, lift the seedlings carefully, disturbing the roots as little as possible, and plant firmly. Water if the weather is dry.

### Spring sowing outdoors

March and April are the usual months for sowing. Rake the soil to a very fine tilth and sow the seed in drills 1 ft apart and ¼ in. deep with no more than three seeds to the inch. Firm the soil so that it is in contact with the seeds. Progressively thin the plants to 6 in. apart, firming the soil back afterwards. Don't leave any thinnings lying about to attract the onion fly – use them as spring onions. As the onions develop they will sit on the surface of the soil and get the full benefit of the sun.

### Sets

But it is much easier to grow onions from sets. They are very small onions that have been partly grown the year before. You can buy them from most seed merchants and get about 100 to the lb. Unpack them as soon as you receive them and spread them out in a cool, dry frost-proof place in full light to prevent them sprouting prematurely.

Plant them out in March or early April. Take out a drill 1 in. deep and place the sets 4–6 in. apart along the drill. Replace the earth making sure the tip of each set is uppermost and just showing above the soil. Firm the soil round each one. The birds like to pull out the sets to check for worms underneath so keep them off with black cotton.

The rows of onions on the Master Plans are only 6 in. apart. This will produce medium sized onions that will keep well. If you want bigger onions have the rows up to 1 ft apart.

### Cultivation

Onions are hungry feeders that require a deeply dug well-manured soil. Hoe carefully and often in the early days to eradicate weed seedlings. If any onion produces a flower head pull it up and use it, as it won't develop into a good keeper.

**Harvesting**

In late August when the onions start to turn brown bend over the tops to hasten the ripening process. A couple of weeks later ease the onions out of the ground with a fork and spread them out with the roots facing the sun. A few days later continue the ripening process by shaking off any earth and laying them out on a path or patio in full sun so that they are golden brown when put away. If the weather is wet put them in the greenhouse or under cloches. They can be stored by making them up into onion 'ropes', but the simplest way is to lay them out in wooden trays or grape boxes which your greengrocer may give you. One layer of onions in each box and each box stacked on another gives good storage with plenty of air circulating between them. Look through them every few weeks and take out any that show signs of rot. They'll keep right through to March if they go into store properly ripe and are kept in a cool dry airy place. Some people store them hung up in nylon tights or stockings which is quite a good way but makes it difficult to remove any that start to rot.

**Summary**

For big onions sow in seed trays of compost in the greenhouse in January and put out the young plants in April, having hardened them off. Or sow in the open from March to May in drills just ¼ in. deep on good rich soil. But the easiest way is to plant onion sets in March or April. For medium sized onions plant 4–6 in. apart with the tips just showing above the soil. Keep the crop clear of weeds and bend over the tops in late August. Ripen off the onions and store in grape or peach boxes which you can get from a greengrocer.

**Recomended varieties**

SOWN IN JANUARY UNDER GLASS: Ailsa Craig Selected; White Spanish-A1.

SOWN IN SPRING: Bedfordshire Champion; White Spanish A-1.

SETS: Sturon; Coranado.

# OTHER ONIONS

There are some other kinds of onions you might like to grow.

## Pickling onions

Little silver skin onions that do well in poor soil. In April scatter the seed fairly thickly in a drill which is 1–2 in. wide and only ¼ in. deep. Replace the soil and keep clear of weeds but do not thin. You will get excellent little pickling onions by July.

## Potato onion

This is sometimes called the underground onion because that's where it grows. It is grown from bulbs which are planted in rows 18 in. apart with 9 in. between each bulb during March, in the same way as shallots. Clusters of bulbs form from the one bulb and these should be earthed up rather like potatoes as the plants grow. Water during the growing season but stop watering when the bulbs begin to ripen. Dig them up in August, dry them on the surface of the soil and store like ordinary onions. They are not always good keepers.

## Spring onions

The well-known salad crop. Sow the seed in March just three to the inch in a drill ¼ in. deep. Thin when they are big enough to start using. Water the row first and then get hold of each onion right at ground level to pull it out intact.

## Recommended variety

White Lisbon.

## Tree onion

An interesting plant which is sometimes called the Egyptian onion. Thick flower stems grow up from the bulbs and these have little onions at the top as well as flowers. Other onions form under the soil. Either may be used to eat or pickle or be used to grow more plants. The stems may also be eaten.

## Plant

Five or six bulbs planted 6 in. apart each way in early April will make a good sized clump but if you want to grow more they should be in rows 18 in. apart and the bulbs 6 in. apart.

## Harvesting

Dig up the whole plant in the autumn and when it has dried off gather the onions from the base and the top, or you may leave the clump in the ground and just use the onions off the top.

**Welsh onion**

Often called the perpetual onion. It grows like a clump of spring onions. Each single onion that is replanted will produce a clump of up to thirty or so that never grow any bigger than large spring onions. They can be eaten raw or used for cooking. If you have a clump near the kitchen door you can dig up a few at a time as you need them – anytime during the year.

## PARSLEY

An essential herb to most cooks for flavouring and garnishing.

**Seed sowing**

To have a long season of use sow half a row in March and the other half in June in a drill ½ in. deep with three seeds to the inch. Parsley can take a long time to germinate, even as long as five weeks. One way to shock it into growth is to pour a kettle of boiling water along the row just after the seed has been planted and covered over with soil in the normal way – it softens the outer skin of the seed. A three-pint kettle will do a 20 ft row. Thin the plants to 3 in. apart once they are up and finally to 6 in.

**Cultivation**

Parsley likes a rich moist soil and will grow in partial shade, which is why it is next to the runner beans in the Master Plans where little else would thrive. Make sure the plants don't dry out in hot weather or they'll go to seed.

**Harvesting**

Pick off individual leaves as you need them. Keep any flower heads cut off to encourage the plant to produce more leaves rather than go to seed. If you want some for winter use just chop up the leaves, spread them out in a normal room temperature indoors and when they are thoroughly dry store in a jar. But parsley will keep its flavour much better if it is frozen rather than dried. Wash the leaves, shake off the surplus moisture, chop them up small and fill small plastic containers without pressing down. Put in the freezer straight away. You will then be able to spoon out however much parsley you want without thawing it first.

## Summary
Sow the seed from March to June $\frac{1}{2}$ in. deep at three seeds to the inch. Cover with soil and then pour a kettle of boiling water along the row to help germination. Progressively thin the plants to 6 in. apart and use the individual leaves as soon as they are large enough.

## Recommended varieties
Moss Curled.
Paramount Imperial Curled.


# PARSNIP

Parsnips have been cultivated since Roman times for their long tapering fleshy roots which go deep into the soil. They are of the order *Umbelliferae* and so are related to parsley, carrots and celery.

The *Guinness Book of Records* mentions one over 4 ft long, a lot of which would presumably be thin tap root. This isn't quite the length most of us want. More like a foot will do and to get that we need a deeply dug rich soil that has had no recent manure.

## Seed sowing
Sow the seed in March or April in drills 1 in. deep and 12 in. apart at 'half stations' putting in two or three seeds every $3-4\frac{1}{2}$ in. The seed is flat and circular and as it's a bit tricky to handle you'll probably find it best to use the fingers rather than try to tap it out of the packet.

Thin the seedlings down to one per half station when they come up and then to the final spacing of 6 or 9 in. when they are established. If you transplant to fill in any gaps be sure to get your trowel or tablespoon right down under the seedling to include all the root.

## Cultivation
Parsnips need a fertile soil that contains no new manure, because this causes the plants to fork in all directions with a tangle of roots that are fascinating to look at but not much use for the cooking pot. A soil that has been well manured for a previous crop is ideal. Keep them hoed and free from weeds, especially in the early stages, but be careful not to get the hoe too near the plants and damage them.

## Harvesting
You can dig the parsnips from September onwards using a spade to get deep down under each root. They will keep very well left in the

soil and the action of frost in the winter months converts some of the starch in the roots into sugar and improves their flavour. You won't get your spade into the ground in very severe frosts so it pays to have some stored in sand. Those remaining in the plot in January should be lifted and stored this way to make way for the next year's cultivation. See 'Storing Your Crops'.

## Summary

Sow in March/April 1 in. deep in drills 1 ft apart in land that contains no new manure. Thin to 6 or 9 in. apart. Keep clear of weeds and use from September onwards. They may be left in the ground or stored in sand. A touch of frost improves their flavour.

## Recommended varieties

SHORT: White Gem.

LONG: Tender and True; Improved Hollow Crown.

## PEAS

Peas are a highly nutritious crop and an important item of food in many countries. The commercial growers and freezers produce an article that is almost as good as the fresh vegetable, but not quite. There is still a certain something about the flavour of a dish of peas newly picked from the garden that makes them worth growing.

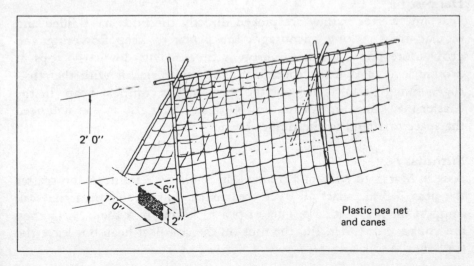

Plastic pea net and canes

## Seed sowing

Sow the seed in March–May. Take out a shallow flat trench 6 in. wide and 2 in. deep and space the seeds 2–3 in. apart in all directions in the trench. Fill in the trench and firm the soil.

Dwarf peas, growing no more than 2 ft high, are easier to stake than the tall ones and can be grown on a pea net supported by a few canes. Or grow them up wire netting or twiggy pea sticks. Put up the support as soon as you have planted the peas.

Peas usually grow away readily but if a spell of cold wet weather after sowing gives poor germination, as soon as the peas are up pop in some more seed in all the gaps using a teaspoon as a little trowel. These will come along just after the others and give you a later picking. What looks like poor germination may of course mean that mice have eaten the seed. A few prickly holly leaves or chopped-up gorse scattered among the peas before you cover them with soil will keep the mice away.

## Cultivation

Peas are quick growers and have only a short time in which to absorb and use plant foods. Those foods need to be in a readily available form and so heavy manuring the previous autumn is necessary for a good yield. Keep that manure or compost one spit below the surface and the peas will go searching for it and build up a good root system which will give you a heavier crop. It's little use just manuring the top few inches of the soil. Peas like a soil with a pH reaction of 6.0–6.5.

## Harvesting

Peas are sweeter if they are picked directly the pods have filled and regular early picking encourages the plants to keep flowering and grow more pods. When the crop is finished cut down the tops at ground level. Leave the roots in the soil to enrich it with their nitrogen fixing nodules and put the tops on the compost heap. In the Master Plans they are not replaced with anything else as you will need the space to attend to the runner beans.

## Summary

Sow in March to May in a trench 6 in. wide by 2 in. deep and scatter the peas 2–3 in. apart all over the trench. Fill in and firm the soil. Support the peas with a pea net or pea sticks and pick them while they are young and tender. Put the tops on the compost heap but leave the roots in the soil.

**Recommended varieties (All early dwarf)**
Little Marvel.
Early Onward.
Vitalis.
Kelvedon Wonder.


## POTATO

The origin of the potato is lost in the mists of time but when the Spaniards invaded South America in 1524 they found a large number of varieties and species already under cultivation. The subsequent introduction of the potato into Europe, North America and almost every important agricultural country in the world has made this a miracle vegetable and a major source of the world's food supplies.

The potatoes we buy from our shops and farms are usually of a very high quality; but the taste of new potatoes straight from the garden when the skin virtually brushes off in your hands is surely one of the great rewards of vegetable gardening, and so a few rows of potatoes have been included in the Master Plans.

### Getting the seed
Do use good seed potatoes that are certified free from disease. The potato is subject to very many potential diseases, usually spread by insects such as aphids or plant lice which don't readily multiply in the cooler climates. This is why the best British seed potatoes are grown in Scotland and parts of Ireland. Seed potatoes are generally about the size of a hen's egg. It doesn't matter if they are bigger except that you won't get as many to the lb.

### Boxing up
As soon as you receive them the seed potatoes should be set up in boxes or trays in a cool, dry frost-proof place in full light with the rose end upwards. (The rose end is where most of the eyes are and is the opposite end to that which was attached to the plant.)

When the shoots start to grow, rub off the weak ones leaving the two strongest on each tuber. If you haven't enough seed you can cut the bigger tubers in half, making sure that both halves have the necessary eyes from which the new plants will grow. Do this cutting at the time of planting, not before. Be very careful these shoots don't get knocked off when you're planting.

*173*

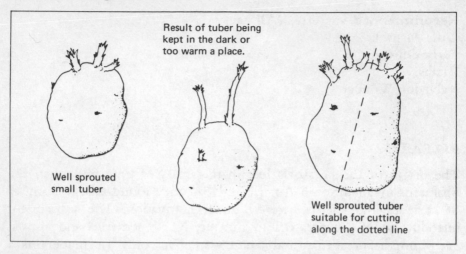

Result of tuber being
kept in the dark or
too warm a place.

Well sprouted
small tuber

Well sprouted tuber
suitable for cutting
along the dotted line

## Planting

The early potatoes should be 12 in. apart, in rows 1 ft 9 in. apart, and the main crop 1 ft 6 in. apart in rows 2 ft apart. Start planting about the middle of March in the south ranging up to the middle of April in the north, most of the country planting the first week in April if the weather is right.

Plant them so that there is about 3 in. of soil above the top of the tuber, either by taking out a drill with a draw hoe or spade, or by digging individual planting holes with a trowel for each tuber.

Directly the potatoes are through hoe the ground between the rows with a cultivator or a draw hoe. If there is any danger of frost bring soil up to the new shoots so that they are just covered: frost could kill them. They will soon grow through again.

## Earthing up

As the plants develop they are earthed up so that any potatoes growing near the surface are covered with soil to prevent them turning green from the sunlight. This soil is drawn up from between the rows with a draw hoe or spade. The earthing up is done when the plants are about 8 in. high, and a few weeks later another inch or so of soil is brought up round the plants. The ridges shouldn't be brought up so steeply that there is any danger of tubers being exposed at the side.

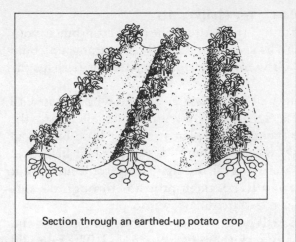

Section through an earthed-up potato crop

Sides too steep, tubers exposed

## The soil

Potatoes will grow on most soils but the ideal is a well-drained deeply dug medium loam that has been manured the previous autumn. Certainly plenty of manure or compost dug in in the autumn will improve all soils. No lime should be used as this might make the potatoes scabby and in any case they like a slightly acid soil with a pH reaction of 5.5. Never grow potatoes in the same place two years running.

## Harvesting

See if your earlies are ready by digging up a root when the plants are in flower. If the potatoes are too small leave them for another couple of weeks and try again. Dig them as you need them: they are best straight from the soil.

If you have any maincrop potatoes still in the ground when the tops have died down in September/October dig them up, let them dry on the surface for a few hours in fine weather and then store them in boxes or hessian sacks in a dark frost-proof place. Any light will turn them green. Don't store them in plastic bags or they'll sweat and go bad.

If the tops are in any way diseased then burn them. If they are healthy they may go on the compost heap but don't use that compost for potatoes or tomatoes next year. You will find it is easier to dig up the crop if you cut off the tops first. Don't leave any tiny potatoes in the soil to grow again next year: they could carry over diseases.

## Growing under black plastic on chalk soils

There is no doubt that earthing up ensures a heavier crop but if your soil is very shallow and on chalk or limestone then earthing up could bring chalk to the surface. Growing under plastic sheets is perhaps the best and easiest way.

Plant the tubers in the normal way, then cover the whole plot with large black plastic sheets weighed down with stones all round the edges. As soon as you see the growing plants making little bumps in the sheeting make a 4 in. slit where the bump is with a razor blade and then another slit forming a cross with the first. Be careful not to cut the new white shoots underneath. Let them protrude through the slits and they will soon turn green and grow away into plants.

Your first early potatoes will be growing just under the plastic and you can lift it up and virtually pick them off the ground. The rain will find its way through the slits. If it rains heavily before you cut the slits you can simply release any big puddles by making a slit where they are. The sheeting may be kept for future years but then you'll need to lay down the sheeting first and then plant the tubers where the slits are.

## Summary

Obtain certified seed potatoes early in the year and set them up in boxes in full light in a frost-proof place with the eyes uppermost. Leave on only the best two or three shoots. In late March or early April plant the earlies 5 in. deep in rows 1 ft 9 in. apart with the potatoes 1 ft apart in the rows. Plant the maincrop at the same depth in rows 2 ft apart with the potatoes 1 ft 6 in. apart in the rows. Earth up the plants as they grow and start to harvest the earlies when they are in flower. Dig up the rest of the maincrop in late September or early October. Burn any diseased tops. Dry the crop and store in hessian sacks or boxes.

## Recommended varieties

EARLIES: Foremost; Maris Peer, Pentland Javelin.

MAINCROP: Maris Piper; Majestic.

## RADISH

Probably the first thing you will gather from your vegetable garden at the beginning of the year will be some tender crisp radishes – and how welcome they are after the long winter wait. Early varieties will be ready for pulling in 6–8 weeks from an outdoor sowing: sow some seed in early March and you will be pulling radishes by the beginning of May.

## Seed sowing

Sow ½ in. deep from March onwards with just one or two seeds to the inch in the drill. Radishes have a high rate of germination so don't be tempted to put in a few more seeds 'just in case': it will only give you the tedious task of thinning them later. Sow half a row at a time with a couple of weeks between each sowing. You can sow them right up to August.

If you have a few cloches put them in position a few days before sowing to warm up the soil and your radishes can be sown and harvested a couple of weeks earlier. Make sure you close the ends of the cloches so that you don't create a cold wind tunnel.

## Cultivation

For sweet, crisp and mild flavoured radishes grow them quickly. They will grow quickly if they are sown on fertile soil containing plenty of organic matter and kept well watered in dry weather.

## Harvesting

Pull them, wash them and eat them all within the hour to have them at their best. Once they are past their best clear the row straight away. Don't leave old radishes in the soil as a home for pests.

## Summary

Sow radishes ½ in. deep, just one or two seeds to the inch from March to August in a fertile soil and keep them well watered so that they grow quickly. Use them while they are young and tender.

## Recommended varieties

They come in a variety of shapes and sizes, most of them bright scarlet or white, and are a delight to the children, especially if you let them pull them.

ROUND: Cherry Belle; Saxerre; Scarlet Globe.

CYLINDRICAL: French Breakfast.

LONG WHITE: Icicle.

## WINTER RADISH

These are large radish that are lifted and used in the winter. They may weigh as much as a pound each.

### Seed sowing
Sow very thinly in July or August ½ in. deep in good fertile ground. If the soil is dry take out a drill, trickle water from a can just along the bottom of the drill, sow the seed and cover with dry soil. Don't water again until they come up. Thin to 6 or 8 in. apart.

### Harvesting
Lift as required in the winter. Sliced or shredded they make an excellent crisp salad.

### Recommended varieties
China Rose.
Black Spanish Round.
Black Spanish Long.


## RHUBARB

Although it is not a 'vegetable' it's worth growing a couple of roots in even the most modest sized garden and more in a big one. It's a valuable crop at the beginning of the year for pies and puddings before other fruit is available and the leaves, which should never be eaten, contain oxalic acid which makes a readily available greenfly killer (see 'Pests and Diseases').

As only a few varieties breed true from seed rhubarb is usually propagated by dividing up existing clumps.

### Seed sowing
If you do grow from seed sow them thinly in April in a drill 1 in. deep and thin the little plants to 6 in. apart. Transplant to their final quarters in autumn or the following spring.

### Plants
If you buy roots, or divide a clump, each root should have one good sound bud at the top. The roots should be planted with the tops just an inch below soil level and there should be 2 ft 6 in. between plants each way.

## Cultivation

Rhubarb likes its roots to be well fed, cool and moist but well drained. As the plants will no doubt spend a number of years in the same place dig the site deeply and incorporate plenty of compost or manure. After planting put a 2 in. layer of compost on top of the soil round the plants and as the worms take it down replace it in January or February each year.

## Harvesting

Don't pull any sticks the first year and be sparing in what you pull the second year. To get an early pale pink crop cover half your plants with large upturned boxes or perhaps even a small dustbin in December or January to 'force' the plants, but remove the covers by May after pulling the early crop. Do any subsequent pulling from the other plants to allow the first ones to recover. And by the way do 'pull' the rhubarb to remove the whole stick – don't cut it off. Stop pulling altogether by the end of July.

## Recommended varieties

FROM SEED: Victoria; Holstein Bloodred.

ROOTS: Timperley Early; Hawke's Champagne.

## SALSIFY

Sometimes known as 'Vegetable Oyster' it is a root crop with slender almost grass-like foliage and a cream coloured tap root about 9 in. long and 2 in. thick at the top. It has a nutty flavour and is very good to eat if it is boiled in salted water until tender and then sliced and fried in butter.

## Seed sowing

Sow during March or April in drills 1 in. deep and 15 in. apart and thin to 9 in. between plants.

## Cultivation

The soil should not have been freshly manured. The ideal is a light deep soil that was manured for a previous crop so this is a good alternative for the Roots Group. Keep the rows cultivated and free of weeds in the normal way.

## Harvesting

The roots should be ready from November onwards, and it may even be worth trying some in late October. Dig up deeply and carefully with a spade so as to get out the full length and not damage them. Salsify is relatively hardy and may be left in the ground for use as required right through to early spring. Or it may be lifted and stored in sand like carrots.

## Recommended varieties
Giant.
Sandwich Island.

# SCORZONERA

This is similar in appearance to salsify but it has black-skinned roots with an unusual delicate flavour. To prepare, scald the roots, scrape off the blackish skin and then cook like salsify. In fact it can be grown and treated like salsify in every way except that the plants need a little more room. They should be thinned to 1 ft apart in the rows and you may have to dig a little deeper to get out the whole root. They may stay in the ground and be lifted for use as required or dug up and stored in sand.

## Recommended variety
Russian Giant.

# SEAKALE BEET

Seakale beet is a kind that is grown for its leaves and not for its roots. It is easy to cultivate and crops abundantly even in dry weather. The green part of the leaf is cooked like spinach and the white mid-rib like asparagus, or both may be cooked together. The outer leaves are picked off as required and the plants will keep producing more leaves throughout the summer and autumn.

## Seed sowing

Take out a drill 1 in. deep and put in one seed every 2 in. and cover over. They are cluster seeds so thin down to one seedling when they come up and then progressively thin to the final distance of 12 in. apart. Protect from slugs and birds until the plants are established.

**Cultivation**

Most soils seem to suit this vegetable although it prefers one with a pH reaction of 6.0–6.5.

If you are short of space a few plants in the flower garden will not look amiss as the plant is a handsome one. But like most leaf crops deep digging and plenty of manure will produce a much better crop.

**Harvesting**

Pull off each leaf and stem right at the base – they come off best with a slight sideways pull. Don't cut them off as this will leave a stem on the plant to inhibit the rapid growth of the remaining leaves.

This vegetable is excellent for freezing. Strip the green leaves away from the stems and freeze them separately.

**Recommended variety**

Silver or Seakale Beet.


## SHALLOTS

The shallot is one of the easiest vegetables to grow and is used for pickling, a pickled shallot having a more nutty flavour than a pickled onion and considered by many a connoisseur to be the better of the two. Plant one shallot bulb and it splits and divides to form a cluster of six to twenty shallots where one was before.

**Planting**

Plant the bulbs as soon as it is possible to get on the soil, which will usually mean February in the south and March in the north. But don't try to plant if the soil is wet and sticky – it's better to wait.

Rake and firm the soil and, using a line as a guide, take out small shallow holes with an old spoon 1 in. deep and 9 in. apart. Put a shallot in each hole, pull the earth back round it and firm it into position with your hands leaving the pointed top half of the shallot showing above the soil. Protect from birds with black cotton and replant any that they dislodge.

The shallots will soon put down roots and send up fresh green shoots from their tips which look very attractive in early spring.

**Cultivation**

Shallots will grow on most soils, preferring them to have a pH reaction of 6.5 and to be deeply dug, well drained, and with plenty of organic material dug in the previous autumn. Keep them clear of weeds by hoeing carefully between the rows so that you don't knock or bury the developing clusters of bulbs. They prefer to grow on the surface with just their roots in the soil.

### Harvesting

On a fine day in July, when the shallot leaves have turned brown, lift them and leave them on the surface of the soil to dry out. After a couple of days move them to a warm paved area for a few days to complete the ripening. They may be stored in open boxes or nets in a cool dry place and used as required.

If the weather has been very wet in the last weeks of growth the shallots may not keep very well and it is then best to pickle them straight away without bothering to try to dry them. But if you store them you must dry them.

### Summary

Plant on a fine day in February or early March 9 in. apart and 1 ft between the rows, setting each shallot so that its top half is just above the soil. Keep them clear of weeds by careful hoeing. Dig up and dry off in late July for putting into store, or pickle them right away.

### Recommended varieties

Giant Yellow.
Long Keeping Yellow.
Or select enough small bulbs from your own crop, about ¾ in. in diameter, for planting the following year. Only plant sound bulbs.

## SPINACH

It is hardy and easily grown but its one drawback is a tendency to run to seed in dry weather.

### Seed sowing

Sow from March to July in rows 1 ft apart and 1 in. deep with just two seeds to the inch. Thin early leaving the plants 9–12 in. apart.

### Cultivation

The soil for spinach must be deep, moist and fertile and the plants must be kept watered in dry weather to stop them going to seed.

**Harvesting**
Pick the leaves as they develop and take out any flower heads as well. This will encourage more leaves to grow.

**Recommended varieties**
Greenmarket.
Viking.
Broad-leaved Prickly. (It is the seeds that are prickly, not the leaves.)

## SPINACH BEET

Sometimes called leaf beet or perpetual spinach as it has a long season of use. It is a type of beet that is grown for its leaves and not its root, and it is rightly popular.

**Seed sowing**
Sow from April to June with just one seed every 3 in. in rows 12 in. apart and 1 in. deep. Progressively thin to 12–15 in. between plants.

**Cultivation**
Like beetroot, spinach beet does not need large quantities of manure or compost and ideally should be grown in ground that is deeply dug and was manured for a previous crop, so the Roots Group of the Master Plan is the right place for it. Keep the plants watered in very dry weather.

**Harvesting**
The bigger leaves must be picked regularly, including their stalks, to encourage fresh leaves to form continually.

**Recommended variety**
Perpetual Spinach.

## SWEDES

Although fully grown garden swedes may weigh more than 5 lb each they have a delicacy of flavour that makes many people prefer them to turnips.

**Seed sowing**
Sow during the first half of May in the north and the second half of

May in the south. Sow the seed in drills $\frac{1}{2}$ in. deep and 1 ft 6 in. apart with just two seeds to the inch. Progressively thin the seedlings until they are 9–12 in. apart. These young seedlings will look very small and isolated at that distance but when they start to put up large leafy tops and the roots start to swell you'll see why those final distances are necessary.

### Cultivation
Swedes like a deeply dug and well-drained soil that has been manured for a previous crop – new manure can make them taste earthy. They need a pH reaction above 6.0. Keep them clear of weeds in the early stages and as they grow their big leaves will cover the soil and make weeding unnecessary. Bear in mind that they are members of the cabbage family so they can pass on club root disease from infected ground.

### Harvesting
Pull them as you need them from late August right through to March. They are very hardy and can be left in the ground through the winter: they sit on top of the soil so don't get frozen in.

If you have swedes in the way of next year's cultivation pull them up with plenty of soil clinging to their fibrous roots and stack them close together in the open in any spare corner; carry on using them as you want them. Never put diseased swedes or their leaves on the compost heap – it won't reach a high enough heat to kill some of their diseases – put them in the dustbin. Healthy leaves or roots may be put on the compost heap but keep them to the centre and bash them up.

### Summary
Sow early May in the north, late May in the south in drills 1 ft 6 in. apart at a depth of $\frac{1}{2}$ in. Thin progressively to 9–12 in. apart. Leave them in the ground for the winter and pull them as you need them.

### Recommended varieties
Any purple or bronze-topped kind.

## SWEET CORN

If you like sweet corn you'll like the home grown variety even more, especially if you eat it within an hour of picking it.

## Seed sowing

For earliest crops sow under glass in April in 2½ or 3 in. pots of potting compost. Sow the seed just one to a pot 1 in. deep. Cover with
plastic film or a sheet of glass until the seeds come up. Then remove
this cover and grow them in full light, potting on into larger pots as
the roots grow and start protruding through the holes in the base of
the pots.

Or start them off in the airing cupboard with the pots covered with
plastic film and directly they come up remove the film and put them
on a south-facing windowsill. Pot on as necessary. Put the plants out
under cloches or in a frame in mid May.

Or sow straight in the open ground in mid May in the south and
late May in the north, putting two seeds 1 in. deep at each 'station'.
Thin down to the best plant.

## Planting out

If you are growing from plants put them in their final positions when
the soil has warmed up, probably in late May to early June, in rows
2 ft apart with the plants 1 ft 6 in. apart in the rows.

The cobs form in the lower leaf axils and need to be pollinated from
the male 'flowers' at the top of the plants. Corn is planted in several
adjoining rows rather than in single rows to give a better chance of
pollen falling on the green silky tassles that grow out from the end of
the cobs.

## Cultivation

Sweet corn needs a good fertile soil containing plenty of organic
matter.

## Harvesting

When the tassles turn brown and start to shrivel it's a sign the cob is
ready for picking. But before you break it off pull back part of the
leafy sheath that encloses the cob to see if it is ready: if you put your
thumb nail in one of the golden grains the contents should be like
thick cream.

They are best cooked immediately. Strip off the husks, put the cobs
in slightly salted boiling water and simmer for ten minutes. Serve hot
well dabbed with butter and with salt and pepper to taste. Marvellous.

But so much depends on the weather. They need a long hot summer to be at their best.

## Summary
Sow the seeds in the open ground in May in rows 2 ft apart with the planting positions 1 ft 6 in. apart. Put two seeds at each station and thin to the best. For earlier crops start under glass in April, or in the airing cupboard. Grow on in full light and plant out in late May to early June in blocks rather than single rows. Protect from frost. Pick when the tassles turn brown and cook within the hour. When you have used all the cobs pull up the plants and put them on the compost heap.

## Recommended varieties
First Of All.
Kelvedon Glory.
North Star.
Aztec.

## TOMATO

A relative of the potato and an important food crop that we get great pleasure in growing. A tomato straight from the greenhouse or the garden is sweet indeed.

Most tomatoes are grown in greenhouses but there are a number of varieties that will succeed outdoors, especially in the south and the midlands. If they are protected by cloches, or grown against a south-facing wall, they will succeed outdoors further north too.

Seed sown outdoors will rarely have a long enough season of growth to ripen the crop, so either buy plants or grow your own plants indoors.

### Time of sowing
The time of sowing will depend on where you live and whether the tomatoes are to be grown in a heated greenhouse (sow January to March), a cold greenhouse (sow March and April), or outdoors (sow indoors or in a greenhouse in April). The seed should be sown in a temperature of 17–23°C (65–75°F) and the young plants should not be planted outdoors until the average temperature is over 10°C (50°F). In most places this means June.

## Seed sowing

Put two seeds ¼ in. deep in potting compost in a 3 in. pot. Cover with clear plastic film or a plastic bag and keep at 17–23°C (65–75°F). Use the airing cupboard if you haven't a heated greenhouse or propagator. Inspect daily. Directly the young seedlings are up bring them into full light and place the pots near the glass on a south-facing windowsill or, of course, in a greenhouse. If you don't do this straight away the seedlings will become drawn and leggy.

Take off the plastic film when the seedlings touch it and if both the seeds have germinated remove the weakest plant. If you are growing them indoors take the plants off the windowsill if there is any danger of frost or if you close the curtains. Don't leave them in the cold air between the curtains and the glass. But be sure to put your plants back on the windowsill during all daylight hours.

## Pot on

As the roots of the plants fill the existing pots move them into larger pots. Use a peat based potting compost. Put a little compost at the bottom of the pot, tap the plant out of the existing pot and place it on the compost in the middle of the new pot. Press compost down the side of the root ball with your fingers so that the new pot is full of compost to within ½ in. of the top and the tomato is planted just a little deeper than it was in the previous pot. Water in. Support each plant with a small cane in its pot and loosely tie the plant to it.

If you have a cold greenhouse the plants should be moved to it some time in May as long as the temperature in the greenhouse never drops below 8°C (45°F), and is normally higher. If you haven't got a greenhouse that south-facing windowsill will be your plants' home until the first week in June. In late May you should put them outside in a sheltered spot during the day to harden them off, but bring them in at night or if there's a frost.

If you are going to grow your plants in pots they will need to end up in 10 in. pots or two plants to a growing bag, whether in a greenhouse or outdoors.

## The soil

Tomatoes need a fertile soil but not one that has been recently manured or you will end up with too many leaves and not enough fruit. Apply no lime.

## Plant out

This will normally be in June outdoors, during May in a cold greenhouse and earlier in a heated greenhouse. Put a strong 6 ft stake at each position and plant close up to it. Make the hole slightly deeper than the pot so that the root ball is covered with an inch of new soil. Be very careful not to damage the stems as you do this. Always hold the plants by the rootball not by the stem.

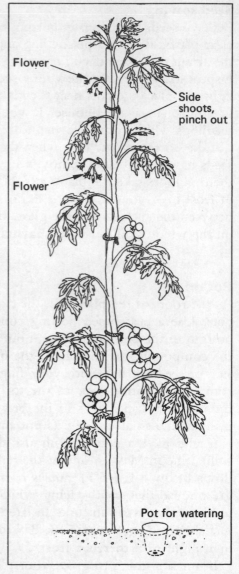

Get the plants out of the pots by turning them upside down, supporting the rootball with one hand with the plant upside down between the fingers and tap the rim of the pot against the edge of a table or tap it smartly with a trowel handle to knock it free.

Sink the pot in the ground a few inches from the plant and keep it topped up with water in dry weather so that the lower roots get watered.

Tie your plants loosely to the stakes with soft string, making sure the stem has room to swell. Tie at intervals as the plants grow.

Remove any side shoots that develop in the plant axils – the place where each leaf joins the main stem – otherwise the plants will become bushy, difficult to manage and the final crop will be less. Do this while the side shoots are still small. This does not apply to varieties described as 'bush type' which are left to grow as they wish. In some ways they are easier to manage if you can get some straw to put on the soil under the plants for the fruit to rest on as they ripen. They don't need staking.

Make sure you don't remove the little bud clusters that develop into the flowers and then the fruit. They grow out of the main stem but not from a leaf axil.

### Stopping the plants
At the end of July or during the first week in August it is advisable to stop the plants from growing further by pinching out the growing tip. Let outdoor plants have four 'trusses' of fruit and plants in a cold greenhouse six trusses. Let bush varieties grow as they will. If you have a heated greenhouse let the plants have more than six trusses if they are growing happily.

### Harvesting
You may either leave the tomatoes on the plants to get fully red or you may pick them as they start to turn and let them ripen off indoors. If the blackbirds and thrushes start to eat them then certainly pick them before they go red.

At the end of September, before the frosts come, pick off the remaining trusses from outdoor plants and hang them up in a cool frost-proof place. Pick off any that show signs of turning and bring them in to the warmth of the kitchen to ripen off. (If you bring them in to the warmth too soon they will shrivel.) In this way your tomatoes will go on ripening for a number of weeks – even up to Christmas.

Do the same with the tomatoes from the cold greenhouse once the weather starts to get chilly, probably in October.

### Plant hygiene
Tomato plants are very susceptible to potato blight, so never touch them after you have been handling potato plants without first washing your hands. Don't touch them if you have been handling tobacco or cigarettes either; although it's a slight risk it is possible to pass on the tobacco mosaic disease.

### Summary
Either buy plants from a nursery or grow your own. For outdoor tomatoes sow two seeds to a 3 in. pot in April. Keep at 17–23°C (65–75°F) until they germinate, then bring in to full light. Thin down to one plant per pot. Pot on into larger pots if necessary. Harden off in May and plant out in June when there are no frosts.

Plants for a cold greenhouse may be started up to one month earlier and for a heated greenhouse any time from January onwards.

Unless they are bush tomatoes support each plant with a strong cane, pinching out any side shoots as they develop, and finally stop the plant at four trusses if it's growing outdoors and six trusses in a cold greenhouse. At the end of the season bring any green tomatoes indoors to ripen off.

### Recommended varieties
Just a few from a large number of good ones.

GREENHOUSE ONLY: Eurocross; Spring Giant (large fruits but not many of them).

GREENHOUSE OR OUTDOOR: Gemini; Extase; Arasta; Alicante.

OUTDOOR BUSH VARIETIES: Sigmabush; Roma; Small Fry (little tomatoes).

## TURNIP

A large group of plants belonging to the *Cruciferae* family and related to the cabbage. Turnips have been used from early history as food for both livestock and humans. There are turnips of many sizes, shapes and colours – white ones, green ones, golden ones and some that are red at the top and white at the bottom. If used when young they are sweet and tender. From an April sowing they are one of the first vegetables to come from the garden – so it's worth growing some. The tops can also be used like spinach.

### Seed sowing
From April to July sow in $\frac{1}{2}$ in. deep drills 1 ft apart with two seeds to the inch, and thin as early as possible to 4–6 in. apart.

### Cultivation
Turnips need a deep and fertile soil to help them grow quickly but one that has not been freshly manured as that would make them taste earthy. Soil that was well manured for the previous year's crop is ideal. In shallow soils over chalk or limestone, or on light soils that

dry out easily, turnips tend to go to seed unless the soils have been well supplied with humus in previous years.

Keep them clear of weeds and water them if the weather is dry.

**Harvesting**
If you leave them to get too big turnips may get fibrous or woody, so unless you are growing one of the really big varieties pull them when they are not much bigger than a billiard ball. Young turnips are delicious if cooked in salted water and served with dabs of butter.

**Summary**
Grow in fertile soil that has not been newly manured. Sow thinly from April to July in $\frac{1}{2}$ in. deep drills 1 ft apart. Thin early to 4–6 in. apart and use when they are small and tender.

**Recommended varieties**
Snowball.
Purple or White Milan.
Golden Ball.


**HERBS**

No garden is really complete without a few herbs. Fortunately many of them make attractive plants for the flower garden. I think most of us would regard the essential ones as mint, parsley and chives closely followed by thyme, sage and rosemary; but again it's all a matter of taste.

MINT is best grown in a bucket with holes in for drainage and buried to its rim near the kitchen door or in a small confined bed of its own, otherwise it spreads too rapidly. Get a friend to give you a root or buy one from a nursery. Grow in semi-shade and renew the soil every second year.

Most of the other herbs can be grown from seed, which is the economical way if you want several plants of one variety. Otherwise buy one plant of each from a nursery.

The following can be grown from seed.

| | Annual renew every year | Perennial | Growing conditions | Comments |
|---|---|---|---|---|
| Balm | | √ | Semi-shade | Lemon scented |
| Basil, bush | √ | | Full sun | Clove-like scent |
| Basil, sweet | √ | | Full sun | Larger leaves than bush basil, scent the same |
| Borage | √ | | Normal | Cucumber taste; pretty blue flowers |
| Chervil | √ | | Semi-shade | Aniseed flavour |
| *Chives | | √ | Normal | A mild taste of onions. Divide clumbs every three or four years |
| Dill | √ | | Sunny | Feathery blue-green leaves |
| Fennel | Grow as annual or perennial | | Normal | Aniseed flavour; will grow 4 ft tall |
| Hyssop | | √ | Sunny | Bitter minty taste |
| Majoram, sweet | √ | | Sunny | Spicy taste |
| Parsley | See p. 169 | | | |
| Rosemary | | √ | Normal | A pretty evergreen shrub with needle-like leaves. Can grow to 5 ft tall |
| Sage | | √ | Sunny | Hardy shrub. Well-known grey-green leaves used in many dishes |
| Savory, winter | | √ | Normal | A little perennial evergreen with a sage-like taste |
| Thyme | | √ | Sunny | Pretty miniature shrub with strongly scented small leaves |

* Use the green tops of chives by cutting to the ground with scissors: this will encourage new growth.

**Winter use**

Chives and parsley can be chopped and frozen. The seeds of dill and fennel can be kept if they are thoroughly dried.

To dry the other herbs gather when they are growing at their best with the flowers still in bud. Hang them up in bunches in an airy place or spread them out in a cool oven for several hours. When they are quite dry rub them coarsely and store in airtight jars. Or you can rub some of them down to a powder for use in sauces and casseroles.

# 14. Indoor Salad Crops

There are several salad crops that can be grown indoors and young children get great pleasure from being appointed the 'indoor gardeners'.

## CRESS

This is the well-known fast-growing plant that is used as a salad, for garnishing or in sandwiches. It is easiest grown in shallow dishes – the white plastic trays used for prepacked foods being ideal. Cut a piece of towelling to fit the container or use folded paper towelling, a pad of cotton wool or a ½ in. layer of compost.

### Cultivation

Wet the growing pad, fit it into the tray and sow the seed fairly thickly on the surface. If you use compost this should be levelled, moistened and firmed before sowing the seed. Keep the container in the dark for two to four days, inspecting it daily. Directly the seeds start to grow bring into full light on a sunny windowsill, in a frame or in the greenhouse. Keep the pad moist at all times with water from a fine spray and cut the crop with a pair of sharp scissors when the stems are 1–2 in. tall. Cress takes seven to ten days from sowing to cropping and should be sown three days before mustard if you want them both ready together.

## MUSTARD

This grows a little faster than cress but otherwise should be grown in the same way. It has a somewhat different taste from cress and is its traditional companion.

## ALFALFA, FENUGREEK AND MUNG BEANS
## (Bean Shoots)

These are three simple-to-grow indoor crops of sprouting seeds. They are ready in three to six days and make delicious crispy salad crops if they are eaten raw. They are grown in a normal kitchen temperature of 12–23°C (55–75°F).

You need a glass jar about 8 in. tall by 3 in. wide with a wide neck, a piece of muslin or nylon stocking, and a rubber band.

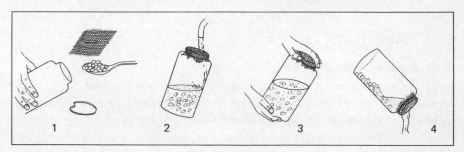

### Cultivation
1. Spoon ½ oz alfalfa or fenugreek or 1 oz of mung beans into the jar.
2. Secure the muslin firmly over the top with the rubber band and quarter fill the jar with clean tepid water through the muslin.
3. Gently swirl the seeds round in the water for ten seconds.
4. Drain off the water without removing the muslin.
5. Repeat this watering and draining every morning and evening until the sprouts are ready to eat.

ALFALFA: ½ oz of seeds yields about 3 oz of salad and it is ready to eat in four to five days when the shoots are about 1 in. long. It has a crisp sweet flavour not unlike fresh green peas.

FENUGREEK: ½ oz of seed produces about 4 oz of salad and it is usually ready in three to four days when the sprouts are about ½ in. long. The flavour tends to deteriorate if they are grown longer than this. It has a tangy sweetness that most people find very pleasant.

MUNG BEANS: what most people know as Chinese bean sprouts. 1 oz of seed will produce about 5 oz of sprouts in about six days. The crisp tasty shoots are excellent eaten raw as a salad dish or they can be steamed or fried for two to three minutes and served as a cooked vegetable.

# 15. Greenhouses, Cloches and Frames

## GREENHOUSES

### Why a greenhouse?

A greenhouse is not necessary in a vegetable garden and very many people cultivate their plots quite happily without one. Frost-tender plants like tomatoes can be obtained from a local nursery, or you can raise your own without a greenhouse if you have a plant propagator or a large airing cupboard, some south-facing windowsills, an understanding spouse and preferably central heating.

A greenhouse is difficult to justify on the basis of saving money. Add up the cost of the greenhouse, the foundations and paths, accessories (such as hose pipe, a water tank, shading, staging), the yearly cost of compost, fertilisers, seeds, plants and pots and then add on the compound interest your money would have earned in, say, a building society. Divide the total by ten or even twenty years to get an average yearly cost and you'll find you will have to grow some pretty good crops each year to get your money back.

But most of us will still be tempted to buy a greenhouse, and why not? There are far worse ways of spending your money. The convenience of having somewhere to raise and harden off plants, the joy of having somewhere warm and snug in which to garden on a chilly wet day and the very welcome fresh crops that come from it make it all worth the money.

### Types of greenhouses

There are four basic types of greenhouse: lean-to, span roof, Dutch light, and circular (octagonal) ones. They may be made with a framework of aluminium, wood or steel and be 'glazed' with polythene sheeting or glass, either right down to the ground or part way, with the lower part being timber, brick, concrete, aluminium sheeting or some other material.

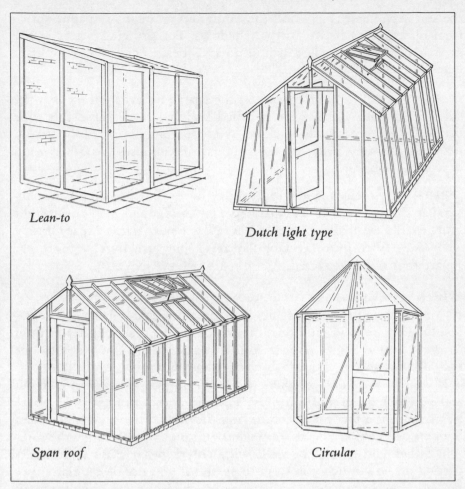

Lean-to

Dutch light type

Span roof

Circular

LEAN-TO: this has a single-sided sloping roof and is built against a wall. The disadvantage is that most of the light can only enter from one side and so it should only be erected on a southerly aspect. The advantages are that the wall absorbs heat during the day and releases it at night, and it is easier to supply water and electricity to the greenhouse if it is built against a wall of the house near, say, the kitchen.

But be careful: if it's not your own house the greenhouse could be classified as part of the house and become the property of the landlord, and you may need to abide by building regulations and get planning permission. Check with your local council.

SPAN ROOF: this is the best shape for a vegetable greenhouse: it has a pitched roof and vertical sides. It should be erected if possible on an east-west alignment as this presents the maximum amount of glass to the sun at the best angles and the minimum amount of opaque structural material which would cast shadows. For growing plants in the greenhouse borders rather than in pots it's best to have one with glass extending all the way down.

DUTCH LIGHT TYPE: the same as the span roof type except that the sides are slightly sloping. It is called Dutch light because this type originally had separate lights fixed to a basic framework. Now usually made in the same way as conventional greenhouses. Another good type of greenhouse.

CIRCULAR: usually made with eight or more 'sides' to give a roughly circular shape. Unusual and attractive to look at and may admit light more evenly to smaller plants in pots. Wasteful of garden space if they have to be fitted into a rectangular area. They usually cost more per square foot of area covered.

## Which type to choose

If you are going to grow plants like tomatoes, cucumbers and vegetables then glass to ground on all four sides is the best. But if you want to grow potted plants as well you might like a greenhouse with one half all glass and the other half clad up to the staging level.

If you choose a design where the panes of glass are easy to take out and put back again you can move earth in and out of the greenhouse by taking out a few panes and having the wheelbarrow outside rather than inside. You'll find this very handy if you have to change the soil.

Whether you have it covered with polythene or glass will largely depend on how much you wish to spend. If you decide on glass price will also have a bearing on whether you choose wood or aluminium. Wood is easier to fix certain kinds of accessories to; aluminium has a very long life and is virtually maintenance free.

Size is something to consider very carefully. The bigger the greenhouse the lower the price of each square foot of usable space. If you buy a very small greenhouse you'll almost certainly wish later on that you had bought a bigger one. Get the best and biggest you can afford, or that will suit your garden, and shop around for a discount off the price.

## Siting the greenhouse

Choose a spot that gets plenty of sunlight and is away from trees, walls or hedges. Remember you may need to get all the way round the greenhouse to maintain it or replace a pane of glass. Avoid low-lying areas that may be frost hollows. The nearer it is sited to the house the less it will cost to run a hose pipe or an electric cable if you should need one. Have a good path leading up to it.

## Laying foundations

If you erect the greenhouse on a paved or tarmac area you may not need to put it on a foundation but you will be restricted to growing plants in pots or in growing bags. So it is better to erect it on a found-ation in the garden, and it is better in the long run to make sure that the foundation is a good one.

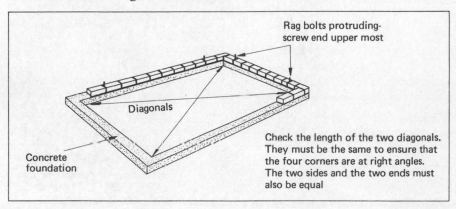

Rag bolts protruding-screw end upper most

Diagonals

Concrete foundation

Check the length of the two diagonals. They must be the same to ensure that the four corners are at right angles. The two sides and the two ends must also be equal

Get exact details of the base dimensions of the greenhouse you are proposing to erect before you start work on the foundations. Measure the area very carefully so that the foundations are level and true. Remember that the greenhouse will need to sit on the outside edge of the brickwork so that the rain runs off down the outside. If the green-house framework is wooden include a damp-proof course. Fasten the base of the greenhouse to the brickwork either by drilling and screwing into the brickwork with masonry plugs or by setting rag-bolts in the mortar joints between the bricks to coincide with predril-led holes in the greenhouse framework. These need to be very care-fully positioned.

One of the worst problems with greenhouses is the back-ache one gets from having to stoop down to ground level to attend to plants in the limited space. You can bring the plants nearer to you if you erect your greenhouse on a low wall just three or four bricks high. That will make all the difference to your comfort when working in it. Some greenhouses are designed specifically for this and have the door stepped down a little lower than the base of the glass. But with most greenhouses the base of the door is level with the framework. In this

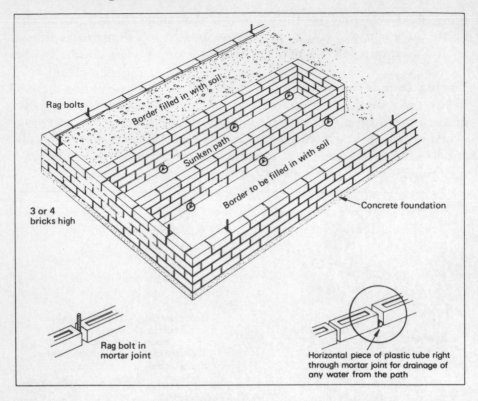

case you can design the foundations to give you a 'sunken' path with the same effect. This will also give you more headroom when standing on the path.

Make sure you build in small drainage holes through the brickwork at path level to let any water that gets on the path seep away. It won't be easy to manhandle a wheelbarrow in the greenhouse so if you do build it this way make sure it is one with panes of glass that are easy to take out and put back so that you can shovel earth out through the sides.

For a 12 ft by 10 ft greenhouse don't make the path more than 1 ft 3 in. wide (that's 2 ft including the width of the bricks) or the borders will be too narrow. Use less space in a smaller greenhouse.

Before you fill the borders with soil decide if you want to grow all or part of your greenhouse crops by the 'ring culture' method (see page 204). If you use soil it will need to be changed every three years.

### Greenhouse accessories

Some accessories can be regarded as essential:

A water tank so that the plants can have water the same temperature as the greenhouse. A plastic dustbin sunk almost to its rim in a corner of the greenhouse by the door serves very well. It can be filled with a hose or, with a little ingenuity, from the greenhouse gutter. Keep a heavy lid on it so that very young children are not at risk.

A hosepipe from the house to the greenhouse.

A minimum-maximum thermometer that tells you what the current temperature is and what it has fallen and risen to.

Some kind of removable staging on which to put seed trays and plants in pots. If the greenhouse is built on a low wall planks of wood laid from wall to wall will do quite well.

You'll also need bamboo canes, string, a knife, scissors, a pencil and labels, a trowel and a watering can.

Other equipment could include:

A propagator – to raise seedlings.

An automatic watering system.

A hygrometer to measure humidity.

Automatic vent controllers to open and shut the windows according to the heat.

Greenhouse shades.

**Shading**

The rays of the sun coming through the glass from a cloudless sky in midsummer may be too intense for young plants and for some established ones too – such as cucumbers. So much depends on the summer we get and also which part of the country you live in.

For most places and for most plants some shading is only necessary in June and July. If your greenhouse is not equipped with shades you can spray or paint the outside of the glass with one of the following:

A proprietary pale green shading made up as a wash.

A lime solution. Mix one tablespoonful of garden lime with a little water and make up to a pint.

A flour solution. Mix two tablespoonfuls of ordinary flour in $\frac{1}{4}$ pint of water to a smooth paste and then make it up to $\frac{1}{2}$ pint. This goes on best if dabbed on the glass with a sponge.

They will all wash off with some warm soapy water and a squeegee.

Shade the top of the greenhouse and just the upper part of the sides. Don't shade the north side.

## Ventilation

Most plants like fresh air but they do not like cold draughts. However, it is always better to give too much ventilation rather than too little.

If the weather is hot and still, open up the ventilators and probably the door during the day in midsummer. Close them at night leaving a top ventilator open away from the windward side.

If the weather is windy keep the ventilators closed on the windward side and open the others as necessary. **The golden rule is, if in doubt give air but not cold draughts.**

## Cleanliness

This is most essential in a greenhouse. Treat it like a hospital. Keep all equipment washed and clean. Weed regularly. Pick off and burn all dead or diseased leaves.

When the greenhouse is empty of plants in winter give the whole place a good wash down both inside and outside with Jeyes fluid. Include the tools and canes. Keep the glass clean to let in the greatest amount of light.

## Heating a greenhouse

A greenhouse without any heating will protect your plants from quite a lot of late frosts, keep off cold winds and give them a generally warmer climate than the one outside. You will get very good crops of tomatoes, cucumbers and other plants without any heating at all.

However, at its simplest level, heating gives you the chance to protect your plants from severe late frosts and at its most sophisticated it enables you to grow earlier crops, later crops and more exotic crops. The simple system might be a paraffin heater that you light when there is a frost warning and a sophisticated system might be an oil-fired thermostatically controlled boiler with hot water pipes backed up with undersoil heating.

Probably the easiest and most reliable form of heating for the small greenhouse is the tubular electric heater. Mounted round the greenhouse walls these heaters make an efficient permanent system and can be controlled by a thermostat. They are simple to operate, not too expensive to install but relatively expensive to run. Do make sure that any electrical installations in greenhouses are put in by a qualified electrician and are checked at regular intervals.

Many gardeners like to strike a balance on costs by running a 'cool' house rather than a hot one. They just make sure that the minimum temperature does not fall below 8°C (45°F). To raise the minimum temperature just another few degrees to 10°C (50°F) would probably double the fuel bill.

Among other types of heating are solid fuel boilers, gas heaters, fan heaters, convector heaters, copper covered heating cables and soil warming cables. One way to minimize running costs is to combine soil warming with minimal space heating.

### Keep the heat in

Lining the greenhouse with PVC or polythene to create a double glazing effect will help to keep the heat in during the colder months. Fix the lining before you start using the heating each year, and remove it when you turn the heating off. Clear PVC admits more light than polythene. Use drawing pins to fix it to the framework of timber greenhouses and specially made suction pads with securing pins to fix it to the glass of metal greenhouses. These hold the sheeting 1 in. away from the glass. Cover the door and ventilators separately and sellotape the joins in the sheeting.

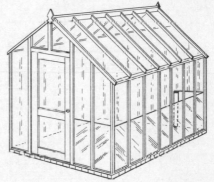

*It's easier to run the sheeting round the greenhouse rather than from top to bottom. Start at the side by the doorway and then let the top layers overlap the lower ones.*

## GREENHOUSE CROPS

Although almost every vegetable may be grown in a greenhouse to produce an earlier or a later crop, in many cases it is not worth the time, effort and cost. Most amateur vegetable growers use their greenhouses at the beginning of the season to house tender plants like marrows and runner beans that will be planted out later on in the garden and then to grow crops that do not do as well outside like tomatoes and cucumbers.

A greenhouse is not essential to the Master Plans but it is certainly an asset. Broadly speaking it may be used in three ways. (For full cultural instructions see 'Culture of Individual Crops'.)

## 1. To raise plants without heat, but so that they are protected from frost, for planting out later in the garden.

| | |
|---|---|
| French bean | Sow seed two or three weeks earlier than outside. |
| Haricot bean | Use 3 in. pots of compost and grow one bean or |
| Runner bean | seed per pot. Harden off and plant out in late May |
| Sweet corn | or early June. |

## 2. To raise plants with heat in March, April or May for planting out in the garden later after they have been hardened off.

| | |
|---|---|
| Cucumber | Choose outdoor varieties. Sow in March, April or |
| Marrow | May, depending on variety, ensuring a minimum |
| Melon | temperature of 15–17°C (60–65°F). Prick out or pot |
| Capsicum | on as necessary and plant out in the garden in May |
| Tomato | or June. |
| Celery | |
| Celeriac | |

## 3. To raise plants in heat and then to grow them on in a cool or heated greenhouse.

| | |
|---|---|
| Aubergine | Choose greenhouse varieties. Sow from February |
| Capsicum | to May, depending on variety, ensuring a minimum |
| Cucumber | temperature of 15–17°C (60–65°F). Prick out or pot |
| Melon | on as necessary and then grow in the greenhouse |
| Tomato | in the borders, in growing bags or in large pots. |

**Ring culture**

One way of growing plants, especially tomatoes, is by ring culture. Before you fill your greenhouse beds with soil you might like to consider this system as it uses a sterile aggregate and not soil.

The basis of the method is to get tomatoes to use the lower half of their root system to take up water and the upper roots to take up plant nutrients. The plants are grown in bottomless pots sitting on a bed of gravel which is flooded with water daily. Once you've got the initial work done it's less trouble to look after the plants, they seem to be more disease free and you can get a heavier crop.

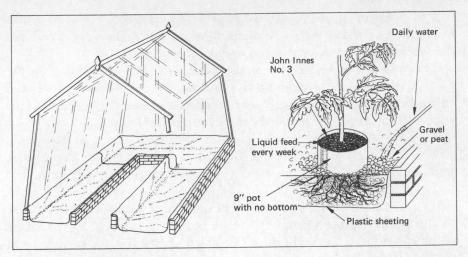

The soil is removed to a depth of about 6 in. The greenhouse borders are lined with 500 gauge (or thicker) plastic sheeting – those low brick walls will be a great help here – and then a 6 in. layer of washed gravel replaces the soil. The gravel should be $\frac{1}{8}$–$\frac{1}{4}$ in. (What is called $\frac{1}{4}$ down will do.) You can get it from many builders' merchants, or you may use peat. Let the water drain away from the gravel each day; don't try to make a join where the plastic sheets overlap.

Place ring culture pots on the gravel where you wish to grow each plant and half fill each one with compost. John Innes No. 3 is normally used. It's easier to put the support canes for the plants in place first, then slip the bottomless pots down over the top of them. Make sure the canes are firmly seated in the gravel.

Place a tomato plant in the centre of each pot and then add more compost round the plant to fill the pot to within an inch of the top. Water the plant in well and thereafter put no more water in the ring culture pot unless the plant shows definite signs of wilting in, say, the first two weeks. The gravel should be literally flooded with water every warm or sunny day. Use a hose and do it at midday so that the gravel can warm up again by nightfall. If the weather is chilly do the flooding every second day so that the greenhouse is not made too cold with a consequent late crop. Or use water with the chill off – say 26°–37°C (80–100°F).

Feed the compost in each pot with $2\frac{1}{2}$ pints of diluted tomato fertiliser once each week after the second truss has set and twice a week when the fourth truss has set. Read the instructions on the fertiliser container in case they differ from this.

Don't worry if the compost appears to dry out between feeds. Remember to flood the daily water straight on to the gravel and put the weekly feed of diluted fertiliser into the pots.

Cucumbers can be grown in the same way but they need bigger pots. A big plastic bucket with the bottom cut out is ideal. Give each cucumber a feed of fertiliser every week but unlike the tomatoes also water the compost in the pot between times if necessary.

If you are growing both tomatoes and cucumbers in the same greenhouse put the tomatoes in the side borders and the cucumbers against the end wall where you can train them up a suitable support.

CHECK THE GRAVEL: tomatoes will not grow well on gravel that is alkaline. If it has been properly washed at the gravel pit there will be no problem but if in doubt do a simple alkalinity test on it with a soil test kit. If the gravel is alkaline sprinkle sulphate of ammonia on the top of it at the rate of 1 lb per 10 sq. yards to lower the pH reaction by 1.0. 10 sq. yards is about the total border area of a 12 ft by 10 ft greenhouse that is built on a brick foundation and has a central path. So if the pH reading is 7.0 in such a greenhouse and you want it to be 5.5 (which is what tomatoes like) 1½ lb of sulphate of ammonia for the whole greenhouse will be enough. For a 6 ft by 8 ft greenhouse with a central path you'd need less than half that amount. Sprinkle it evenly on the surface of the gravel and water it in before planting the tomatoes.

## CLOCHES

They're a very worthwhile addition to the garden. Cloches protect seedlings and young plants from cold winds; they warm up the soil and produce earlier crops; and they can be made from glass, plastic or polythene tubing.

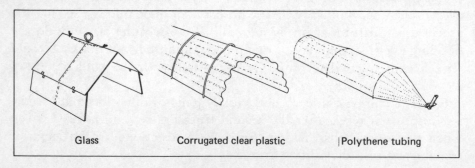

Glass           Corrugated clear plastic          |Polythene tubing

Generally speaking the more solid they are the easier they are to handle and move from one crop to another – and the more they cost, with the glass ones being the most expensive. I prefer the corrugated clear plastic ones as they are light to handle and easy to store away when not in use.

Use them to bring on early crops at the beginning of the season and to protect late crops in the autumn or to ripen off shallots and onions. If you have just one row of cloches you could use them, say, to bring on an early row of lettuce from a February sowing, then to cover sowings of sweet corn, marrows or cucumbers from April to June, then to ripen off shallots in August and onions in September, and lastly in September to cover a late row of French beans that you sowed at the end of July.

The following crops can be sown about a month earlier if they are covered with cloches:

| | | |
|---|---|---|
| Broad beans | Celery | Peas |
| French beans | Cucumber | Radish |
| Runner beans | Leeks | Spinach |
| Beetroot | Lettuce | Sweet corn |
| Brussels sprouts | Marrows/Courgettes | Turnips |

Tomato seed may be sown outdoors in April if covered with cloches.

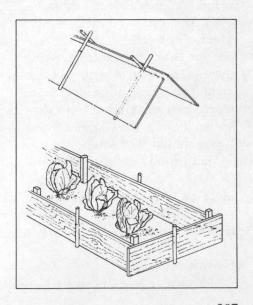

*You may be able to make your own cloches with sheets of glass or plastic and canes to support them.*

*Side protection can do a lot to keep cold winds off plants like lettuce and radish and bring them on earlier from normal sowings.*

With frost-shy plants like runner beans, celery, cucumber, marrows, sweet corn and tomatoes the cloches must stay in place until all danger of frost is past, which will normally be in June.

Close the ends of the row so that you don't create a wind tunnel, and put the cloches in place two weeks before seed sowing to warm up the soil. Make sure they butt up to one another so that the row is continuous. Don't worry that the rain won't reach the roots. It will run down the sides of the cloches and reach the roots that way as long as there is plenty of humus in the soil to absorb and transfer the moisture.

## FRAMES

### Cold frames

A portable frame is very useful for growing an early crop of, say, lettuce or radish, for bringing on runner beans or French beans in pots, or as a halfway stage between the greenhouse (or windowsill) and the open air – a hardening-off area that can be kept open during the day and closed at night in case of frost.

If you make your own frame it can be quite simply done by contructing an open 'box' from wooden boards 12 in. high at the back and 9 in. high at the front. It's quite easy to retain the glass or corrugated clear plastic you may use as a 'light'. If these are not enclosed in a framework then keep them in place with a weight or some other device so that a gust of wind doesn't dislodge them. The slope of the frame should face south.

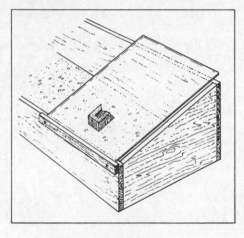

Don't molly-coddle the plants. Give them plenty of air by opening or taking off the lights during the day but put them back in place at night or in very cold or frosty weather. During a severe frost the whole frame may be covered over with sacking, which should be removed when the danger has passed.

### Hot frames

These were used extensively by skilled gardeners in the days of horses and the large estates to grow melons, cucumbers and other plants that needed a longer summer than we sometimes get.

In late winter or early spring a frame is placed on top of a 'hot bed' – a fermenting pile made from equal quantities of partly rotted strawy horse dung and partly rotted compost turned a couple of times until it has lost the first intense heat of fermentation and the strong smell of ammonia. It is put in a pile over 1 ft deep with 9 in. of good soil

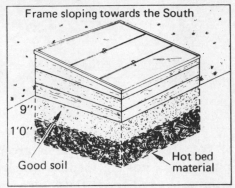

Frame sloping towards the South

9"
1'0"
Good soil
Hot bed material

on the top and the seeds are sown in the soil as the temperature drops to about 35°C (80°F). It will continue to lose its heat gradually until by the late spring the warmth of the sun has taken over. The pile may either be retained by brick walls or a pit may be dug and the hot bed material placed in that so that the frame ends up at ground level. At the end of the season you can sift the old hot bed to use as the 'soil' layer for next year's hot bed and then in late winter get some more horse dung to start again.

It's a skilled operation but you can grow a number of crops this way including early lettuce, young carrots, melons, cucumbers, peppers and aubergines. You can also raise seedlings of celery, leeks and onions which are later planted in the garden.

It is, of course, much easier to get an electric under-soil heating kit to warm your frame but you will find it rather expensive to run. It's better to make friends with a horse and end up with well-rotted manure instead of an electricity bill.

## Propagators

Basically a propagator is a box with soil at the bottom heated by under-soil electric heating and with a glass top. It can be a worthwhile investment if you wish to grow your own tomato, cucumber, marrow or celery plants – or, of course, many others. But if you only need a few plants this will be an interesting but expensive way to rear them.

Don't buy a very small one. It can be frustrating only to have room for a couple of seed-trays.

Do be sure you have somewhere to bring on the plants afterwards – a greenhouse, some warm south-facing windowsills or a hot frame.

# 16. The Potting Shed

If you had a whole range of greenhouses no doubt they would be linked by a potting shed in which you kept all the tools, fertilisers, composts, seed trays, pots, canes and other things to cultivate your greenhouse crops. If you have room in the garden for a proper potting shed then by all means build one, have water and electricity laid on to it and site it near the greenhouse if at all possible. An extension off the kitchen is ideal as you can be tempted to get on with the necessary tasks in winter without braving the elements.

But for most people the 'potting shed' has to be a corner of the garage, part of the garden shed or even the kitchen itself. It's worth organizing this space to the best advantage to make things as convenient as possible for yourself. You should have a place to put the tools, a portable potting bench and a storage unit.

## THE TOOL RAIL

Hang up your garden tools so that they can't easily be dislodged and their sharp edges are out of harm's way. I would recommend a length of 3×2 in. timber with 5 in. nails driven in at an angle of 20° from the horizontal with 3 in. of the head end of the nails left protruding. Big draw hoes and cultivators may need longer nails.

This tool rail should be firmly screwed to the wall at a height of 7 ft in a place where people will not brush against the tools and the garage or shed door will not hit them. One nail every 6 in. will accommodate most sizes of rakes, hoes, forks and spades provided the latter have D-shaped handles. If they have T-shaped handles then you will need two nails for each such implement instead of one.

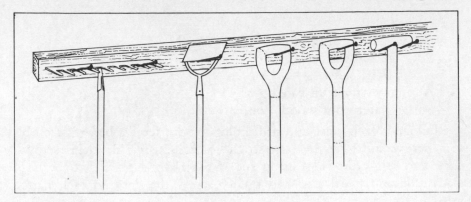

Hang the spades and forks up by their handles with their prongs and blades facing in towards the wall. Hang the Dutch hoe by the blade with the blade facing inwards, the draw hoe by the crooked part behind the blade and the cultivator by the uppermost prongs. Hang up rakes by their heads in most cases with the teeth facing outwards. But do try each of your own tools individually to see which is the safest way. Remember they can be very dangerous if someone falls against them or they become dislodged.

Screws, nails or hooks in the handles of tools are not to be recommended. They can be a nuisance when using the tools.

Hang up an oily rag near the tool rail so that you can give the blades and prongs a wipe over before putting the tools away.

## A PORTABLE POTTING BENCH

Make a simple portable bench for doing your seed sowing, pricking out and potting up in the spring. Use it on a bench in the garage, on the greenhouse staging, or even on the kitchen table. Keep it on top of the Storage Unit in summer.

Cut it out from a 3 ft by 3 ft sheet of ½ in. thick waterproof plywood using a fine-toothed saw. Mark out the curves using an ordinary plate and a pencil.

You will also need:

Two 1 ft 6 in. lengths of 2×1 in. wood.
Six 1 in. screws.
Eight 1½ in. screws.
About twenty 1 in. panel pins.
Some waterproof wood glue.

Sandpaper each piece and drill holes for the screws before assembling. Screw and glue the base to the battens using the 1 in. screws. Glue and screw the sides using six of the 1½ in. screws. Fix the back with glue and panel pins and finally screw the back to each batten with a 1½ in. screw.

Sandpaper the finished potting bench and give it at least two coats of clear polyurethane inside and outside.

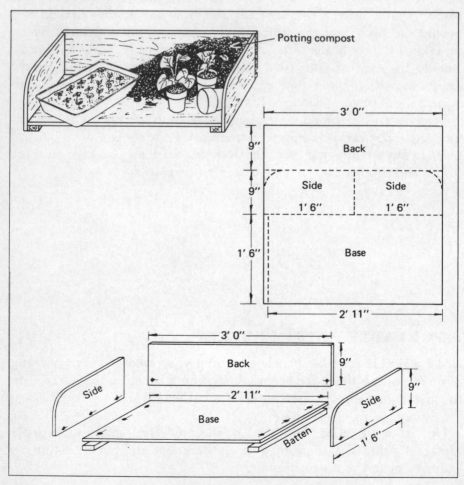

## THE STORAGE UNIT

Measure all the things you have to store and then design a rack to take them. Make it from timber or Dexion slotted angle. Clad the sides so that things don't fall out, and fix the unit back to the wall.

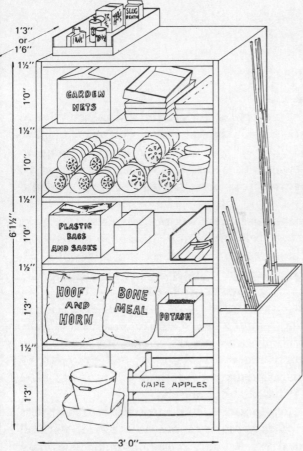

Insecticides and poisons on the top out of reach of children — in a box so they don't fall off.

Lightweight items like seed trays at the top of the rack. Garden nets in a cardboard box.

Flower pots stack very well on their sides. Why not standardize mainly on 3 in. and 5 in. pots?

There will be items like plastic bags, plastic sheeting and small hand tools to store.

Put the heavier items like fertilisers and composts here. Easier for you and gives the rack more stability. Don't store them on the floor where they might get wet.

Buckets, boots and boxes on the floor, with canes in compartments at the side.

### Firming tool

Make a simple tool for firming and levelling compost in seed trays from a few pieces of wood:

    1 piece  4×1 in. − 8 in. long
    2 pieces 1×1 in. − 4 in. long
    1 piece  1×1 in. − 8 in. long

Sandpaper the pieces before assembly, then glue and screw them together. Lastly round off the four corners to use with modern plastic seed trays.

# 17. Pests and Diseases

**Prevention is better than cure**

If you had a whole array of pesticides, fungicides and insecticides to eradicate every known plant pest or disease would you want to have to bother to use them? Would you be sure that you were doing no permanent damage to the balance of nature and would you always be happy for your family to eat the crops after they had been sprayed and treated?

I don't say we should never use these drastic measures. I'm quite sure that if it was a choice between losing my entire crop to a swarm of locusts or eliminating them with a 'safe' insecticide I would reach for my spray gun. But I would keep by fingers crossed that the insecticide really was safe, in the long term as well as the short term.

With synthetic insecticides it is a question of doing just that – keeping our fingers crossed. The manufacturers aim to make them safe. Very carefully detailed and controlled tests are carried out before they are released on to the market and no doubt most will prove to be completely safe. But very occasionally the odd one will prove to have unforeseen faults, like DDT and thalidomide did.

Nature breaks down natural poisons, like nicotine, into harmless substances within a couple of days but it cannot do the same with all synthetic materials. Unnatural and possibly poisonous substances may remain in the plant, the pest or the soil. That's problem number one.

Problem number two is that animals, birds or predator insects sometimes eat the treated pests. Occasionally they will be harmed by them – either immediately or by a gradual build-up of noxious substances in their body fats.

Problem number three is that we run the risk of producing strains of pests and diseases that are resistant to these cures, like the malaria mosquitoes found in many tropical countries that are resistant to DDT.

But if we use insecticides that are of plant origin, even though some are poisonous in the short term, nature will break them down into harmless substances and we won't need to go around with our fingers crossed.

## INSECTICIDES OF PLANT ORIGIN

### Nicotine
Extracted from tobacco and used to kill caterpillars and aphids. It breaks down within forty-eight hours so does not build up in the soil and spares hoverflies, ladybirds and their larvae, but it is very poisonous so keep it out of reach of children and pets and make sure none gets in the fish pond or bird bath. Wear rubber gloves and wash your hands, gloves and utensils after using it.

Make up a spray of $\frac{1}{4}$ fluid oz of pure nicotine to 3 gallons of water with 4 oz soft soap mixed in to act as a spreader. Or get your nicotine from cigarette ends which, having filtered the smoke contain a high concentration of nicotine. Use a ratio of 2 oz of ends (this can include filters) to 1 pint of water. Boil for half an hour. Strain through a stocking and add 4 pints of soapy water. Keep an old saucepan especially for this purpose.

Wet the plants thoroughly making sure the undersides of the leaves are soaked as well as the top surfaces.

### Derris
A powdered tuberous root that is harmless to warm-blooded animals if used sensibly. Effective against aphids, caterpillars and some other pests and remains toxic for forty-eight hours. Unfortunately it will kill bees, fish and ladybird eggs and larvae. This means you could be cutting down on future generations of ladybirds – which is a pity as they do a good greenfly-eating job.

Use as a spray or a dust following the instructions on the container.

### Pyrethrum
Made from a variety of chrysanthemum and does much the same job as derris except that it only remains toxic for about twelve hours. If you use it in the evening, about an hour before sunset when the bees have gone back to their hives, you won't do them much harm. But it does kill ladybirds, their larvae and some other helpful predators.

Follow the instructions on the container.

**Rhubarb leaves**

Rhubarb leaves contain oxalic acid, which will kill aphids if used in the early stages of an attack, when there aren't too many of them. So directly you see blackfly or greenfly pick a pound of rhubarb leaves, cut them up and boil them in 2 pints of water for half an hour. Treat them as poison and use an old saucepan solely for this purpose. Dilute the liquid with a further 4 pints of water and spray it on the aphids within twenty-four hours of making it. It won't harm bees and will soon break down in the soil.

**Elder leaves**

These can be used in the same way as rhubarb leaves. They contain hydrocyanic acid. Treat as a poison.

## OTHER SIMPLE INSECTICIDES

**Permanganate of potash**

Buy from the chemist and keep it in a screw-topped jar, tightly closed. Simply mix 1 oz of the permanganate in 2 gallons of water and use as a spray against aphids. It will also control powdery mildew. It breaks down in about four hours and seems to be harmless to almost everything except aphids.

**Soapy water**

The caustic soda in ordinary soap will act as a mild caterpillar killer, but it is better to use soft soap which contains potassium carbonate. Dissolve 1 oz in 4 pints of hot water and use when cool. Use it as a spray against caterpillars and whitefly larvae on brassicas.

## SOME COMMON PESTS THAT ATTACK MANY PLANTS

The things from which plants may possibly suffer would fill several volumes, rather like our own human ailments. But if you build up a good soil structure containing the correct plant nutrients and keep strictly to the rotation plans you will avoid most of them. There are a few you may have to deal with separately.

## Ants

Ants feed on the sticky fluid given out by aphids, which they will 'farm' by transferring them like milking cows from one plant to another. Controlling the aphids will, of course, help to control the ants but if they are a real nuisance you can kill them with a mixture of equal parts of borax and icing sugar. Borax can easily be obtained from the chemist. Mix the two ingredients thoroughly together and treat as a poison in case someone thinks it's just icing sugar. Put some on a tile, or a piece of wood or glass near where the ants run and cover it with another piece propped up with stones to keep the rain off. The ants will take some back to their nest where it will kill off others. It's possible to kill off the whole nest this way.

## Aphids

There are very many species of blackfly, greenfly and whitefly which suck the sap from plants. They can multiply several times in a day and badly infected plants can become a black or grey-green mess of flies which sap their vitality. But there are other insects which feed on aphids and the great trick is to avoid using sprays that would kill these predators as well. Use only weak sprays like the rhubarb leaf one and use it early, at the first sign of attack. Pick off any badly infected shoots and put them in the dustbin.

The two important predators of aphids are the hoverfly and the ladybird. Hoverflies lay their eggs among the aphids and a hoverfly larva can eat its way through up to 600 or so aphids before itself becoming a hoverfly. They look like little wasps that hover in one place and then dart off to another to hover again. There are many species and they feed off pollen and nectar as adults – so there is a benefit in having your vegetable plots near the flower garden.

Ladybirds and their larvae are the other well-known eaters of aphids, although the larvae eat at random and will quite happily eat ladybird eggs as well as aphids.

## Millipedes

These can be confused with centipedes.

CENTIPEDES are carnivorous and do a great deal of good by eating harmful insects. They have flattened bodies and each segment of the body has only one pair of legs. Don't destroy them.

MILLIPEDES eat into roots and stems and eat pea and bean seeds.

They have round bodies and are between ½ in. and 1 in. long. The first four segments of their bodies have one pair of legs each, all the other segments have two pairs of legs.

Hedgehogs are very partial to them. If you've no hedgehog in your garden and you suffer from millipedes put down traps to catch them. Make the trap from a piece of perforated zinc 9 in. long wrapped round a broom handle to form a cylinder. Stitch it with wire, close the bottom and fit a handle to the top. Fill it with pieces of carrot or potato peelings and bury it in the ground with the handle sticking up in the part of the garden where the millipedes are. Pull it up once a week. Shake out the contents and kill the millipedes. Have several such traps.

## Slugs

Slugs are a great nuisance and can severely damage a row of seedlings in one warm moist night – and of course they feed on more mature plants as well. Manure can contain quite a number of them. Metaldehyde slug baits are an effective killer but they are poisonous to cats and dogs. They are also poisonous to the hedgehog which is nature's best controller of slugs. So if you do use slug bait cover the pellets with domes of wire netting securely fixed down and remove all dead slugs as they are as poisonous as the bait.

A much safer way to dispose of slugs is with beer traps. Sink a soup plate in the ground so that its rim is level with the soil and fill it with beer. The slugs come for a drink and drown. Use a normal glazed plate and not a plastic one or the slugs may 'walk' out again. You can dilute the beer if you like with an equal quantity of water. Have a number of these traps permanently round the garden. Keep them clear of leaves, clean them out occasionally and recharge with more beer. Or you can sink bottles a quarter full of beer up to their rims in the soil and replace them when they are full of slugs. It's cheaper if you make your own beer.

## Wireworms

These are a pest of newly dug grassland but can be an occasional nuisance in established gardens. They are the larvae of the click beetle and are up to ¾ in. long, light brown, shiny and slender with a group of legs at one end. They will eat into potatoes, carrots and other root crops.

In established gardens catch them in millipede traps in exactly the same way. Put a couple of traps by your tulip bulbs as well because wireworms will have a nibble at them and other bulbs.

If you're going to dig up new grassland to make a garden then tackle the problem in a different way. Wireworms go deep down into the soil in winter but in March and April most of them are in the top 2 in. of soil among the grass roots. So strip off the turf 2 in. deep during these two months and make a careful search for wireworms. If you find any then stack the turf upside down on a thick sheet of polythene, or anything impervious like sheets of corrugated iron. The wireworms will stay in the heap eating the grass roots during the summer and then attempt to burrow deep down into the soil in late October and November but find that they can't. You can let the stack decay into good loam or put the top three-quarters of it into the trenches as you dig in November, being careful to remove perennial weed roots. You can then sterilize the bottom layer that has the wireworms in it.

## SOME PESTS AND DISEASES OF INDIVIDUAL CROPS

### Asparagus

THE ASPARAGUS BEETLE and its larvae may eat the foliage of the plant and completely strip it if they are not controlled. There are several broods of the small blue-black or greenish beetles in a season and they may spend part of their time in piles of rubbish so make sure there is none. Spray with nicotine solution or with derris. Cut down and burn any foliage that has been infected as soon as it starts to yellow in the autumn.

### Beans

BLACKFLY attack broad beans, French beans and runner beans as well as other vegetables like spinach and beetroot by sucking the sap from leaves and stems. If you see a distorted leaf turn it over and you will almost certainly find a group of blackfly. They multiply quickly so keep a watchful eye and spray with rhubarb leaf extract, or nicotine, or permanganate of potash solution as soon as you see them. Do this in the evening to reduce the possible damage to bees. Pick off any badly infested leaves or shoots and put them in the dustbin.

Keep an especially careful eye on your broad bean plants and pick out the tender tops as soon as they have a good set of flower. It's on these tender tops that the blackfly attack starts and it will spread to the young beans if you don't literally 'nip it in the bud'.

Spraying runner beans with the water hose during the day will wash off some of the fly.

## Beetroot

THE BEET FLY lays little groups of white eggs on the underside of the leaves. They hatch into little maggots which tunnel through the leaves, making long slim blisters. Spray with nicotine or pick off damaged leaves and put them in the dustbin.

BLACKFLY will attack beetroot leaves (see under 'Beans').

RUST: beetroot and spinach beet or seakale can suffer from rust, which shows as dark brown or light brown spots on the leaves. When you pull beet you can help to control rust by cutting off the beetroot leaves over the compost heap and putting them in the middle of the pile so that they really heat up. A temperature of over 48°C (120°F) will kill rust.

## Brassicas
A large family that includes cabbage, broccoli, Brussels sprouts, kohl rabi, swede, radish and turnip.

CLUB ROOT: the worst disease of the whole cabbage family, caused by a fungus. The roots swell into a club-like mass and have a distinctive sour smell. The plants are reduced in vitality or may die. It is because cauliflowers are the brassicas worst affected by club root that I have left them out of the Master Plans. They are best left to the farmer who can grow them in different land each year.

Club root spores can live as long as nine years in the soil so if your whole garden is badly infected you may have to give up growing members of the cabbage family for as long as this, or keep getting useless crops.

Otherwise keep strictly to the rotation plans, check for correct lime level and always dig up brassicas rather than pull them up so that you can get out all the roots, which must be burnt or put in the dustbin. They must not be put on the compost heap, whether they look diseased or not. If any plant seems to be suffering from club root then burn the whole plant or dump it in the bin.

CABBAGE ROOT FLY is probably the next worst pest of brassicas. These are like large house flies and lay their eggs on the surface of the soil round the stems of cabbages, broccoli and sprouts. Maggots hatch out and eat into the stem which turns the leaves blue-grey from starvation. Plants often topple over and many will be of no use.

As the flies need soil near the stems on which to lay their eggs the best trick is to deprive them of it by putting a shield round the young plant. Collect enough plastic yoghourt or cream cartons to have one for each plant. Put out your plants as usual and water them in. Straight away make the shield for each one by cutting a slit up the side of the carton with a pair of scissors and then carry on cutting to take out a 1 in. wide round hole in the bottom of the carton. Turn it upside down, open it up and carefully place it round the plant

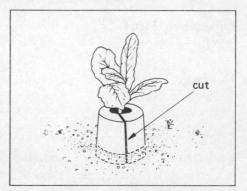

with the leaves poking through the hole. Close it up again and push the rim of the carton about an inch into the soil. A perfect shield. As the plant grows its stem will open up the hole to the room it needs, or you can remove the carton.

CATERPILLARS: several butterflies lay their eggs on members of the cabbage family – the Large White, the Small White, the Green-veined White Butterfly and the Cabbage Moth. If you see clusters of little yellow eggs on your plants then squash them or pick off the leaf before they turn into caterpillars.

The best control is to kill the butterflies before they lay their eggs and the easiest way of doing this is to swipe them with a badminton racket – or tennis if that's your game. A whole family chasing white butterflies round the garden with rackets on a summer's day is a merry sight indeed – but leave the other butterflies alone.

Inspect your plants regularly for caterpillars and either pick them off or, if the cabbages are not yet at the eating stage, spray them with a nicotine solution. If you are soon going to eat them then spray with a solution of 1 oz of ordinary salt in 4 pints of water to slow the caterpillars down.

THE CABBAGE GALL WEEVIL makes galls on the roots of cabbage

and these may be mistaken for club root. The galls are round and firm and if you cut through them with a knife you will find a maggot inside. The plants will almost certainly be stunted and useless. The same procedure as before – put diseased plants in the dustbin or burn them.

### Broccoli
See under 'Brassicas'.

### Brussels sprouts
See under 'Brassicas'.

### Cabbage
See under 'Brassicas'.

### Carrot

THE CARROT FLY is like a small house fly with a greeny–black body. It also attacks celery, parsley and sometimes parsnips, but you rarely see it. It multiplies in road verges and hedgerows so it's useless trying to kill it. It lays its eggs on the surface of the soil by the carrots and the small maggots go down into the soil and then bore into the carrots. The outer leaves of infected carrots tend to turn a maroon colour.

The fly is attracted to the carrots by their smell and thinning them fills the air with carroty perfume. The trick is to sow *very* thinly and then leave the carrots strictly alone until July. Don't touch them or thin them at all till then. When you do thin dispose of the thinnings immediately, don't leave any lying about.

If your carrots do get infested carefully dig up any that you suspect are maggoty and pop them into a plastic bag so that no maggots fall on the soil. Sort them out indoors using the good bits of carrot and putting the rest in the bin. Any maggots that do get in the soil will pupate and become another batch of flies, laying eggs in August and September. They may not lay them in your garden but in case they do, welcome the robins at the November dig. If they spot the pupae they'll eat them up for you.

### Celery

THE CELERY LEAF MINER lays eggs on the underside of celery and parsnip leaves from April to June. The larvae hatch out and tunnel between the leaf surfaces leaving blisters and light brown lines. A nicotine spray will penetrate the leaf tissues and kill them.

## Kale
See under 'Brassicas'.

## Kohl rabi
See under 'Brassicas'.

## Leeks

THE LEEK MOTH lays eggs in April and May at ground level on leeks and onions. The maggots tunnel up the leek or onion leaves. These tunnels show as white streaks. Spray with nicotine as soon as you see them. Don't forget to wash your hands after using nicotine.

## Lettuce

PEMPHIGUS BURSARIUS is a root aphid that sometimes attacks lettuce. They may spend the winter on poplar trees or on artichokes and in July move to the roots of lettuce, feeding on the root just below the soil. If you see any lettuces wilting it may be for this reason. The aphids are yellow and covered with a white wool-like substance.

Soak both sides of the row with nicotine solution from a watering can with a rose on. There is no need to water the leaves, just the roots, but make sure that the solution gets to the area where the root joins the plant.

## Onion

THE ONION FLY looks rather like the ordinary house fly. It is attracted by the smell of onions at thinning time and lays its eggs on the surface of the soil by the onions. The maggots tunnel into the base of the onion, sometimes as many as twenty or thirty of them, and reduce the onion to a rotten mess. Dig up any unhealthy onions as soon as you spot them and put them in the dustbin. If you grow onions from sets you should get no trouble from the onion fly, but still look out for any unhealthy onions and deal with them accordingly.

See also under 'Leeks'.

## Parsnip
See under 'Celery' and 'Carrot'.

## Peas

THE PEA MOTH lays its eggs on the plant and on the flat little pods from the middle of June to the middle of July. These hatch out into the familiar pea maggots. The simple answer is to keep to the Master Plan and sow an early row of dwarf peas in March or early April which will mature by July so that you'll be eating the peas before the maggots can.

THE PEA AND BEAN WEEVIL *(Sitona lineatus)* is another pest that attacks peas. It is a light brown beetle with pale stripes and is about ¼ in. long. It eats the leaves, starting at the edges, and can seriously damage the plants when they are young. The weevils are nocturnal and spend the day resting among weeds or surface pieces of soil. Hoeing between the rows keeps the weeds down and disturbs the weevils making them easy prey for the robins. Or alternatively put down a mulch of grass mowings. The weevils will hide in the dried surface of the grass and a watering with nicotine solution will kill them.

## Potatoes

POTATO BLIGHT is perhaps the most serious potato disease. It creates dark brown patches with rounded edges on the leaves of the plants starting round the tips and the sides of the leaves. There is often a white mould on the underside of the leaves as well. The disease kills the foliage which halts the growth of the crop reducing the yield. Directly you see any signs of the disease spray with 'Bordeaux Mixture' which you can obtain from most garden centres. If the disease has gone too far spray the entire crop with 'Burgundy Mixture' to disinfect and kill the foliage. When it has withered carefully cut it off and put it in plastic sacks, in situ, so that it is not carried round the garden. Burn the sacks of foliage. Dig up the crop making sure you get up every potato. The potatoes can be stored and eaten but look them over every two weeks for the first two months and remove any that are going bad.

As always the best answer is prevention. The disease over-winters in small infected potatoes left in the ground so continually search your garden for any 'wanderers' from the previous year and dig up these stray potato plants as soon as you see them. One small infected plant can start an epidemic. If you live near a farm that grows potatoes be especially watchful. Always grow varieties that are resistant to blight. Remember it can spread to tomatoes.

POTATO EELWORM is a serious pest that is prevalent where potatoes have been grown too often in the same place. The female eelworms are just visible to the naked eye looking like white dots on the fibrous roots and on the tubers. They cause the plants to have stunted foliage which turns yellow and dies off early reducing the crop and giving very small tubers. The eelworm cysts will fall off into the soil and the eggs in them will hatch into larvae to infect the next year's crop. If your plants have got eelworm dig them up early, carefully putting the potato stems and foliage and the fibrous roots into plastic sacks right where you've dug them up so that you don't shake off any eelworms back into the soil. They will not be killed in the compost heap – it doesn't get hot enough – so burn them or put them in the dustbin. Don't put the potato peelings of this crop on the compost heap either. In future grow resistant varieties like Pentland Meteor (early) or Maris Piper (a good maincrop), and make sure you keep to the rotation plan. The eelworm eggs are contained in cysts and they can infect the soil for up to ten years.

A CALCIUM SHORTAGE will also stunt the growth of potato plants but the Master Plans take care of this by growing potatoes on soil that has been limed in previous years.

COMMON SCAB is a widespread disease that creates scabs on the skin of potato tubers. It is especially prevalent on alkaline soils, on those that have been recently limed and on light sandy soils deficient in organic matter. Follow the Master Plans and ensure the potato patch gets its ration of compost or manure but no lime. Keep dry soils watered – especially in the early stages of growth when the new tubers are just forming.

WART DISEASE is now rare but this is only because farmers and gardeners grow varieties that are resistant to this disease. It creates large black raised warts on the tubers and round the base of the stems. If you see them you must inform the local office of the Ministry of Agriculture as the disease is notifiable. It is very virulent and the spores can stay in the ground for up to thirty years. Be certain to grow varieties that are immune to this disease.

CORKY SCAB: if your potatoes develop smaller brown warts instead of black ones this is corky scab, which is fairly common in gardens where potatoes have been grown too many years running in the same place. With a six year rest the disease will die out. If you don't want to wait that long spread flowers of sulphur over the plot at 2½ oz to the square yard and dig it in before planting potatoes again. After that keep to the rotation system.

There are several other pests and diseases of potatoes which are fortunately fairly rare. Always dig up and destroy any potato plants that are stunted or unhealthy in any way, then wash your hands. I don't think it's worth the risk of saving your own potatoes for 'seed'. Only use seed that is certified as inspected by the Ministry of Agriculture and conforming to government regulations. Choose varieties that are resistant to disease and keep to the crop rotation in the Master Plans.

## Radishes and turnips

Both are members of the cabbage family (see 'Brassicas'), but if you keep to the Master Plan you should avoid the brassica diseases. Radishes and turnips should be grown quickly and used when they are young and tender. No unused plants should be left in the ground.

FLEA BEETLE: in some years either of them can be attacked by one of the many varieties of flea beetle which appear in the gardens from the hedgerows during May and nibble holes in the leaves of brassicas. They lay eggs in June which hatch out as a second generation of beetles after pupating and attack plants later in the year. If you see leaves with holes in them then dusting with derris is the best answer, but these little small black or dark grey hopping beetles can do a lot of damage to young plants in a very short time. Make sure you have no heaps of rubbish in the garden for them to over-winter in.

## Seakale beet
See under 'Beetroot'.

## Spinach
See under 'Beetroot'.

## Spinach beet
See under 'Beetroot'.

## Swede
See under 'Brassicas' and 'Radishes'.

## Tomato
Those grown in the open don't suffer from many of the diseases and pests that afflict tomatoes grown in the greenhouse.

POTATO BLIGHT can severely damage them (see under 'Potatoes') so if there are any signs of blight or if the summer is wet and cold spray the plants with 'Bordeaux Mixture' (which you can get from a garden shop) every two weeks from the beginning of August. As with potatoes do take up and burn any badly diseased plants and avoid touching the rest till you've washed your hands.

If you see any **caterpillars** on the plants just pick them off by hand. If they wilt when they are obviously not short of water it may be that **wireworm** are eating at their roots so water round the base of the plants with nicotine solution.

## Turnip
See under 'Radishes and turnips' and 'Brassicas'.

# PREVENTION

I'm sorry to go on at such length about things that might go wrong. The best type of control is 'prevention' – it's so much easier. Let's look at a few basic prevention measures.

## Rotate
The crop rotation in the Master Plans will in itself do more to prevent a build up of pests and diseases than anything else. Getting your soil into a good fertile state and keeping down the weeds will produce strong vigorous plants that will quite happily survive a few pests. If starting at Year 1 in the Master Plans means that a particular crop will be grown yet again in the same place then start your rotation at Year 2, or 3, or 4; whichever is the best starting place for *your* garden.

## Clean up
Keep your vegetable garden clean and tidy at all times. Don't have any rubbish, weeds or dead plants lying around which can act as a haven or breeding ground for pests. Rake up all tree leaves and put them on the leafmould heap. Clear away all plants as soon as they have finished cropping and put them on the compost heap. Leave the roots of all legumes (peas and beans) in the soil but burn the roots of all brassicas (cabbages, sprouts, broccoli, etc.). If you can't burn rubbish straight away, let it dry out for a couple of days and then store it in properly sealed plastic sacks. It's better to burn it straight away, but having bonfires in the summer is a bit rough on the neighbours. You

may be lucky enough to have a local rubbish tip. Keep your hedge bottoms clean and tidy.

## Heat up
Make sure the compost heap is made properly and is protected from the rain and snow so that it heats up enough to kill off pests, diseases and weed seeds.

## Hose off
Use the hose for washing blackfly off the runner beans, French beans and other crops. You'll water them at the same time and they'll like that. Be careful how you use the hose, though, don't be too rough on the more tender plants.

## Pick off
If you see a single shoot of a plant that's badly infected with aphids or any other pest then pick it off and burn it. Dig up any plant that's obviously badly diseased and burn that too before it infects the others.

Pick off any caterpillars you see on the brassicas but kill the 'cabbage white' butterflies if you can before they lay their eggs. Swiping them with badminton rackets is the best way – but it's not easy – it requires a good eye and a nimble action.

## Wash
If you've been handling diseased plants wash your hands before you touch other plants and don't handle tomato plants after you've been handling potato plants unless you've washed your hands first. And don't let the tobacco handlers fondle your tomato plants. There's a very slight chance they could pass on tobacco mosaic, just a very slight one.

## Select
If one variety of plant seems to suffer from a particular disease then change to another variety. Seed catalogues are helpful in nominating varieties of plants that are resistant to some diseases. This applies to your whole garden. If one variety of rose suffers badly from mildew don't spend your life trying to treat it. Dig it up and plant another variety that is resistant to mildew. Some open varieties of lettuce get covered in greenfly but the more tightly growing ones like Little Gem only seem to have greenfly on the outer leaves. So grow several varieties and see which ones do best in your garden.

## Hoe
Keep the weeds down in the early stages by regular hoeing. This will prevent pests like aphids getting established on them ready to move on to your crops when they come up. In any case if you keep down the weeds there will be more moisture and nutrients to build up strong vigorous plants that can put up with a few greenfly.

## Attract the birds
By all means make rude noises at the pigeons to stop them eating your brassicas, and tell that beautiful bird the bullfinch to push off because he'll strip the buds off a fruit bush in a matter of hours or even minutes. But otherwise most birds do more good than harm. Tempt them into the garden with scraps of food and they'll probably eat some greenfly or greenfly eggs as well, especially the sparrows and tits. Of course if you spray the greenfly with synthetic insecticide the birds may stop eating them. I mean would you want to eat greenfly with insecticide on them? It spoils the taste.

When you're digging the plot in November a pair of robins and a blackbird will almost certainly join you. They may pinch a few worms but the robins will eat a lot of pests as well.

## Protect from the birds
Having said all that in defence of the birds it's true that they'll also have dust baths in your finely raked seed beds, they'll pull out your onion sets to see if there are any worms underneath and they'll help themselves to some of your new seedlings. So protect your rows of young plants with black cotton. It won't keep the birds off altogether but it will enable most of your plants to survive. Just one strand of black cotton over each row will often do the trick. The birds can't easily see it and find it a bit off-putting. You may have to increase your defences to several strands if they're very determined. (By the way use cotton and not nylon. Nylon fails to rot down and is a nuisance in the soil in future years.)

If black cotton doesn't put them off then you may have to cover

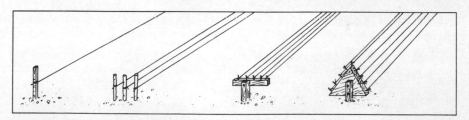

your plants with cloches or wire netting and in very extreme cases put a fruit cage over the plot – but that's a very expensive answer and it doesn't just stop the birds eating your crops, it stops them eating the pests as well.

## Friends and foes

Some insects feed off your plants and other insects eat those insects or their offspring. The former we call pests and the latter we call friends. Quite selfish of us, of course. But there it is: we want the vegetables for ourselves rather than let the insects have them. How do we tell which insects are doing what we want them to and which are doing what we don't want them to?

There's one rule of thumb that's not infallible but is a general kind of guide. If an insect moves slowly it probably eats plants and if it moves quickly it probably eats other insects. So don't kill the latter until you're sure what they are. But it's only a general rule. Some insects that move quickly and do no harm themselves, like the cabbage white butterfly, lay eggs that turn into caterpillars that move slowly and do do harm by eating up your cabbages.

One great friend of the gardener moves very slowly indeed as it spends its time improving the structure of the soil: the earthworm. Keep your soil rich in humus and free from chemicals and the earthworm will thrive and multiply and further improve your soil. Worms drag leaves and surface particles of organic material underground, doing a general tidying-up job. Their burrows improve the aeration of the soil and permit drainage of surface water which helps to prevent waterlogging and assists root growth. The presence of worms decreases putrefaction of the soil. Organic material is broken down by their digestive juices as they eat it and the soil is enriched by their excretory products. And when they've finished all that work their dead bodies further improve the soil. What a friend!

## SUMMARY CONTROL CHART

*Note.* 'Destroy' means burn or put in the dustbin. **Do not put on the compost heap.** Treat all sprays as poisonous – nicotine is especially so.

| Pest or disease | Plants mainly affected | Remedy |
|---|---|---|
| **Ants**<br>They transfer aphids from one plant to another | Bean crops<br>Beet crops<br>Lettuce | Put an equal mixture of borax and icing sugar in little heaps where the ants run |
| **Aphids**<br>Whitefly, blackfly and greenfly that suck sap from plants and multiply prodigiously | Bean crops<br>Beet crops<br>Lettuce | Being eaten by ladybirds and their larvae and hoverfly larvae.<br>Pick off and destroy badly infected shoots. Hose off.<br>Spray with:<br>Rhubarb leaf solution<br>Elder leaf solution<br>Soapy water<br>Permanganate of potash<br>Nicotine spray<br>Derris or pyrethrum – these two will kill bees and ladybirds |
| **Asparagus beetle**<br>A black and red beetle whose larvae eat the foliage | Asparagus | Have no piles of rubbish.<br>Spray with:<br>Nicotine solution<br>Derris solution<br>Cut down and burn foliage as soon as it yellows in the autumn. |
| **Cabbage gall weevil**<br>Maggots create a gall on roots | Brassicas | Dig up and destroy roots of diseased plants |

| Pest or disease | Plants mainly affected | Remedy |
| --- | --- | --- |
| **Cabbage root fly**<br>Fly lays eggs which become maggots and eat into stems and kill plants | Brassicas | Put plastic cartons round stems when planting out. Dig up infected plants, put straight into bucket or plastic bag and destroy |
| **Carrot fly**<br>Maggots of fly eat into roots | Carrots<br>Celery<br>Parsley<br>Parsnips | Sow seeds very thinly to avoid early thinning. Dig up infected plants, put straight into bucket or plastic bag and destroy |
| **Caterpillars**<br>Eat stems and leaves | Brassicas | Kill the cabbage white butterflies and the cabbage moth. Squash or remove their eggs. Pick off individual caterpillars or whole leaves. Spray with: Soapy water Salt water Nicotine solution Derris or pyrethrum – these two will kill bees and ladybirds |
| **Celery leaf miner**<br>Larvae tunnel between leaf tissues | Celery<br>Parsnip | Remove infected leaves and destroy. Spray with nicotine solution |

| Pest or disease | Plants mainly affected | Remedy |
| --- | --- | --- |
| **Club root**<br>A disease which causes large swellings on roots which turn into a club-like mass. Severely weakens plants. They may recover during the evenings but wilt during the day | Brassicas<br>All brassicas may be affected by or transmit this disease. Cauliflowers are particularly affected | The only real cure is to grow no brassicas for as long as nine years and to use no manure that has come from club-root infected farms.<br>Prevention:<br>Make sure the ground is properly limed.<br>Dig up and destroy all brassica roots.<br>Practise proper crop rotation |
| **Flea beetles**<br>They nibble holes in leaves of young brassica seedlings | Cabbage<br>Radish<br>Swede<br>Turnip | Keep the garden clear of rubbish – especially under hedges.<br>Dust with derris (which can kill bees and ladybirds) |
| **Leek moth**<br>Lays eggs which become maggots | Leeks<br>Onions | Dig up infected plants and destroy |
| **Lettuce root aphid** | Lettuce | Water the soil round the roots with nicotine solution |
| **Millipedes**<br>Eat roots and stems | Various | Being eaten by hedgehogs.<br>Keep garden clear of rubbish.<br>Use millipede traps |
| **Onion fly**<br>Maggots of fly eat into the bulbs | Onions | Use sets rather than seeds.<br>Avoid bruising leaves and creating onion smell.<br>Dig up unhealthy plants and destroy |

| Pest or disease | Plants mainly affected | Remedy |
| --- | --- | --- |
| **Pea and bean weevil**<br>Eats leaves | Peas and beans | Keep weeds down.<br>Hoe regularly.<br>Put down a mulch of grass mowings – let it go dryish – then water with nicotine solution to destroy the weevils hiding in it |
| **Pea moth**<br>Eggs become maggots which eat the peas | Peas | Grow an early variety |
| **Potato blight**<br>Dark brown patches on leaves which destroy foliage and hence stop the plant growing | Potatoes<br>Tomatoes | Grow resistant varieties.<br>Use 'Bordeaux Mixture' at first signs of disease.<br>Cut off and burn diseased foliage.<br>Dig up your crop thoroughly – never leave tiny potatoes in the ground to grow the next year |
| **Potato eelworm**<br>Plants don't grow properly – have stunted yellow foliage early on | Potatoes | Practise proper crop rotation.<br>Dig up infected plants into buckets or plastic bags and destroy.<br>Grow resistant varieties |
| **Potato scab**<br>Makes scabs on tubers | Potatoes | Make sure soil contains plenty of humus and does not dry out.<br>Use no lime |

| *Pest or disease* | *Plants mainly affected* | *Remedy* |
|---|---|---|
| **Rust**<br>Brown patches on leaves which reduce vitality of plants | Broad beans<br>Beetroot<br>Spinach beet<br>Seakale beet | Keep land well drained.<br>Cut off leaves over compost heap putting them in centre to heat up well and kill spores |
| **Slugs and snails**<br>Eat stems, leaves, shoots and young plants | Brassicas<br>Lettuce<br>Beet crops<br>Celery<br>Young marrow plants<br>Potatoes | Being eaten by hedgehogs and birds.<br>Keep garden clear of all rubbish.<br>Use beer traps.<br>Use metaldehyde slug bait but cover it with wire mesh to stop other creatures eating it.<br>Poisonous |
| **Wireworms**<br>Grubs of the click beetle which eat roots and stems of plants | Various | Use millipede traps.<br>Stack newly dug turf on polythene or corrugated iron sheeting to stop grubs re-entering soil |

# 18. Storing Your Crops

You'll eat most of your vegetables at their very best straight from the garden on the day they are picked but many of them will store well and will be useful in the leaner months of the year. The home freezer gives us the chance to enjoy vegetables in the middle of winter nearly as good as the fresh ones and many vegetables will store well without a freezer.

## SOME CAN BE LEFT IN THE GROUND

BROCCOLI – purple sprouting. Support the plants with stout sticks to stand the winter gales, protect from the pigeons and you'll be enjoying new broccoli spears in March and April. Freeze them then if you wish.

BRUSSELS SPROUTS. Support the plants and leave in the ground until the sprouts are ready for picking. If you have more than you need the surplus may go in the freezer.

CURLY KALE. Withstands the hardest weather. Leave in the ground and pick the leaves and shoots as required. Freeze them if you have a good supply.

LEEKS. Leave in the ground and dig up as you need them but remember that if the soil is frozen hard you may not get them out. If there's a warning of severe frost dig up a supply and keep them in the bottom of the fridge.

PARSNIPS. They taste sweeter after the first frosts: the low temperatures convert some of the starch into sugar. Leave them in the ground and dig as you want them. Or store them in a simple clamp out in the open near the kitchen door – a layer of parsnips, a 2 in. layer of soil over them, another layer of parsnips covered with a further layer of soil and so on.

SAVOY CABBAGE. Leave them in the ground and use as required while the hearts are still firm.

SWEDE. They can stand quite severe weather so leave them in the ground right through the winter. If they get in the way of next year's cultivation ease them up with a fork with plenty of earth clinging to their fibrous roots and stack them standing up close together on any spare patch of garden. If it's near the kitchen door so much the better.

WINTER RADISH. Leave in the ground and pull as required or they may be dug up and stored in sand.


## SOME ARE STORED DRY

GARLIC. Ripen off thoroughly and store in slatted boxes like onions.

HARICOT BEANS. Put the dried plants in a sack and beat with a stick to extract the beans, then spread them out on paper until they are completely dry. Store in boxes or jars in a dry frost-proof place.

MARROWS. They are best used, or frozen, at the courgette size but fully grown ripe marrows can be stored in an airy, cool, frost-proof place till January or February. Put them on a shelf or hang them up singly in nets.

ONIONS. Ripen off thoroughly and store them in an airy frost-proof place but not in the garage as they may absorb the smell of petrol. Inspect them every couple of weeks and discard any that are showing signs of rotting.

They can be stored in slatted grape or peach boxes with a single layer of onions in each and the boxes stacked one on top of another. This is a very good way to store them as the air can circulate freely and it's easy to pick out any that are rotting.

Or you can store them as onion ropes. The simplest way to do this is to tie a knot in the end of a piece of stranded rope or thick string

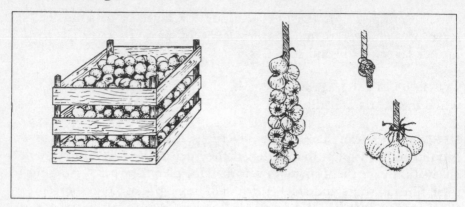

about 2 ft long and then tie three onions to the rope just above the knot with some thin string. Now simply add the other onions by pushing their stalks between the strands of the rope. The onions need a few inches of dried stalk left on them for this purpose. Hang up the ropes.

Onions may also be stored hanging up in nets or in old nylon stockings. This serves quite well but you'll have to tip the onions out of the stockings from time to time to discard any that are going bad. If you have just a small crop you might think it worthwhile to tie a knot in the stocking between each one, so that you can just snip out any bad ones.

POTATOES. When the tops have died down cut them off with shears and if they are in any way diseased burn them. Dig up the potatoes and dry them off for a few hours on the surface of the ground or on a path in fine weather. Store in hessian sacks or a wooden storage bin in a cool dry airy place away from the light and protected from frost. Leave the top of the sack or the box open for a couple of days until the potatoes have 'sweated', then cover them over. Don't store any damaged or diseased ones.

SHALLOTS can be stored like onions as soon as they have been ripened off, or they can be pickled straight away. If the summer and autumn has been wet the latter course is perhaps the wisest as they may go bad in store. But they'll certainly keep if they've been properly dried and ripened and in any case you may wish to keep a few for next year's 'seed'.

By the way, if shallots and onions make you 'cry' peel them in the garden in the open air or do them under water.

TOMATOES. In October, before the frosts come, pick any remaining green tomatoes on outdoor or cold greenhouse plants. Store them in single layers in grape boxes in a cool dry frost-proof place. This might be a spare bedroom with no heating on. As they start to turn colour bring them into the normal warmth of the kitchen to finish ripening. If you bring them into the warmth too soon they tend to shrivel.

## SOME CAN BE STORED IN SAND, PEAT OR DRY EARTH

BEETROOT, CARROT, CELERIAC, PARSNIP, SALSIFY, SCORZONERA, SWEDE, WINTER RADISH: these may all be stored in containers of sand, earth or peat in a cool frost-proof place. Plastic dustbins, large plastic buckets or strong wooden boxes are all suitable containers.

Cut off the leaves, leaving about an inch of stem on the roots. Put a 2 in. layer of sand in the container, then a layer of roots, then another layer of sand and so on right up to the top.

Parsnips, salsify, swede and winter radish may also be left in the ground.

## MOST CAN BE FROZEN

To get the best results vegetables must be picked when they are young and tender, before they come to full maturity, and frozen 'within the hour'. Pick them first thing in the morning, wash and prepare them as if you were going to cook them, removing all traces of soil, and then 'blanch' them before freezing.

## Blanching

This halts enzyme activity which would make the vegetables age. Without blanching they would lose their colour, their flavour and some of their vitamin C. You have to scald the vegetables for a strict period of time and then quickly chill them in cold water for the same period (see 'Freezing Chart').

## Equipment

You'll need: a timer, a large pan (6–9 pint capacity), a wire basket, a colander, a big bowl for really cold water (to make sure that water is cold have plenty of ice cubes ready in polythene bags in the fridge); polythene storage bags, closure tags, labels and a few drinking straws.

You'll also need a deep freeze!

## Method

Have enough boiling water in the large pan to accommodate the wire basket containing the vegetables so that they can move about freely in the water. The water must return to the boil within one minute of putting in the vegetables, or they may go mushy. If it takes longer reduce the quantity of vegetables for the next go. Put in the basket of vegetables and start timing the very second the water reboils. Take out the basket directly the time is up. Plunge straight into the cold water for the same length of time you scalded them. Keep the water really cold by having ice cubes in it and letting the cold tap gently run into it.

Drain thoroughly, pack into polythene bags and suck out as much air as possible – you can do this with a straw – before sealing and labelling. Put in the freezer straight away.

You'll retain a bit more of the vitamin C if you do up to six consecutive loads in the same 'boiling' water but always change your 'chilling' water to keep it cold.

Store your vegetables in the right sized helpings for one meal for your family, with a few small make-weights for the odd visitor. It's best to blanch no more than a pound at a time.

# FREEZING CHART

| *Vegetable* | *Blanching and cooling time. (Both the same: in minutes)* | *Preparation, type and size* |
| --- | --- | --- |
| Asparagus | | Don't freeze thick stalks or the lower |
|   Thin stalks | 2 | tough ends. Grade into thicknesses and |
|   Medium stalks | 3 | cut into even lengths. |
| Aubergines | 4 | Cut into ½ in. thick slices and put into salted water before blanching to avoid colour change. |
| Beans | | |
|   Broad | 2 | Use young beans no larger than a man's thumbnail. |
|   French | 2 | Freeze whole tender beans that 'snap' easily. |
|   Runner | 1 | Sliced. Use tender beans. |
|     ,, | 2 | Cut into pieces. Use tender beans. |
| Broccoli | | |
|   Purple sprouting | 3 | Use tender shoots and cut off any tough stalks. |
|   Calabrese | 4 | Ditto. |
| Brussels sprouts | 3 | Use small firm sprouts. Take off any loose leaves. |
| Carrots | 3 | Either freeze whole young carrots or sliced larger ones. |
| Cauliflower | 3 | Cut into small sprigs or 'florets'. |
| Celeriac | 4 | Peel and cut into 1 in. cubes. |
| Celery | 3 | Cut into 2 in. long pieces for use in cooking. |
| Chives | None | Don't blanch. Just chop up and freeze with no water. |
| Courgette | 1 | Use small ones. Cut in half lengthways or into ½ in. thick slices. |
| Cucumber | | Make into cucumber soup in the normal way and freeze that. |
| Curly kale | 3 | Use the fresh young leaves and shoots and trim off the stalks. |
| Kohl rabi | 2½ | Use young ones. Peel and cut into quarters. |
| Leeks | | |
|   Thin ones | 4 | Freeze whole. Do make sure all the soil is washed out. |
|   Thick ones | 2 | Cut into 2 in. long pieces. Do make sure all the soil is washed out. |

*241*

| *Vegetable* | Blanching and cooling time. (Both the same: in minutes) | *Preparation, type and size* |
|---|---|---|
| Mint | None | Chop up tender fresh mint, add a little water and freeze as cubes in an ice-cube tray in the freezer. |
| Parsley | None | Same as chives. |
| Parsnip | 2 | Peel and cut into small cooking pieces or dice. |
| Peas | 1 | It's better to eat your own fresh from the garden and buy any frozen ones. If you freeze your own use young ones and blanch in a muslin bag. |
| Rhubarb | None | Cut tender young rhubarb into 1 in. long pieces and freeze raw. |
| Salsify | 2 | Use young roots cut into 2 in. long pieces. Cool in the air not in water. |
| Seakale beet | | |
| Ribs | 3 | Cut the mid ribs into 2 in. long pieces. Only use tender ones. |
| Green leaf | | Deal with the green part of the leaf the same way as spinach. |
| Spinach or spinach beet | 2 | Strip leaves off stalks. After cooling, drain and press out excess moisture. |
| Sweet corn | | |
| Small cobs | 4 | Take off husks and silk and sort into |
| Medium cobs | 6 | sizes. Blanch and freeze whole or cut |
| Large cobs | 8 | kernels off cobs and just freeze them. |
| Kernels only | 3 | |
| Tomatoes | None | Freeze small to medium tomatoes whole, for use in casseroles. Wash and dry, don't blanch. Or freeze tomato puree. |
| Turnip | 3 | Use young ones. Peel and cut into quarters. |

# 19. Monthly Reminders

Use these reminders as memory joggers.

In deciding exact dates for sowing and planting be guided by the weather, the state of the soil and where you live.

The garden year has no beginning and no end. Tasks lead from one month to another and there are always crops of some kind in the ground. But we'll start these reminders in November – the month of preparation and planning for the year ahead.

## JOBS FOR NOVEMBER

FROM THE GARDEN use Brussels sprouts, cauliflowers, celery, celeriac, chinese cabbage, endive, Jerusalem artichokes, leeks, parsnips, salsify, scorzonera, Savoy cabbage, sugar loaf chicory, swede, winter radish.

FREEZE cauliflowers, celery and celeriac.

STORE celeriac in sand instead of freezing if you wish. Or in the south leave it in the garden.

FROM STORE use beetroot, carrots, marrows, onions, potatoes, shallots. Use other vegetables from the freezer.

CLEAN UP. Have a good clear up round the whole garden. Leave no places for pests and diseases to over-winter. Clear out under any hedges. Take down the runner bean structure, put the old bean plants on the compost, but leave the roots in the soil. Pull the yellow leaves off the brassicas. Put these and all other plant material that will rot on the newest compost heap. Cover it against the winter rain and snow. Put leaves on the leafmould heap. Burn all rubbish.

PLAN. Decide in general what vegetables to grow and where to grow them, you can decide on varieties later – and send for seed catalogues. Allocate the right groups of plants to plots A, B, C and D according to the rotation dance and draw up your own sowing and cropping plan or use one of the Master Plans exactly as it is.

MANURE AND DIG. Wait until the trees have dropped most of their leaves and clear them away before starting to dig so that they don't litter up your newly dug plots. Share out your supplies of manure and ripe compost in small heaps round the garden according to the crops to be grown. The plots where the peas and beans and the onions and brassicas are to go will be clear of last year's crops so get on digging and manuring these two plots. Then dig and manure as much of the potato plot as you can and lastly dig any available space where the root crops will go. Remember this last plot gets no manure.

If this is the first time you're using the Master Plans adapt your digging to any crops still in the ground. If the ground is completely clear get on and dig the lot.

But do your digging at a gentle steady pace. There's no rush. Make sure you leave the soil rough for the winter frosts to do their work.


## JOBS FOR DECEMBER

FROM THE GARDEN use Brussels sprouts, curly kale, endive, Jerusalem artichokes, leeks, parsnips, salsify, scorzonera, Savoy cabbages, swede, winter radish.

FREEZE sprouts, kale and leeks.

FROM STORE use beetroot, carrots, marrows, onions, potatoes and shallots. Use other vegetables from the freezer.

LOOK OVER onions, potatoes and other vegetables in store and remove any that show signs of rotting.

GET CATALOGUES and prepare your seed list for the coming season.

CLEAN and sterilize last year's row markers in a bucket of Jeyes fluid solution, or make some new ones. Clean up and sterilize the greenhouse.

REPAIR AND OIL all tools.

SWEEP UP any leaves and put them on the leafmould heap.

CONTINUE DIGGING AND MANURING where this hasn't been done.

## JOBS FOR JANUARY

FROM THE GARDEN use Brussels sprouts, corn salad, curly kale, Jerusalem artichokes, leeks, parsnips, salsify and scorzonera, Savoys, swedes, winter radish.

FREEZE Brussels sprouts, kale and leeks.

STORE. Parsnips may be left in the ground or dug up and stored either in containers of sand or in a clamp – the nearer the kitchen door the better.

FROM STORE use beetroot, carrots, marrows, onions, potatoes and shallots. Use other vegetables from the freezer.

LOOK OVER vegetables in store and remove any that show any signs of rot.

PLANT rhubarb roots. Sow summer cauliflowers under glass.

ORDER seeds if you haven't already done so. Unpack onion sets and shallots as soon as you get them and put in a light airy frost-proof place.

CLEAN and sterilize all bamboo canes, plant pots and seed trays.

CLEAR UP any more leaves that have blown into the garden and put them on the leafmould heap.

CONTINUE DIGGING the plots as the roots and brassicas get used up.

MAKE SURE the sprouting broccoli is well supported against the winter winds and protect it from pigeons with nets.

TEST your soil for lime, decide how much you need and obtain in readiness for spreading in February. It's also a good idea to test the soil for nitrogen, phosphorus and potash content. (You'll need a soil test kit, obtainable from most garden shops.)

## JOBS FOR FEBRUARY

FROM THE GARDEN use purple sprouting broccoli, corn salad, curly kale, leeks, parsnips, swedes, winter radish.

FREEZE broccoli, cauliflower, kale and leeks.

STORE remaining parsnips in sand or a clamp. Lift remaining leeks and heel-in in an odd corner (or freeze). Lift remaining swedes with earth on and stack together in a vacant spot to clear the ground for digging.

FROM STORE use beetroot, carrots, onions, parsnips, shallots and swede. Use other vegetables from the freezer.

LOOK OVER vegetables in store and clear out any rotten ones.

SET UP seed potatoes in trays with the eyes uppermost in a *light*, frost-proof and airy place.

DIG UP all brassica stumps where the crops have been gathered, dry and burn.

DIG any remaining vacant ground.

APPLY LIME to those plots that need it. Choose a day with no wind.

PLANT Jerusalem artichokes and shallots.

SOW broad beans, lettuce under cloches (which were put in place at least a week before to warm the soil) and in a heated greenhouse sow aubergines, capsicum, cucumbers, melons and tomatoes.

## JOBS FOR MARCH

FROM THE GARDEN use corn salad, curly kale, purple sprouting broccoli and winter cauliflower.

FREEZE broccoli, cauliflower and kale.

FROM STORE use beetroot, carrots, leeks, onions, parsnips, shallots and swede. Use other vegetables from the freezer.

LOOK OVER vegetables in store.

DIG UP all remaining cabbage or sprouts stumps early in the month, dry and burn them and dig over the area where they were.

SPREAD FERTILISERS early in the month if tests show they are needed.

COVER rhubarb with pots or boxes to force it.

SOW Brussels sprouts and leeks in a seed bed and in the garden sow broad beans, early lettuce, parsley, parsnips, peas, radish, spinach, spinach beet and spring onions.

PLANT onion sets and garlic and in the second half of the month early and maincrop potatoes.

PLANT OUT new asparagus beds.

IN THE HEATED GREENHOUSE SOW aubergine, capsicum, celery and celeriac, cucumber, melon and tomatoes if not already sown.

STAKE peas or put up pea nets as soon as they are sown.

HOE between all growing crops whenever conditions allow – at least once every two weeks.

EARTH UP existing asparagus beds.

247

# JOBS FOR APRIL

FROM THE GARDEN use asparagus, remainder of the broccoli, chives and forced rhubarb.

FREEZE broccoli.

FROM STORE use beetroot, carrots and onions. Use other vegetables from the freezer.

DIG UP broccoli plants and dig over ground vacated. Bash up the tops with a hammer to put on compost. Burn stumps and roots.

SOW (if not already sown in March) early beetroot, broad beans, broccoli, Brussels sprouts, carrots, cauliflower, celery, curly kale, garlic, leeks, kohl rabi, lettuce, onion seed, parsley, parsnips, peas, radish, salsify, Savoys, summer cabbage, scorzonera, seakale beet, spinach, spinach beet and turnips.

PLANT Jerusalem artichokes, onion sets and potatoes.

UNDER GLASS SOW French beans, runner beans, capsicum, celery, marrows or courgettes, sweet corn, outdoor tomatoes. These may all be sown in a cold house but the temperature should not drop below 8°C (45°F). In cooler districts don't sow till May.

IN A HEATED GREENHOUSE sow aubergine, capsicum, celeriac, celery, cucumber, marrows, melons, tomatoes. These may all be germinated in warmth indoors and brought on on a south-facing windowsill.

PLANT OUT summer cauliflower and, in the second part of the month, Brussels sprouts.

THIN all young seedlings except carrots.

HOE regularly between all crops.

REMOVE forcing pots or boxes from rhubarb.

STAKE peas, or put up pea net, if not already done.

PUT DOWN slug traps or pellets.

# JOBS FOR MAY

FROM THE GARDEN use asparagus, chives, early lettuce, radish, spring onions.

USE vegetables from the freezer.

FREEZE chives.

CARRY ON SOWING dwarf broad beans, French beans, runner beans, haricot beans, maincrop beetroot, broccoli, cabbages – summer and Savoy, carrots, cauliflowers, outdoor cucumber, curly kale, garlic, kohl rabi, lettuce, marrows or courgettes, onions, parsley, parsnips, radish, seakale beet, spinach, spinach beet, swede, sweet corn, turnip.

UNDER GLASS SOW French, haricot or runner beans, capsicum, marrows, sweet corn and outdoor tomatoes. These may also be sown in the garden, depending on where you live and the weather.

IN A COLD GREENHOUSE now is the time to plant out capsicum, cucumbers, melons and tomatoes, but make sure the night temperature does not drop below 8°C (45°F).

PLANT OUT Brussels sprouts, summer cabbage, curly kale, celery, celeriac and, at the end of the month, French beans, runner beans, haricot beans and sweet corn plants. You can also plant out cucumbers, marrows, melons and tomato plants but protect them with a frame or cloches unless you live in a sheltered area.

THIN ALL YOUNG SEEDLINGS (except carrots) as soon as you can handle them and then progressively thin them to their final distances.

HOE regularly between all crops.

ERECT the framework for the runner beans. This is best done before sowing the seeds or putting out the plants.

DRAW A LITTLE earth over potato shoots, as they appear at the beginning of the month, to protect them from frost and then continue to earth them up as they grow.

COMPOST all possible material. Gather vegetable matter, lawn mowings, young hedge trimmings, grass cuttings, annual weeds – anything that will rot down.

PROTECT seedlings from birds and slugs.

## JOBS FOR JUNE

FROM THE GARDEN use asparagus, cauliflower, chives, courgettes, lettuce, peas, early potatoes, radish, spinach, spring onions, turnips. Use cucumbers from the greenhouse.

USE vegetables from last year's crops in the freezer.

FREEZE asparagus, cauliflower, chives, courgettes, spinach and turnips.

SOW (if you haven't already done so) runner beans and French beans, maincrop beetroot, carrots, sugar loaf chicory, outdoor cucumber, endive, kohl rabi, lettuce, marrows/courgettes, parsley, radish, spinach, spinach beet, turnips.

PLANT OUT French and runner beans, calabrese broccoli, purple sprouting broccoli, Brussels sprouts, summer and Savoy cabbage, capsicum, cauliflowers, cucumbers, curly kale, leeks, marrows/courgettes, cantaloupe melons, sweet corn, outdoor tomatoes.

IN THE COLD GREENHOUSE plant out capsicum, cucumbers, melons and tomatoes.

THIN all crops where necessary, but still leave the carrots alone.

HOE at least once every two weeks.

EARTH UP potatoes.

SHADE GREENHOUSE when the sun gets too strong.

WATCH OUT for blackfly, greenfly and other pests. Spray where necessary.

*250*

PINCH OUT the growing tips of broad bean plants when they have plenty of flowers to deter blackfly.

COLLECT material for the compost heaps.

## JOBS FOR JULY

FROM THE GARDEN use broad beans, French beans, runner beans, early beetroot, summer cabbage, carrots, cauliflower, courgettes, kohl rabi, lettuce, parsley, peas, potatoes, radish, seakale beet, shallots, spinach, spinach beet, spring onions, turnips.

FROM THE GREENHOUSE use aubergines, capsicum, cucumbers, melons, tomatoes.

FREEZE broad beans, French beans, runner beans, cauliflower, courgettes, kohl rabi, parsley, peas, seakale beet, spinach, spinach beet, turnips. Freeze these crops at their very best when they are young and tender and within an hour of picking them.

LIFT AND STORE shallots towards the end of the month or pickle then straight away.

SOW sugar loaf chicory, Chinese cabbage, kohl rabi, endive, lettuce, radish, winter radish, spinach.

PLANT OUT calabrese broccoli, purple sprouting broccoli, cauliflowers, curly kale, leeks, Savoy cabbage.

THIN the carrots and use them to eat. Don't leave any lying around to attract the carrot fly. Cover any on the compost with grass cuttings to hide the smell. Thin other plants where necessary.

TIE UP tomato plants and remove any side shoots, unless they're a bush variety.

HOE between all crops. Use the Dutch hoe and just skim below the surface. You'll lose moisture from the ground if you hoe deeply.

KEEP the garden tidy and continually add to the compost heap.

WATER celery, marrows, runner beans and other vegetables if necessary. If possible do the watering at midday so that the soil can warm up again by nightfall.

## JOBS FOR AUGUST

FROM THE GARDEN use broad beans, French beans, haricot beans, runner beans, beetroot, calabrese, summer cabbage, capsicum, carrots, courgettes, cucumber, garlic, kohl rabi, lettuce, marrows, melons, onions, parsley, peas, potatoes, radish, seakale beet, shallots, spinach, spinach beet, spring onions, swede, sweet corn, tomatoes, turnips.

FROM THE GREENHOUSE use aubergines, capsicum, cucumbers, melons, tomatoes.

FREEZE calabrese, broad beans, French beans, runner beans, courgettes, kohl rabi, parsley, peas, seakale beet, spinach, spinach beet, sweet corn, tomatoes, turnips.

LIFT AND STORE shallots if not already done. Bend down tops of onions as they begin to turn yellow and lift about two weeks later to let them ripen off.

SOW corn salad, lettuce and winter radish.

REMOVE pea and broad bean plants as soon as they have finished cropping and put on compost. Hoe over the vacant ground.

REMOVE SHADING from greenhouse about the middle of the month.

WATER all plants where necessary but especially celery, cucumbers, marrows and runner beans.

STAKE broccoli, kale and Brussels sprouts against the winter winds.

HOE between all crops.

STOP outdoor tomatoes at four trusses and those in the cold greenhouse at six trusses.

KILL the cabbage white butterflies with a badminton racket. Pick off any caterpillars on the brassicas – nibbled leaves will tell you where they are.

DIG UP stumps of summer cabbages, dry and burn them.

COLLECT material for the compost heaps.

## JOBS FOR SEPTEMBER

FROM THE GARDEN use French beans, haricot beans, runner beans, beetroot, calabrese, capsicum, carrot, autumn cauliflower, courgettes, celery, outdoor cucumber, garlic, kohl rabi, lettuce, marrows, melons, onions, parsley, parsnips, potatoes, radish, seakale beet, spinach, spinach beet, swede, sweet corn, tomatoes.

FROM THE GREENHOUSE use aubergines, capsicum, cucumbers, melons, tomatoes.

FREEZE French beans, runner beans, calabrese, cauliflower, courgettes, celery, kohl rabi, parsley, seakale beet, spinach, spinach beet, sweet corn, tomatoes.

STORE haricot beans, garlic, onions. Dig up and store maincrop potatoes if the tops have died down. At the end of the month store any ripe marrows.

SALT DOWN runner beans if you have no freezer.

SOW corn salad.

HOE between all crops.

WATER celery, marrows and runner beans if necessary.

EARTH UP base of broccoli, Brussels sprouts and kale to give added anchorage against the winter winds.

PULL UP outdoor tomato plants at the end of the month with the green fruits attached. Hang up the whole plants, or the bunches of fruit, away from frost danger but in a cool place to finish off ripening. As soon as the fruit start to turn pick them off individually with the green calyx attached and take them into the normal warmth of the house.

CUT OFF and burn potato tops if diseased.

PICK OFF any caterpillars on the brassicas.

COLLECT material for the compost heaps.

## JOBS FOR OCTOBER

FROM THE GARDEN use runner beans, beetroot, calabrese, cauli-flower, carrots, celeriac, celery, Chinese cabbage, sugar loaf chicory, courgettes, endive, kohl rabi, lettuce, marrows, parsley, parsnips, potatoes, seakale beet, spinach beet, swede.

BLANCH endive before using by covering with pots, boxes or darkened cloches.

FROM THE GREENHOUSE use aubergines, capsicum, cucumbers, melons, tomatoes. When frosts threaten pick off the bunches of green tomatoes in the cold greenhouse and hang them up in a frost-proof place to ripen. When they start to turn take them into the warmth of the house.

FREEZE runner beans, calabrese, cauliflower, celeriac, celery, courget-tes, kohl rabi, parsley, seakale beet, spinach beet.

FROM STORE use haricot beans, garlic, onions.

STORE beetroot, carrots, marrows, potatoes.

SALT DOWN runner beans if you have no freezer.

HOE round the remaining crops, cutting off all weeds to stop them flowering and seeding.

PROTECT winter cauliflowers from frost by breaking a leaf over the curd.

INSPECT all brassicas. Dig up any that are stunted or diseased and burn them. Make sure the others are securely staked and have extra soil piled round their roots to give them better anchorage for the winter.

CUT DOWN asparagus plants to just above ground level when the foliage changes colour.

PULL UP tomato, cucumber and melon plants in the cold greenhouse at the end of the month and generally tidy up – removing all leaves and weeds. Pull up all spent plants from the garden. Put them on the compost or burn if diseased. Put all other available material on the compost heap and protect from the rain.

COLLECT all sound canes, plants supports and nets. Store in the dry for the winter. Collect leaves for the leafmould heap.

DOUBLE DIG any grassland where you propose to extend your vegetable plot. It shouldn't need manure the first year unless the soil is known to be poor.

HAVE a good clear up generally and burn all rubbish.

# 20. Some Useful Information

## THE BOTANICAL FAMILIES TO WHICH VEGETABLES BELONG

**Chenopodiaceae**
Beetroot. Spinach beet. Seakale beet. Spinach.

**Compositae**
Lettuce. Chicory and endive. Globe artichoke. Jerusalem artichoke. Salsify (vegetable oyster) and scorzonera.

**Cruciferae**
Cabbage. Kohl rabi. Broccoli. Cauliflowers. Kale. Brussels sprouts. Radish. Turnip. Swede. Cress. Coleworts (collards). Chinese cabbage.

**Cucurbitaceae**
Marrow. Courgette. Cucumber. Melon.

**Gramineae**
Sweet corn.

**Leguminosae**
Peas. Runner beans. French beans. Broad beans. Haricot beans.

**Liliaceae**
Onions. Welsh or perpetual onions. Leeks. Shallots. Garlic. Chives. Asparagus.

**Polygonaceae**
Rhubarb.

**Solanaceae**
Potatoes. Tomatoes. Capsicum (sweet peppers). Aubergines (egg plants).

**Umbelliferae**
Parsley. Celery and celeriac. Parsnip. Carrot.

**Valerianaceae**
Corn salad (lambs lettuce).

# IMPERIAL TO METRIC CONVERSIONS

## TEMPERATURE

| C | F |
|---|---|
| 100 | 212 |
| 90 | 200 |
| | 190 |
| 80 | 180 |
| | 170 |
| 70 | 160 |
| | 150 |
| 60 | 140 |
| | 130 |
| 50 | 120 |
| | 110 |
| 40 | 100 |
| | 90 |
| 30 | 80 |
| | 70 |
| 20 | 60 |
| 10 | 50 |
| 5 | 40 |
| 0 | 32 Freezing |

## LENGTH

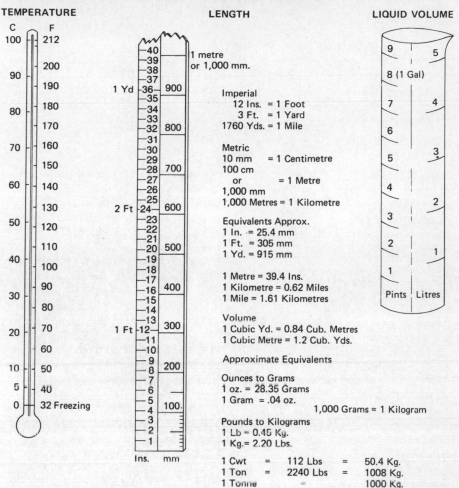

1 metre or 1,000 mm.

Imperial
12 Ins. = 1 Foot
3 Ft. = 1 Yard
1760 Yds. = 1 Mile

Metric
10 mm = 1 Centimetre
100 cm
 or = 1 Metre
1,000 mm
1,000 Metres = 1 Kilometre

Equivalents Approx.
1 In. = 25.4 mm
1 Ft. = 305 mm
1 Yd. = 915 mm

1 Metre = 39.4 Ins.
1 Kilometre = 0.62 Miles
1 Mile = 1.61 Kilometres

Volume
1 Cubic Yd. = 0.84 Cub. Metres
1 Cubic Metre = 1.2 Cub. Yds.

Approximate Equivalents

Ounces to Grams
1 oz. = 28.35 Grams
1 Gram = .04 oz.
1,000 Grams = 1 Kilogram

Pounds to Kilograms
1 Lb = 0.45 Kg.
1 Kg. = 2.20 Lbs.

| 1 Cwt | = | 112 Lbs | = | 50.4 Kg. |
| 1 Ton | = | 2240 Lbs | = | 1008 Kg. |
| 1 Tonne | = | | | 1000 Kg. |

## LIQUID VOLUME

## WEIGHT

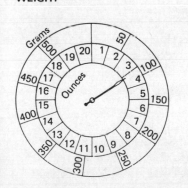
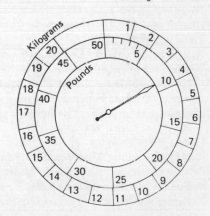

257

# Index